*(Continued from front flap)*

valuable historical material was lost, a portion of which is restored in this volume.

Thus in tracing the written references to Jesus from Jewish sources through the centuries, Dr. Goldstein not only gives us more of the historical background of Christ's life but he has also written a history of the relationship of Judaism and Christianity — a history almost unique in its fairness and accuracy. The book closes with an appeal to the common brotherhood of Christian and Jew.

Since this book is a pioneer work in its field it should appeal to both Jews and Christians, to all students of comparative religion, to all concerned with the building of religious freedom in accordance with the democratic spirit.

# JESUS
## IN THE
# JEWISH
# TRADITION

THE MACMILLAN COMPANY
NEW YORK · BOSTON · CHICAGO · DALLAS
ATLANTA · SAN FRANCISCO

MACMILLAN AND CO., LIMITED
LONDON · BOMBAY · CALCUTTA · MADRAS
MELBOURNE

THE MACMILLAN COMPANY
OF CANADA, LIMITED
TORONTO

MORRIS GOLDSTEIN, Rabbi, M.A., D.H.L.

# JESUS

## IN THE

## JEWISH

## TRADITION

New York : The Macmillan Company : 1950

TO

*Adeline and Joyce*

THERE is no book, strangely enough, in our language which tells with continuity through the centuries, from the first century of the Christian Era until modern times, the story of what is known regarding Jesus in Jewish life and literature. To supply that want this volume is presented, simply and humbly.

It is the expansion of a thesis, *The Record Concerning Jesus in Rabbinic Judaism*, written as a partial requirement for the degree of Doctor of Hebrew Letters received at the Hebrew Union College of Cincinnati, Ohio.

The research was conducted with the scholarly guidance of Professor Samuel S. Cohon, to whom I am profoundly grateful. It required the assembling of the original Hebrew and Aramaic source-material, with all the variant readings of manuscripts and early printed editions which had escaped censorship—and the translation, interpretation and evaluation of these texts.

Acknowledgment is expressed herewith to President Nelson Glueck and the Faculty of the Hebrew Union College; to President Ronald Bridges and my colleagues of the Faculty of the Pacific School of Religion of Berkeley, California, which for three years now, with the cooperation of the Jewish Chautauqua Society, has invited the author, a rabbi, to teach in a Christian seminary the course on Judaism during the formative period of Christianity; to Professor Walter J. Fischel, of the University of California; to the libraries of these three institutions; to Professor Solomon Zeitlin and Mr. R. Travers Herford for correspondence on this theme; to Congregation Sherith Israel of San Francisco for encouragement to engage in this type of work in conjunction with an active rabbinate; to Professors Israel Bettan and Alexander Guttmann; to Dr. Lou H. Silberman; to Mr. Eugene B. Bloch; to Mr. Harold Wachter; and to publishers and copyright owners of the works cited here.

There are various systems of transliterating Hebrew words into

English. The one here employed is that used in the *Universal Jewish Encyclopedia*. It is chosen because this newest Jewish Encyclopedia, in English, is readily obtainable for reference purposes.

The Literature Analysis is an integral part of the subject and might have come immediately after Chapter I, for it evaluates the work done in this field; it deals with the original sources from which the texts, subsequently discussed, were assembled; further, it supplies the key wherewith to identify the text-sources. However, in order not to interrupt the flow of thought the relevant literature is given after the concluding chapter.

Technical terms are usually explained in these pages when first mentioned. In the way of further assistance, the index specifies where definitions may be found.

The notes are placed at the end of the book, and not at the foot of each page, in order to enhance the readability of the text, since it is believed that the record concerning Jesus in the Jewish tradition is of interest to the general reader as well as to the scholar.

In Jewish tradition there is a phrase spoken by the congregation at the completion of the reading of a Book of the Torah. It is *hazak, hazak, venis'hazek.* It means: "Be strong, be strong; may we strengthen one another." So, it is our prayer that this work may strengthen our relations to fellowmen and to God—and thus that we be strengthened.

MORRIS GOLDSTEIN

# CONTENTS

CHAPTER I

# IMPORTANCE OF THE INQUIRY

IN whatever way we regard the phenomenon, the role of Jesus in the scene of human events is such as to cause us to wonder whether we really know all that can be known concerning him.

The Christian tradition, derived from the New Testament, is available and accessible. It tells us that Jesus was born into a Jewish home, studied with Jewish teachers and, in a sense, lived a Jewish life and died a Jew. It is natural, therefore, to ask: "What is the record concerning Jesus in the Jewish tradition?" This is not generally known. It is not easily to be found. Yet it is exceedingly important to ascertain. Four groups of reasons prompt an accurate and painstaking search of the record for the facts.

1. *For a clearer understanding of Judaism, past and present.*

Inquiry into this theme requires, before aught else, an examination of the early Jewish literature of the first five centuries of the Christian Era where mention of Jesus might be found. This early record is contained primarily in the Talmud and the Midrash, and these are difficult documents. To read them in the original and share the wealth they contain requires considerable preliminary training. Even the translations into English puzzle the novice, for there are baffling technical terms, unexpected transitions in subject-matter, serious discussion interrupted by the play of imagination, abbreviated allusion and reference inadequate for proper identification, as well as tiring redundancies and repetitions.

That being the case, consider how much more perplexity is added to the passages purportedly dealing with Jesus, for these have been severely censored during blighted centuries at the instigation of hostile authorities. Whole paragraphs have been deleted; words have been expunged or substituted; spellings have been changed, thoughts mutilated and manuscripts seized and burned. Wherever in these rabbinic writings it was thought by the Church-appointed censor that a reference might possibly allude to

Jesus or Christianity it became the target of attack.[1] Therefore, as Hermann Strack reports in his valuable guide to the study of the Talmud and Midrash: "In consequence of the repeated confiscations and foolish destructions of Jewish manuscripts by fire only a very small number of ancient Talmud copies are extant." [2]

As though this were not enough difficulty, it was compounded by a self-imposed censorship on the part of the Jewish communities as a practical means of confining within limits the vicious persecution of their books *and their lives*. Thus, in 1631 the Jewish Assembly of Elders in Poland declared: "We enjoin you under the threat of the great ban to publish in no new edition of the Mishnah or the Gemara anything that refers to Jesus of Nazareth. . . . If you will not diligently heed this letter, but run counter thereto and continue to publish our books in the same manner as heretofore, you might bring over us and yourselves still greater sufferings than in previous times." [3]

At first, deleted portions or words in printed Talmuds were indicated by small circles or blank spaces but, in time, these too were forbidden by the censors.[4]

As a result of the twofold censorship the usual volumes of rabbinic literature contain only a distorted remnant of supposed allusions to Jesus. The vast Midrashic material still requires considerable critical editing.[5] The first task, therefore, is to ascertain the correct text, as indicated by the few early manuscripts and printed editions which escaped the destructive fury of censorship.

Diligent textual study has been made by those who have given their lives to this one objective,[6] but the material is scattered and not accessible. The best work of restoring the censored material has been done with the Babylonian Talmud and the most recent censor-free edition is that of Lazarus Goldschmidt, published between 1897 and 1935, giving also the variant readings, a German translation and brief comment.[7] The Soncino English translation [8] likewise calls attention, in footnotes, to the censored passages.

However, our inquiry regarding Jesus in Jewish tradition covers a field, even in the early centuries, which goes beyond the Babylonian Talmud. The field is so wide and the material is so disputed as to impose the necessity of assembling all the relevant passages, in the original Hebrew or (often) Aramaic language of the text. This was done in the initial phase of this research in order to establish a foundation upon which to build. The full and accurate original texts, with every variant reading, of the Talmudic and Midrashic references to Jesus [9] were gathered and recorded—both those which will be found really to refer to him and those erroneously believed to have alluded to him.

Closely related to this is the need for an accurate translation of the text. Because the original has been tampered with and required restoring there is greater latitude for error. Furthermore, inasmuch as the subject of inquiry is a controversial one and rarely is approached with sufficient objectivity, the temptation to see certain meanings in certain words is almost irresistible, a temptation encouraged by the very nature of rabbinic expression—the words without vowels, the absence of punctuation, the several meanings of a particular term, the injection of an incident or thought independently of the context. As we move into the analysis of the specific passages we shall become increasingly aware of the dangers of mistranslation. "The texts which must be cited," W. Bacher, careful expert on the Talmud, cautioned, "again and again require fresh critical examination, however often they have already been interpreted before." [10] One of the primary purposes in this study, then, is the determination of the exact and true translation of the text.

Thus, the gathering, recording, translating and—finally—interpreting of the relevant material may result in an improved knowledge of the Talmud and Midrash insofar as these highly important documents of Jewish tradition disclose the rabbinic attitude to Jesus.

Also of significance in an understanding of Judaism is the two-part question often asked, as expressed by Joseph Klausner in *Jesus of Nazareth*: "Why did Jesus arise among the people of Israel? And why, in spite of that, did the people of Israel repudiate his teaching?" [11] One way of answering the question is to examine the New Testament and the history of Christianity in the light of Jewish history and teaching. This way alone is not sufficient, for, as we shall soon observe,[12] the students of the New Testament and of the Patristic writings themselves seek external confirmation for the events and opinions there recorded.

Moreover, the demands of scholarly inquiry caution against accepting without utmost scrutiny a piecing together of Jewish life from reports of its nature contained in polemic literature in opposition to it. R. Travers Herford[13] and George Foot Moore,[14] for instance, have demonstrated convincingly the inadequacies in the New Testament portrayal of the Pharisees. James Parkes,[15] in telling of the early conflict between the Church and the Synagogue, warns against accepting at face value the greater part of the Patristic accounts of Jewish acts of hostility.

In *The "Dialogues With the Jews" as Sources for the Early Jewish Argument Against Christianity*,[16] Amos B. Hulen gives particular attention to the classic *Dialogue with Trypho* by Justin Martyr, because of the importance attached to it as a source of information regarding the Jewish attitude toward Jesus during the middle of the second century. He brings to light the fact that only comparatively recently has it been admitted on both sides, Christian as well as Jewish, that this *Dialogue* is not a faithful representation of Judaism in the second century,[17] for, he argues, "We do not look with confidence to a document against Judaism for a faithful account, at least in details, of what Jews believe";[18] it "may have been written for the sake of wavering Christians."[19] Hulen doubts that any of the "Dialogues" of the Church Fathers were *actual* debates. Together with George F. Moore[20] and A. C. McGiffert,[21] he reaches the conclusion that if we truly wish to learn the attitude of the Jews toward Christianity we must search elsewhere than in the Christian writings directed against them. This is the testimony of Christian scholars of recognized standing.

One of the reasons for not using Jewish sources in reconstructing the Jewish attitude to Christianity in the early Christian centuries is the paucity of Jewish material or, at least, the obstacles in getting to know that material.[22] While the thesis of our study here is the Jewish attitude toward Jesus, and not the larger question of the attitude toward Christianity, it may nevertheless yield a certain amount of information on the larger question as well.

At all events, it should prove instructive to search in the Jewish literature closest to the lifetime of Jesus for expressions of attitude and viewpoint regarding him and his activity. In these expressions we may find the clue, *in Jewish sources,* as to why the main stream of Judaism flowed on without Jesus—even though Julius Wellhausen,[23] the Christian, and Joseph Klausner,[24] the Jew, and a good part of Christian and Jewish scholarship of the past two centuries have agreed: "Jesus was not a Christian: he was a Jew."

In seeking the answer to this question there necessarily will be discovered, concurrently, the distinctive characteristics of the Jewish way of life. As we come to learn why Jesus was not accepted by Jewish tradition we shall become aware—by comparative study—of the fundamentals of the religion which precluded the acceptance of him.

The theme of this book is urgent in the elucidation of Judaism, in the third place, because for many centuries the Talmud and other rabbinical writings were not only condemned and censored but disgracefully confiscated and burned in public[25]—because of presumed insults to Jesus and Christianity which they supposedly contained. On these grounds, one Jewish community after another suffered bitter hostility and tragic persecution. Therefore, in addition to the challenge of objective scholarship, the ideal of humanity expressed in the phrase, "God is Truth," demands that the record regarding Jesus in rabbinical literature be made manifest, that the truth be known and understood.

What are the facts? *Are* the references insulting? So much of the misery in Jewish history is related to the answers we shall seek to these questions! It is important that we *know!*

It is surprising to discover that the explorers of our day in this much-contested field have been mainly non-Jewish scholars—at least, those who have published complete works upon it.[26] Heinrich Laible, R. Travers Herford and Hermann Strack were Christians.[27] It is natural that their thinking be influenced by their religious convictions.

Thus, Laible transmits to the modern reader a polemic spirit inherited from the Middle Ages, when the discussion of religious problems was not as disciplined by the desideratum of objectivity as we seek to apply in our times, and he avowedly points his study of *Jesus Christ in the Talmud* to the goal of converting Jews to Christianity. It is his prerogative to do this but can he be accepted as an unbiased witness?

Herford, as a striking contrast, demonstrates in his comprehensive work a remarkable spirit of appreciation of Judaism. He does not attempt to impose his own point of view. Yet, his *Christianity in Talmud and Midrash,* in the portion which recites the record concerning Jesus, is so definitely based on Laible's book (as he frankly admits) that he cannot entirely escape its faults, although he greatly modifies them.

Strack has dealt more recently with the theme than these two others. His qualification in terms of Talmudic scholarship is of a high order. Indeed, in the Preface to his *Jesus, die Häretiker und die Christen nach den ältesten jüdischen Angaben* he specifies his intention in compiling the material as being the hope that he might thereby help alleviate some of the injustice done to the Jew. There is no reason to doubt his avowal. Nevertheless, he participated also in missionary efforts among the adherents of Judaism. For example, he wrote the Preface to *A Manual of Christian Evidences for Jewish People,* by A. Lukyn Williams,[28] a handbook of arguments wherewith to convert Jews to Christianity, in which he indicated that he himself had wanted to write such a book. Strack had a right to this expression of his religious principle but it is inevitable that it would condition his exposition of the tradition of the Jews among whom he was seeking to make converts.

The plain fact is that as we would turn **to an** earnest Protestant for an appraisal of Protestantism and to a convinced Roman Catholic for an explanation of the Roman Catholic Church so it would be normal and logical to look to one who is persuaded of the validity of Judaism to deal with a phase of Jewish tradition which has been surrounded with so much argument, misunderstanding and even violence.

Dean Inge of England was correct in his assertion that Christianity can be understood only from inside. So also Judaism can be understood best from the inside.[29] It would seem mandatory that a Jew, who rightly counts the Talmud and Midrash as his inheritance as does the author of this volume, who thinks as a Jew, who is part of the tradition and history under discussion—the glory and the suffering—that a disciple of Judaism should concentrate upon a complete examination of the evidence.

**2.** *This subject is likewise of value to the student of Christianity.*
In the study of Christianity there is that school of thought which argues that there is no historical Jesus, that he never actually lived on earth, that he is a myth created by the writers of the New Testament.

When David F. Strauss in 1835 pioneered the critical examination of the life of Jesus,[30] he opened the road which led to the doubts of Jesus' existence expressed by his fellow-German, Bruno Bauer; [31] by the Dutch School of daring theologians; by the Scotsman, John M. Robertson; [32] by the American, William Benjamin Smith; [33] by the German, Arthur Drews; [34] by the Frenchman, Paul-Louis Couchoud; [35] by the Danish author, Georg Brandes.[36]

To quote but one of these and other less known proponents of the myth theory, Arthur Drews in his Introduction to *The Witnesses to the Historicity of Jesus* [37] asserts that as historic evidence regarding Jesus the New Testament is vulnerable. Because of its shortcomings and obscurities a search has been made from the earliest times for other evidence—non-Christian evidence. Certainly, if Jesus really existed, some references to him should be found in the writings of the Jews or Greeks or Romans who lived in his century or shortly thereafter. But, according to Drews and the others who follow this school of thought, no indisputable reference is to be found. Of the possible "Jewish Witnesses" to confirm the existence of Jesus he finds nothing in Philo Judaeus who lived from 30 B.C.E.[38] to about 54 C.E., visited

Palestine,[39] wrote on many matters at great length and would have been expected to mention Jesus; nothing in the Jewish historian, Justus of Tiberias, who was a contemporary of the period of Jesus' activity and actually lived near Capernaum, and whose records Photius, ninth-century Patriarch of Constantinople, long ago searched in vain for mention of Jesus; nothing in Josephus, who lived from about 37 to approximately 100 C.E. and who wrote profusely on events of his day, nothing genuine, nothing but later interpolations; [40] nothing in the Talmud, excepting material of so late a date as to be of no historical value. To this, Drews adds with approval the comment contained in Justin Martyr's *Dialogue with Trypho*, dated between 135 to 150 C.E., "Ye follow an empty rumor and make a Christ for yourselves. . . . If he was born and lived somewhere, he is entirely unknown." [41]

On this question the Jewish scholar, Solomon Zeitlin, writes: "The main witnesses to the historicity of Jesus are the Gospels. The statements of Josephus concerning him are not taken seriously by the most conservative scholars; the Talmudic statements are also rejected by many scholars as not having any historical bearing. The data of pagan historians, Suetonius and Tacitus, regarded as proofs of the historicity of Jesus are considered doubtful. Even Paul's epistles have awakened the question, Does he speak of a real historical personage or of an idea? The main sources for the historicity of Jesus, therefore, are the Gospels." Having analyzed the Gospels on the basis of the Halachah there reported, Zeitlin continues: "So we are right to assume that even the Gospels have no value as witnesses of the historicity of Jesus. The question therefore remains: Are there any historical proofs that Jesus of Nazareth ever existed?" [42]

The opposing school of thought—which includes scholars of the calibre of Johannes Weiss, Maurice Goguel, Charles A. Guignebert, Edward Meyer, Frederick C. Conybeare, B. S. Easton, E. F. Scott, Vincent Taylor and Joseph Klausner—offers vigorous refutation to the myth theory. In establishing the historical reality of Jesus there are those who, like Klausner, make use of the Talmudic evidence and invest it with reliability.

In his authentic summary of the main trends in the study of

the life of Jesus, C. C. McCown, having presented the divergent viewpoints, comments: [43] "What new sources or new methods may be discovered to throw light upon the dark period when the New Testament literature was taking shape no one can say." Mentioning archeology as one new source, he goes on to add: "The Talmud is a vast sea of materials which have hardly been touched by careful criticism, a great treasure cave whose forbidding aspect has frightened Christian scholars away." It is important to realize that this observation is dated as recently as 1940.[44]

An added purpose, therefore, of our careful examination of the Talmudic record concerning Jesus is to bring some added light—if it be possible—to the question of the historicity of Jesus.

One step further, in the clarification of the early rabbinic allusions to Jesus there may result not only new knowledge on the historicity of Jesus but, if the Talmudic mention be substantiated and proven of early date, there may come also authentic material wherewith to compare the Gospel accounts, wherewith to add confirmation or to raise doubts on specific recorded details.

If Jesus existed he existed as a Jew who lived and taught and died among his people; his people, therefore, would be expected to remember him most clearly. Also, the language of Jesus was Hebrew or Aramaic, or both, and not the Greek of the New Testament. It therefore stands to reason that what is recorded in the Hebrew or Aramaic of the Talmud might be closer in accuracy to the actual event or original intent.

Of further significance to students of Christianity would be a mirroring of early Christianity as reflected by the nature of reference to Jesus in Jewish sources. A word of warning, though: the same caution in the matter of judging Judaism by references derived from Christian literature applies equally in reverse.

It will be found that careful scrutiny, translation and interpretation of the purported rabbinic allusions to Jesus will lead to findings somewhat different from those generally accepted on the basis of R. Travers Herford's *Christianity in Talmud and Midrash*. Herford's volume, being the only full-sized treatment of the subject in the English language (with the exception of the English translation of H. Laible's *Jesus Christus im Thalmud*, whose value is impaired by reason of bitter bias) has become, since 1903, the source-book for Christian students and authors whenever reference must be made to the rabbinic attitude to Jesus. Yet, with all commendation for his sympathetic approach, scholarship and fairness, it is evident that Herford was in error in several important regards.[45] He mistranslated certain crucial passages.[46] Most of these he subsequently corrected in his article on "Jesus in Rabbinic Literature" published in 1942 in the *Universal Jewish Encyclopedia*.[47] But it is only a sketchy article, without original text, without elaboration, lost in ten volumes of the *Encyclopedia*; nor does it recognize all the points that call for correction.

The unfortunate fact is that the *Encyclopedia* article cannot be appended as an amendment to all copies of the author's book now extant. Nor can he withdraw all that has been written on the basis of his now disproved findings. For example, in his own widely used volume, *Judaism in the New Testament Period*,[48] he wrote of Jesus: "He spoke to the multitude as to his friends; he spoke to the Pharisees as to suspicious critics who might, and who in fact very soon did, become active opponents. Each was seen by the other in the least favorable aspect. . . . To him they were the representatives of hidebound pedantry, enemies of all the working of the free spirit. To them he was a dangerous revolutionary, threatening to undermine the very foundations of their religious system." For what reason does Herford state that the Pharisees regarded Jesus as "a dangerous revolutionary"? By reason of a wrong translation of a Talmudic phrase, as will be shown later.[49] His *Encyclopedia* article admits the error. But the harm done is not thereby erased! And this is only one illustration of others which will be indicated later.

This is not to condemn Herford. On the contrary, he has done valiant work in this field; he has helped us gain increased knowledge of what the Talmud and Midrash contain of Jesus and Christianity; he has correctly reinterpreted for Christians many an unfavorable attitude regarding the Pharisees; he has shown friendship for Judaism. In calling attention to the unfortunate results of his earlier errors, committed in good faith, the purpose is rather to show how analogous the circumstance is to the story of the gossip who wished to retract the false reports he had spread and was reminded that true retraction demanded that he get in touch with each and every one to whom he had spoken, like feathers which had been scattered about and now had to be gathered up, to the last one.

A book on this theme, Jesus in Jewish tradition, must be written. It must be accurate and complete. It must be in the English language. It must be circulated in those circles where a comprehensive up-to-date record is desired as a standard reference. As such it may prove useful in filling in some of the details in the history of Christianity. It is hoped that this volume may serve such a purpose.

**3.** *A third area of significance in this inquiry is its importance in the relationship of Christian and Jew.*

Day by day, Jews and Christians associate with one another. The chances are that exchange of thought will lead, some time or other, to the question of the Jewish attitude to Jesus and the Christian attitude to the Talmud. Whatever information is made available for intelligent discussion should be as exact as possible, especially the earliest Jewish mention of Jesus.

"Even at the present moment," Hermann Strack reported in the Foreword to the Fourth Edition, in German, of his *Introduction to the Talmud and Midrash*,[50] "certain ignorant agitators (most of them are at the same time malevolent) seek to make the Christian-German people believe that the Jews are solicitous, with every possible means at their hands, to keep the Talmud a secret book: for fear lest its contents should become known, indeed."

Although this was written in 1908, it is still to be observed that anti-Semitic agents hint menacingly at nefarious Talmudic and post-Talmudic slander of Jesus. For the sake of complete understanding it is well that the record be brought into the clear. Is there any validity in such assertions? How and why did they originate? Let the truth speak for itself.

It is not unlikely that when the entire story is known a clearer and truer understanding will come between Christian and Jew. The discovery of how closely the ethical teachings of Jesus parallel those of the Talmud—shown by many, but especially by Strack and Billerbeck,[51] Christian scholars, and Montefiore [52] and Loewe,[53] Jewish scholars—has already produced considerable good. What there is to tell of the mention of Jesus in the Jewish tradition is yet uncompleted. In the pages which follow, let us see whether the factual search for truth will lead of itself to new attitudes for Christian and Jew.

4. *It is almost unbelievable that there has not yet appeared in our day a volume giving a continuous historic account of the Jewish viewpoint on Jesus.*

To be sure, in the recital of Jewish history there is to be found mention of Jesus in one period, in another period; in one connection, in another connection; but no continuous treatment. There are books on: As a Jew Sees Jesus; Study of the Background, Life and Teachings of Jesus from the Standpoint of Judaism; Jesus in the Talmud and Midrash; Medieval Polemics, Legends, Apologetics; Contemporary Jewish Writings on Jesus. There is no Jewish Thoughts on Jesus from His Day to This.

Would it not seem that the time has come for a comprehensive study of the full range of Jewish tradition—of the literature within the first two centuries after Jesus, which we know as the Tannaitic period; to be followed by the literature of the next three centuries, which is the Amoraic period; to be followed by the history, literature, legends, disputations, philosophy, folklore and worship of the Middle Ages; to be concluded with the many Jewish writings on Jesus in the modern period?

Interestingly enough, Joseph Klausner mentions as a footnote in *Jesus of Nazareth*: [54] "An important work still remaining to be done is a book on all that has been written about Jesus in Jewish literature from the close of the Talmud period until Jacob Emden.

At present we have only the important article by J. Broydé: *Polemics and Polemical Literature* (*Jewish Encyclopedia*, X 102–109)." [55]

This, however, is only a part of all that is required. The Talmudic period itself (which includes the Tannaitic and Amoraic), as has already been shown, calls for fresh study. Even Klausner, in his otherwise excellent use of the Talmudic references, hastily brushes aside the allusions to Jesus credited to the Amoraim,[56] but these too have their significance in the total picture, for the post-Talmudic development cannot be understood without them.

Beyond the period of the Talmud there is no unitary treatment whatever to carry the story from the sixth century to our modern period, the Era of Democracy.[57] This is a vast area and the modern cannot be seen in proper perspective without reference to the medieval. This volume, therefore, sets out to present the record of the entire Jewish tradition concerning Jesus, from the first century up to and including the eighteenth century.

With the close of the eighteenth century unprecedented forces, inside and outside of Judaism, interacted in such a way as to create new Jewish viewpoints regarding the subject of our inquiry—and the response to these forces has been so variegated and extensive as to require separate attention.

With this study on Jesus in the full range of Jewish tradition the foundation will have been laid for a companion volume on Jesus in Modern Jewish Thought.

# CHAPTER II

# TANNAITIC PERIOD

# II

O UR search begins with the oldest portion of the Jewish
record which might contain mention of Jesus. We examine now
that segment of historic Judaism which is closest to the date
ascribed to the lifetime of the foremost figure in Christianity.

In rabbinic literature the completion of the Mishnah in 220 C.E.[1]
presents to us the first definitive culmination of the comprehensive teaching, opinion and incidental recording of facts and events
in the rabbinic tradition—a tradition beginning with Ezra the
Scribe, in the middle of the fifth century B.C.E., and continuing
uninterruptedly until the time of Judah the Nasi or Patriarch
(called "Rabbi" *par excellence*), in the first quarter of the third
century C.E. It is within this time-area that Jesus appeared on the
scene of human events.[2] His dates are generally given as 2 B.C.E.
to 29 C.E.[3]

Therefore, whatever might be found in the Mishnah regarding
Jesus would be the most significant as historic evidence of his
existence, of the facts of his life and death, of the objective
validity of the New Testament and Patristic recital of events. It
would provide us with knowledge of the earliest Jewish attitudes
toward Jesus, of the roots whence later Jewish attitudes sprouted
up, of the initial reasons for Jewish refusal to accept the religion
concerning Jesus, of the basis for the cleavage which led to a
differentiation between Jews and Christians.

Chronologically, the second layer of rabbinic tradition is the
Gemara—which, added to the Mishnah, as an outgrowth of it,
comprises the Palestinian Talmud (*Yerushalmi*), whose completion is dated at about 425 C.E., when the school in Tiberias,
Palestine, finally came to a close,[4] and the Babylonian Talmud
(*Babli*), completed in Babylonia at the close of the fifth century C.E.,[5] Rabina II bar Huna, the latest sage quoted therein,
having died in 499 C.E., with finishing touches continuing into
the middle of the sixth century.[6]

Because of its later date the Gemara, in both developments of
the Talmud, does not possess the same importance as the Mishnah
in supplying evidence regarding Jesus. Even Judah the Nasi,
compiler of, and one of the latest to be mentioned in, the Mishnah, was born in 135 c.e.,[7] which is a relatively early date in
relation to the generation of Jesus.

Accordingly, in studying the record we must first differentiate
between that which is discernible in the times of the Mishnah and
that which we discover in the Gemara. The teachers and scholars
of the Mishnah period are known as Tannaim. Therefore, this
chapter is designated: The Tannaitic Period. The next chapter
will deal with the centuries of the Gemara; and, inasmuch as the
post-Tannaitic authorities are called Amoraim, that chapter is
titled: The Amoraic Period.

In this introductory explanation it should be stated, further,
that the Tannaitic period includes valid contemporary documents
in addition to the Mishnah. We have passages in the two Talmuds which are quotations of Tannaitic teachings, not found in
the Mishnah compiled by Judah the Nasi but taken from other
authentic Mishnah collections. This is called Baraitha.[8]

There also is the Tosefta,[9] a compilation of the teachings of the
Tannaim, similar to the Mishnah, and of the same time-area.[10]
Then there are the Midrashim, some Halachic (legislative), mostly
Haggadic (inspirational), exposition of Scripture; while the date
of composition of the Midrashim presents difficulties, we may at
least place the Mechilta, Sifra and Sifre in the Tannaitic period,[11]
while the later Midrashim belong in Chapter III.

This chronological division of the material recommends itself
from the standpoint of accuracy as superior to a procedure [12]
which would present the Talmud passages selected at random
from the wide range of centuries and arranged in the sequence of
the life of Jesus. In this chapter we shall attend only to the Tannaitic references to Jesus. In each instance, wherever possible, we
shall give the precise date of the conveyer of the fact or
spokesman of the opinion.

Even so, the question is often raised as to whether the rabbinic
teachings, not intended as history, have any historic value what-

ever. We may concur, though, in the estimate of Herford: "Neither Talmud nor Midrash was intended primarily to teach history; but from the manner of their origin and growth, they could hardly fail to show some traces of contemporary history."[13]

The important caution, when examining the record, is to make use of the well-established principles of literary and historical criticism, to discriminate between that which is factual and that which is legend, anecdote or flight of the imagination, between that which is hearsay and that which is first-hand, and, in the Talmud, between that which is Halachah—authoritative and direct—and that which is Haggadah—which must stand or fall on the prestige and experience of him who offers it.

Furthermore, it must be understood that in the analysis of a text which may or may not allude to Jesus the burden of proof is on him who seeks to make a positive identification. In other words, there must be convincing evidence that the reference *is* to Jesus.

Finally, in this preliminary setting up of procedure it remains but to state that to avoid confusion we shall consider first those allusions to Jesus which appear to be genuine and can be substantiated. Thereafter, we shall deal with those references which, at some time or other, have been identified with Jesus but which we shall demonstrate could *not* have referred to him, during the Tannaitic period. Then we shall take under advisement those sayings and teachings of the Tannaim which may be regarded as indirectly pertaining to the Jewish tradition as regards Jesus, even though his name is not mentioned.

## SECTION A

## AUTHENTIC REFERENCES TO JESUS

The Mishnah itself contains no direct reference to Jesus, nothing which can be proved beyond reasonable doubt.[1]

Nothing is to be found in the Tannaitic Midrashim; nothing, in fact, which might be regarded even as a possibility.

This leaves for consideration in the Mishnah time-area the Baraitha and the Tosefta. Here we discover five allusions where the weight of evidence favors positive identification.

### 1. BARAITHA—B.* SANHEDRIN 43a.

TEXT:—It has been taught (in a Baraitha): [2] On the eve of Passover [3] they hanged Yeshu.[4] And an announcer went out, in front of him, for forty days (saying): "He [5] is going to be stoned, because he practiced sorcery [6] and enticed [7] and led Israel astray. Anyone who knows anything in his favor, let him come and plead in his behalf." But, not having found anything in his favor, they hanged him on the eve of Passover.[3]

DISCUSSION:—This appears to be definite testimony in the early rabbinic data. It does not entirely exclude those who would argue the negative side, namely, that this does not truly refer to Jesus.[8] The passage is not found in the later (censored) editions of the Talmud and is restored from old manuscripts and early printed editions.

Yeshu is not an unusual name. On the contrary, we come upon it rather frequently, either in its fuller form as Yehoshua, which is rendered in English as Joshua, or in the shortened form, Yeshu. When transmitted through the Greek tongue, the name becomes *Jesus* in English—and we must bear in mind that a good part of the non-rabbinic tradition of Jesus reaches us through the medium of the Greek language.

How commonplace a name this was is indicated, for example,

* Abbreviations of references are explained on page 246.

22

by Flavius Josephus, the Holy Land historian of the first century of the Christian Era,[9] who records that among the twenty-eight high priests who held this responsible office during the one hundred and seven years from the days of Herod to the day when the Roman invader Titus destroyed the Temple and ravaged Jerusalem,[10] there were those who bore the names: Jesus son of Phabet; Jesus son of Damneus; Jesus son of Gamaliel.[11] Furthermore, Josephus writes of Jesus son of Sapphias, a general for Idumea [12] and Jesus son of Thebuthus,[13] a priest—of the same century. He expatiates upon the attempted treachery of a Jesus, "the captain of those robbers who were in the confines of Ptolemais." [14] The prevalence of the name Jesus in those times is confirmed by the archeological discoveries of our day in Palestine.[15] Therefore, the possibility of the Jesus named in the Talmud being someone other than Jesus of Nazareth, and identified as such only because of confusion, cannot be entirely dismissed.

While it is true that the Munich manuscript of the Talmud reads "Yeshu *the Nazarene*," nevertheless what is contained in only one manuscript is not as convincing evidence as when there is confirmation by at least a second witness.

There is nothing here of the charge against Jesus which, according to the Gospels, was the cause of his death. There, his crime is his reply to the high priest: "Hereafter shall ye see the Son of man sitting on the right hand of power, and coming in the clouds of heaven"; [16] this manner of reply the high priest pronounces blasphemy and his council judges it punishable by the death penalty. According to another New Testament version, Jesus is deemed guilty unto death because he had made himself the Son of God: "We have a law and by our law he ought to die, because he made himself the Son of God." [17] Yet another accusation against Jesus is indicated by the Gospels, that of the Roman authorities who hold him to be a rebel, one who pretended, or was thought, to be "King of the Jews." [18]

If the New Testament record is historically accurate it adds to the difficulty of accepting the passage under consideration, for it tells of three accusations against Jesus punishable by death —that of blasphemy, that of claiming to be Son of God and that

of assuming the role of King of the Jews—but not that of practicing sorcery nor of enticing and leading Israel astray, as stated
in this Baraitha.

The participation of the Romans is not mentioned in this
excerpt from Sanhedrin 43a either, nor the crucifixion. Furthermore, the penalty exacted is not made too clear; the announcer
proclaims that Yeshu is going to be stoned but the passage tells
that he was hanged. Finally, the precaution of delaying forty
days for the finding of favorable evidence is an entirely new
element, not found in the Christian tradition.

As against these negative arguments we place on the other side
of the scales the factors which, in our opinion, give value to this
passage.

(a) Yeshu is the name used elsewhere in the Tannaitic literature to refer to the New Testament Jesus.[19] It is a shortened
form for the older spelling, Yehoshua,[20] as Yose, for example,
is a later abbreviation of Yosef (Joseph);[21] hence, no slur is
necessarily intended by this spelling of the name.[22]

It may be argued that one would have difficulty in finding another instance of one named Yehoshua or Yeshua being called
Yeshu *invariably*; does this not prove intent to cast aspersion?
The obvious answer is that Jesus became known mainly through
the Greek form of his name, *Jesu*, and that it would be natural
to select that variation of his Hebrew name which bore the
closest resemblance to the name as commonly spoken: hence,
Yeshu.

The second part of the name as given in the Munich manuscript—*Hanotzri*—is translated "the Nazarene." What is the origin
of this designation? It might refer to *netzer*, as in Isaiah 11:1, to
mean "a branch," used in Christian tradition with a messianic
connotation. It might allude to Jesus as the source of the Nazarene sect. It might be a derivation from *noter*, which would
describe those who *keep* the (new) Law of Jesus.[23] It might
mean, as is generally understood, "of Nazareth." Elsewhere in
the Talmud there is no mention of the town of Nazareth; its
earliest appearance in Hebrew literature is about the year 900;
further, there is a philological problem in seeing *Notzri* as re-

ferring to a resident of *Natzereth* (Nazareth); nevertheless, there may easily have been another pronunciation of the name of the town [24]—since Kefar Sechanya was known also as Kefar Sichnin —and there is not sufficient reason to discard this probable meaning of *Hanotzri*.

At this stage of our analysis the important point is that *Yeshu* in this Baraitha *could* refer to Jesus of Nazareth.

(b) The exaction of the death penalty on the eve of Passover is strong verification that Jesus, the Christ of Christianity, is meant. The Florence manuscript of the Babylonian Talmud, whose date is as early as 1176, adds that it was also the eve of the Sabbath. This, too, agrees with the Gospel documents.[25]

The question remains, how to reconcile the discrepancy between the statement of the Gospel according to John [26] that Jesus was crucified on the eve of Passover, which precedes the day, with the recital of the Synoptic Gospels [27]—Matthew, Mark, Luke—which make it appear that he was executed on the first day of Passover. (Both accounts do agree that it was also the eve which begins the Sabbath day.) This problem has been extensively debated. An entire volume, in fact, has been written upon it [28] and nearly everyone who seeks to elucidate the details of the life of Jesus must deal with it. It involves the further inquiry as to whether the Last Supper was indeed a Passover meal, also as to the manner of observing the Passover festival in those days; such inquiry has led certain scholars to see in the story of the Synoptic Gospels a sequence of events which would likewise indicate crucifixion on the eve of Passover. In our analysis here of the Tannaitic record concerning Jesus it is but necessary to comment that the Sanhedrin 43a passage of the Babylonian Talmud, if it possesses historic value, does lend support to the tradition that it was the eve of Passover (Nissan 14), as well as Sabbath eve, when the penalty of death was exacted.[29]

(c) Now, what of the charges brought against Jesus?

First let us examine those given in the New Testament. What of the claim to be "the Christ, the Son of the Blessed"? [30] What of the assertion, "Ye shall see the Son of man sitting on the right hand of power, and coming in the clouds of heaven"? [31] *Is* this blasphemy, calling for the death penalty?

Investigation of the Jewish law, as taught in the Mishnah,[32] shows that it is not. One is not guilty of a capital crime of blasphemy unless he has spoken the *name* of God blasphemously and has seduced others to practice idolatry. While it is true that the Mishnah law, as we now have it, was not compiled in definitive form until the early part of the third century,[33] and, further, that the court which tried Jesus was composed mainly of Sadducees [34] (not the Pharisees whose teaching resulted in the Mishnah), nevertheless there is no positive evidence that the replies of Jesus rendered him guilty of death, even according to the circumstances of his day.[35] On the contrary, the assumption of the role of Messiahship was not blasphemous; [36] there were quite a few in that century [37] who sought to become Messiahs, without incurring the death penalty, and in 132 c.e. Bar Kochba assumed this role with the blessing of Akiba, the leading rabbi of that generation.[38]

Use of the phrase, "Son of the Blessed" or "Son of God," was no capital crime, either; no, not in Mishnah nor in pre-Mishnah law; it is an expression found often in apocalyptic literature.[39] The reference to sitting at the right hand of *Power* is not greatly different from King David's allusion to himself as sitting at the right hand of God; [40] at all events, it is nowhere indicated as blasphemy.

The credible offense which led to the crucifixion by the Romans is revealed in the question put by Pontius Pilate, the Roman Procurator, "Art thou the King of the Jews?" [41] and in the superscription on the cross, "King of the Jews," [42] which described the reason for the penalty. Modern analysis, historical and literary, of the New Testament reconstructs many of the details of the trial and crucifixion: out of it comes the well-founded opinion, with considerable agreement among the scholars, that Jesus was brought to trial as a political offender against Rome and punished as such, in accordance with Roman practice, by order of Pontius Pilate.[43]

Now we are ready to seek an understanding of the charges

against Jesus as preserved in the Jewish tradition. In this text, Sanhedrin 43a, he is accused of practicing sorcery and of enticing and leading Israel astray.

That the Jewish people of that time regarded Jesus as a sorcerer is reflected in the Synoptic Gospels [44] and in the report of Justin Martyr [45] who wrote in the middle of the second century. Yet, the practice of sorcery or magic was not uncommon in those days.[46] It is, in fact, told in the Talmud: "Into the Sanhedrin are brought none other than those wise and acquainted with magic." [47] Rashi in his interpretative comment, many centuries later, explained the requisite: it was in order that the members of the Sanhedrin should be capable of exposing magicians and sorcerers.

Does not this comment point up the distinction which explains the accusation of sorcery? When done within the scope of one's own religion, acts of healing and magic are miraculous; when done outside the boundaries of the religion in which one believes, they are sorcery. This, therefore, was but another way of saying that Judaism in Tannaitic times did not accept the religion based on Jesus. The very counterpart is given from the Christian standpoint in Chapter 13 of Acts which states that Paul (Saul) and Barnabas, being sent forth by the Holy Ghost, had gone unto Paphos, where "they found a certain sorcerer, a false prophet, a Jew, whose name was Bar-jesus." [48]

Sorcery, so called, was not punishable by stoning *and* hanging, according to Jewish law. We read in the Mishnah: " 'All who are stoned are hanged,' R. Eliezer taught; but the Sages say: [49] 'One is not hanged (as well as stoned) unless he is a blasphemer and indulges in false worship.' " [50] We have already given attention to the reasons why Jesus could not be regarded a blasphemer. That he did not indulge in false worship is made clear in the Sermon on the Mount wherein he proclaims: "Think not that I came to destroy the Law or the Prophets: I came not to destroy but to fulfil," [51] and in his confession that the first of all the commandments is, "Hear, O Israel, the Lord our God, the Lord is one: and thou shalt love the Lord thy God with all thy heart and with all thy soul." [52]

What now remains is the charge that he enticed and led Israel astray. What does this mean? Let us survey the literature of the first and second centuries of the Christian Era and discover how the terms "entice" and "lead astray," or their equivalent, were used.

In the New Testament, Matthew tells that "many false prophets shall rise, and shall deceive many," [53] elaborating as follows: "For there shall arise false Christs, and false prophets, and shall shew great signs and wonders; insomuch that, if it were possible, they shall deceive the very elect." [54]

In describing the cause of the Roman attacks upon Jerusalem, Josephus relates that "these impostors and deceivers persuaded the multitude to follow them into the wilderness, and pretended that they would exhibit manifest wonders and signs that should be performed by the providence of God. And many that were prevailed on by them suffered the punishment of their folly: for Felix (the Roman Procurator) brought them back, and then punished them." [55] Even more specific is Josephus' reference to such men "as deceived and deluded the people under pretence of divine inspiration, but were for procuring innovations and changes in the Government; and these prevailed with the multitude to act like madmen, and went before them into the wilderness, as pretending that God would there shew them the signals of liberty. But Felix thought this procedure was to be the beginning of a revolt; so he sent some horsemen and footmen both armed, who destroyed a great number of them." [56]

Is there not a striking parallel between some, though not all, aspects of these references and the way a non-Christian might regard the role of Jesus? He had come upon the scene of history as a savior; to many it meant a savior from the yoke of Rome. He had not succeeded in bringing the salvation which was expected. By the power of Rome he had been put to death, even as in the following generation the Roman authority—Felix this time, like Pilate previously, destroyed those who seemed to be beginning a revolt, "under pretence of divine inspiration." As these who had failed against Felix are called "deceivers and deluders," so, in retrospect, the people who were disillusioned with Jesus might have called him "one who led Israel astray." [57] It was, indeed, when Jesus' earthly career had ended on the cross that, according to the account in Matthew, the chief priests and Pharisees made mention of him as "that deceiver." [58]

In retrospect, also, the adherents of Judaism saw a new religion arise, built upon the person of Jesus. To them it appeared to be "false worship." Therefore, they appiled to Jesus the charge "enticer." The same Hebrew word, *massith*,[59] is used here as in Deuteronomy 13:7-12 which tells that if one as close to you as your own brother or wife or child "entice thee secretly, saying, Let us go and serve other gods, which thou hast not known, thou, nor thy fathers . . . Thou shalt not consent unto him, nor hearken unto him"; such a one must be stoned.

But, so far as we know, Jesus did not in his lifetime act as an enticer in the sense of persuading alien forms of worship, saying, "Let us go and serve other gods." This was indicated in our mention above of the Jewishness of Jesus.[60] Therefore, we must assume that this Baraitha, Sanhedrin 43a, of whose date we know only that it originated prior to 220 C.E., was written at a time when early Christianity had already come to regard Jesus as a Person in the Divinity, in the concept of either Duality or Trinity. To teachers of Judaism it appeared to be the worship of *gods.*

Therefore, in retrospect Jesus was held responsible for the worship of himself, perhaps also for certain disapproved forms of worship which had arisen. From this resulted the legend that, in accordance with the Tannaitic law regarding one who indulges in false worship,[61] Jesus went forth to be stoned and, afterwards, hanged.[62]

This legend was intended, in all likelihood, to strengthen adherence to Judaism, to the service of One God, to the Jewish way of life and worship. As such, this Talmud text concerning Jesus possesses value. It reveals something of the relationship between Judaism and Christianity in the early period. It discloses what Jewish teachers could not accept in Christian theology. It shows where the emphasis was placed in Judaism of the first two centuries of the Christian Era. It indicates the early Jewish attitude regarding Jesus. While it is of no help one way or the other in the question of the historicity of Jesus, it does support certain details in the Gospel account regarding him.

This Tannaitic record is not historic, in an exact sense. It is rather historic tradition. The same, however, may be said of a considerable part of the Christian record, in the New Testament, in the Apocryphal New Testament, and in the works of the Church Fathers.

Typical of modern Christian scholarship is the summation of M. S. Enslin, in *Christian Beginnings:* "Contrary to many popular notions, the new religion produced its book; the book did not produce the religion. Again, these writings which eventually came to be called the New Testament, were written for purely practical purposes: to meet specific needs felt in those days. They were not prepared to edify or to instruct subsequent generations which might desire historical insights into the past. Hence many points about which we would appreciate information are glossed over or omitted entirely." [63]

One thing more remains to be noticed regarding this Tannaitic passage under consideration. Why was it originally included?

We find it introduced into the discussion relating to the introductory Mishnah law that if one is found guilty of an offense, and about to be stoned for it, the herald precedes the convicted person and announces the nature of the wrongdoing; he names the witnesses; he invites anyone whosoever who knows anything in favor of the condemned to come forth and state it.[64] In connection with this procedure the Baraitha regarding Yeshu is inserted, to tell that in his case the herald proclaimed his announcement for forty days, that the execution of the sentence was delayed forty days to allow the fullest time for favorable evidence to come to light. All else in the passage is incidental to this point. There is implied a hope that something favorable *would* turn up.

Nothing of this nature is mentioned in the Gospels. Is this, then, altogether fiction? Various suggestions have been offered as to how the idea of a period of forty days may have come to the mind of the author of the passage.[65] Yet it need not be entirely fictitious. Inasmuch as the New Testament, as indicated above, was not written as a book of history, it is conceivable that some events may have taken place which are not there recorded. If the New Testament is *Christian tradition*, this item is *Jewish tradition*. As the Gospels [66] tell of hurry and eagerness on the part of the Jewish priests and scribes to deliver Jesus to the Roman authorities for trial and punishment, so this Baraitha, as Jewish tradition, tells of deliberateness, of extreme caution, that there be no miscarriage of justice. Each of the two traditions had its purpose, a purpose deeply rooted in the religion itself.

## 2. BARAITHA—B. SANHEDRIN 43a (*bottom*)

TEXT:—Our rabbis taught (in a Baraitha): Yeshu had five disciples —Mattai, Nakkai, Netzer, Buni, and Todah.

DISCUSSION:—In the Talmud, this immediately follows the preceding Baraitha.[1] A long explanation of these five names is then given by the Amoraim. Being of a later date, the longer passage will be presented in Chapter III.[2]

Is there value in this one sentence? After all, it is a Baraitha. It cannot be later than just beyond the second century.

Why only five disciples instead of twelve? [3] The Gospels may have selected twelve as the arbitrary number to correspond to the Twelve Tribes of Israel, as, in one place, Luke [4] mentions the appointment of seventy disciples, which would correspond to the traditional seventy nations.[5] Yet, as Klausner suggests,[6] Jesus may have deliberately chosen for disciples a number to correspond to the Twelve Tribes, in which case it would be historically true that the disciples were twelve in number. The number twelve may have been chosen by Jesus or in retrospect by his biographers to teach that, as the Messiah, he would gather together the Twelve Tribes—for this thought is present in Matthew 19:28 and Luke 22:30. Still, he *may* have had only five disciples.

It is to be observed that there are differences, though minor ones, in the four listings [3] of the disciples. Further, of the twelve, only with regard to five (the brothers, Simon Peter and Andrew; James and John, sons of Zebedee; Matthew or Levi son of Alphaeus) are the specific circumstances given depicting their selection.[7]

Origen, writing in the third century, mentions ten or eleven apostles.[8] Thus, in *Christian Beginnings*, Enslin expresses doubt that Jesus formally called twelve men upon whom to confer especial powers, the greater probability being "that in the course of time some of his hearers came into more intimate fellowship." [9] It is quite possible that Jesus had more than five disciples but that only five were known to the anonymous author of the Baraitha. At the same time, when we read in the Talmud of five disciples of Yohanan ben Zakkai [10] and five students of Akiba ordained by Yehudah ben Baba,[11] we become suspicious of a select number of *five*.[12] Still, this observation does not preclude the possibility that only five happened to have been known in a particular locale by a particular rabbi.

Who are these five? Herford [13] believes that what is meant is, simply, five followers of Jesus, namely, five Christians, but this seems unlikely, as will be shown when the later addition to the Baraitha is discussed.[2] There appears to be a valid connection between Mattai and Matthiah *or* Matthew, Todah and Thaddeus; and conjecture identifies Buni as John *or* Nicodemus, Nakkai as Luke, Netzer as Andrew.[14]

Still another theory suggests that each of the five words may be a description of Jesus—Netzer, the Nazarene; Nakkai, the innocent one; etc.[2] However, this one sentence, when detached from that which follows, would not support such a view; later,[2] of course, new meanings were easily put into these names.

In any event, we have here an early passage naming Jesus and his five disciples.[15]

### 3. TOSEFTA—HULLIN II, 22, 23

(supported by P. Shabbath 14d; P. Abodah Zarah 40d, 41a; B. Abodah Zarah 27b)

TEXT:—It happened with R. Elazar ben Damah,[1] whom a serpent bit, that Jacob, a man of Kefar Soma,[2] came to heal him in the name of Yeshua ben Pantera; but R. Ishmael did not let him. He said, "You are not permitted, Ben Damah." He [3] answered, "I will bring you proof [4] that he may heal me." But he had no opportunity to bring proof, for he died. (Whereupon) R. Ishmael said, "Happy art thou, Ben Damah, for you have gone in peace [5] and you have not broken down the fence of the Sages; since everyone who breaks down the fence of the Sages, to him punishment will ultimately come, as it is in Scripture: 'Whoso breaketh through a fence, a serpent shall bite him.' " [6]

DISCUSSION:—The text P. Shabbath 14d is practically the same. It adds: "The serpent bit him, solely in order that a serpent might not bite him in the future. And what could he [7] have said? 'Which, if a man do, he shall live [8] by them.' " [9] A cognate passage follows, but it belongs to the Amoraic period.[10]

The text in P. Abodah Zarah 40d, 41a is the same. It merely adds, "He said, 'We will speak to you in the name of Yeshu ben Pandera,' " after the reading, "he came to heal him."

The Babylonian Talmud version of the incident (B. Abodah Zarah 27b) does not actually include the mention of Jesus; but the words, "in the name of Yeshu ben Pandera," are contained in the repetition of this passage in the post-Tannaitic Midrash, Koheleth Rabbah on 1:8.[11] Strictly, therefore, the account in the Babylonian Talmud cannot be considered a germane allusion, although the circumstantial evidence points to a follower of Jesus.

Now then, this reference, whose original presentation in all probability is the one found in the Tosefta (the text given above), tells of an incident in the life of Elazar ben Damah. Rabbi Ishmael, who protested the attempted healing in the name of Yeshua ben Pantera, is R. Ishmael ben Elisha.[12] A contemporary of R. Akiba, he lived in the first half of the second century C.E. and, in his boyhood years, had been released from captivity in Rome by R. Joshua ben Hananiah. R. Elazar ben Damah (according to the Babylonian Talmud version of the story) [13] was his nephew.

The reference to R. Ishmael gives the clue to dating the incident. But it is not too specific a clue. All we know is that if R. Ishmael was a boy at the time of the 70 C.E. conquest by Rome, and this happening is between him and an adult nephew, he must then have been along in years. Herford sets the date at 130 C.E. and does so because R. Ishmael went that year to the rabbinic assembly in Usha, in Galilee, and Herford surmises that in Galilee he would be likely to meet a disciple of Jesus.[14] Chwolson sets the date at 116 C.E.[15] This latter date is more probable, possibly an even earlier one (though no earlier than 90), as will be shown in the next Tannaitic passage to be analyzed in this section, where there will be further discussion on the ascertaining of dates.[16]

Tentatively accepting this earlier date, we now can place in the first part of the second century the practice of healing in the name of Jesus. It is significant that there is a difference of opinion between two Tannaim as to whether this is permissible. We learn from the incident two things at least: first, that in Jewish circles Jesus was known in particular as one who, having performed magic in his lifetime,[17] now, a generation or two later, could heal through one's use of this name;[18] secondly, that at this time Jesus had not been completely outlawed, that there still was a temptation for a nephew of the great Rabbi Ishmael to try to be healed in the name of Jesus, although Ishmael strongly condemned this impulse.

That healing was performed by Jesus is vouched for in the Gospels.

We read, for example, in the Gospel according to Mark: "And they bring unto him one that was deaf, and had an impediment in his speech; and they beseech him to put his hand upon him. And he took him aside from the multitude, and put his fingers into his ears, and he spit, and touched his tongue; And looking up to heaven, he sighed, and saith unto him, Ephphatha, that is, be opened. And straightway his ears were opened, and the string of his tongue was loosed, and he spake plain."[19]

In the following chapter we read: "And he took the blind man by the hand, and led him out of the town; and when he had spit on his eyes, and put his hands upon him, he asked him if he saw aught. And he looked up, and said, I see men as trees, walking. After that he put his hands again upon his eyes, and made him look up: and he was restored, and saw every man clearly."[20]

Similarly, the Gospel according to John tells of Jesus curing a man blind from his birth: "He spat on the ground, and made clay of the spittle, and he anointed the eyes of the blind man with the clay, And said unto him, Go, wash in the pool of Siloam . . . He went his way therefore, and washed, and came seeing." [21]

The charge against Jesus in the Baraitha which told of his execution,[22]—"he practiced sorcery"—could logically refer to such practices as here quoted from the New Testament. Thus, the value of that Baraitha is reinforced and this particular phase of the Gospel record is supported. In addition, the Tosefta now being analyzed gains in validity, for it becomes understandable that the followers of Jesus would attempt to perform cures in his name.

Our Tosefta passage under consideration brings to notice the appellation of Jesus: Yeshua (or Yeshu, in abbreviated form) ben Pantera. This name definitely refers to Jesus, although the explanation of its origin is none too certain.

There are variant spellings of Pantera—Pantira, Pandera, Pantiri, Panteri.[23] It is said to be the surname of the father of Jesus of Nazareth; or, it may be the family name of Mary the mother. We shall examine several of the theories concerning the name and determine upon the most likely one.

Herford [24] calls attention to Strauss' suggestion that it may be the Greek word *pentheros*,[25] which means "son-in-law." We must agree with Herford that there is no point to this guess.

He mentions another theory,[24] namely, that "Pandera" might be a garbling of the Greek *parthenos*,[26] "virgin," and allude to the allegation of a virgin birth. Although Klausner [27] accepts this as the most probable explanation, we agree with Herford and others [28] that the Greek word could easily have been transliterated accurately into Hebrew. While it is true that words often do become distorted when imported from one language into another, and one could cite many instances of its happening to Greek words when transmitted into Hebrew, nevertheless, the recognized authority on the linguistic relations between Greek and Hebrew—Samuel Krauss in *Lehnwörter* [29]—states that, whatever other letters of the alphabet may become garbled in the process of transliteration, the Greek *r* sound retains the *r* sound in

Hebrew,[30] the Greek *n* sound retains the *n* sound in Hebrew;[31] not a single variation in this regard could Krauss find in the entire field of rabbinical loan-words. In that case, how can one see *Pandera* as a Hebrew version of *parthenos*?[32]

Finding no answer to the puzzle, the best Herford can conclude is that the designation, Pandera, is a relic "of ancient Jewish mockery against Jesus, the clue to whose meaning is now lost."[33] This is a bold and dangerous assertion, particularly when no substantiation is cited. Certainly, in this Tosefta selection, no mockery is intended or implied.[34] Yes, Eusebius of Caesarea and Epiphanius of Constantia had heard derogatory remarks on the name; but these are relatively late sources, the former having died in 339 and the latter in 403—by which time much has changed in the relations between Christianity and Judaism.[34] Strack[35] agrees with Zahn that there is no historic value in these comments of Eusebius and Epiphanius. That later the name may have been used derisively is not now the question. The history of languages teaches that words not infrequently change their meaning and flavor over the centuries. What we desire to know is the derivation of Yeshu ben Pandera as the name of Jesus, as it is used so casually in this early Talmudic reference.

Still another theory is the guess that there might be some relationship to Pandarus in the *Iliad*, of Greek mythology,[36] but it is only a guess, for there is nothing in the story of Pandarus to establish a comparison to Jesus other than (as the spokesman of the theory maintains) that Jesus broke, by his acts, the truce with Rome, as, in the *Iliad*, Pandarus broke the armistice.

There is also the assumption[37] that Pandera refers to a Roman soldier in Judea, named Panthera, who became the extra-marital father of Jesus. This is mentioned by Origen[38] in c. 248 c.e., who quotes it from the pagan philosopher Celsus (c. 178 c.e.), who claims that he heard it from a Jew.

We know practically nothing of Celsus excepting what Origen quotes in answering him; through this medium we learn that Celsus despised Christianity and Judaism too.[39] How cunning, therefore, it would be for him to manufacture a fictitious spokesman of one religion, which he held in no high regard, wherewith to strike a blow at the other contemporary religion which he argued was unworthy.

Even so, Origen turns the attack to the defense by claiming that Celsus' report of identifying the father of Jesus as a Roman soldier, Panthera, does at least indicate "that it was not by Joseph that the Virgin conceived Jesus"—that Celsus thus unwittingly lends support to the doctrine of the miraculous conception by the Holy Spirit. We must realize that in these early religious disputations the patterned discussions probably never took place, the views attributed to so-called spokesmen of the "other religion" are inaccurately reported, the spokesmen are fictional devices, and we must be on guard against blind acceptance in our search for truth.[40] Herford [41] and Klausner [42] and others definitely reject this theory that Pandera refers to a Roman soldier who was a paramour of Mary.

Even Laible, who ignores few opportunities to cast aspersions upon the Jewish tradition, concludes a lengthy discussion with a negative 'vote on this interpretation.[43] His own preference is to take the Greek word [44] in its literal meaning, "panther." As a panther is promiscuous, so he believes it was intended to imply sensuality on the part of Mary.[45] However, this opinion has not held up. This and similar guesses seem far-fetched.[46]

The last two opinions given above do have some relevancy to the acceptable solution to this problem.

In our search for a probable explanation we are helped by the discovery of a tombstone at Bingerbrück, Germany (now on display in the Museum at Kreuznach), which has inscribed on it: "Tiberius Julius Abdes Pantera, an archer, native of Sidon, Phoenicia, who in 9 C.E. was transferred to service in Germany." [47] This is strong evidence that Pantera is an actual name, used in the Palestine area during the time of Jesus. A. Deissmann has shown, in fact, that the name Pantera occurs several times in Latin inscriptions of the period from the first to the third centuries of the Christian Era.[48] He was led to the conclusion: "Taken in conjunction with the other inscriptions, this epitaph from the Ger-

man frontier shows with absolute certainty that Panthera was not
an invention of Jewish scoffers, but a widespread name among the
ancients." [47]

It is a known fact that Greek personal names are identical frequently with those that denote animals. There is nothing unusual,
then, in one having the name which means "panther," any more
than—by analogy—someone in our own day possessing the name
Wolf or Fox. There is no need whatever to apply to the bearer of
the name the qualities of the animal. Even if there were originally
some such association, the name Panthera could have been chosen
because of the swiftness or the power of the panther. Moreover,
the fact that Roman soldiers, among others, chanced to have that
name is no reason for jumping to the conclusion that Mary had
a Roman soldier as a paramour.[49]

Would a Greek name be used by a Jewish family? Study of the
Hellenic influence during the three centuries before the Christian
Era gives a clear, affirmative answer.[50] Is there in the Jewish
record a name similar in form to Ben Panthera? There is. Josephus
writes of the high priest, Simon Cantheras, and his son Elioneus,
a high priest. One would expect the son to be called Bar Simon;
instead, he is Elionius bar (son of) Cantheras [51]—like Yeshu ben
Pantera, the name of Jesus.

How this name came into the ancestry of Jesus has stimulated
interesting speculation, as in Schonfield's *According to the
Hebrews*.[52] Of immediate significance in our present investigation
is the fact that the Church Fathers, too, regarded it as a family
name. Unsupported, their statements would not have particular
cogency. On the basis, though, of what already has been ascertained it is noteworthy that Origen himself is credited with the
tradition that Panther was the appellation of James (Jacob), the
father of Joseph, the father of Jesus.[53]

In the Christian document, *The Teaching of Jacob*, written in
Greek in 634 c.e., a Jewish teacher of the Law at Tiberias is
quoted as giving the following genealogy of Jesus: his mother
Mary is the daughter of Joakim, who is the son of Panther, a
brother of Melchi, of the seed of Nathan, the son of David.[54]
Thus, if Joseph is not to be regarded as the father, this polemic

writing demonstrates Jesus' Davidic descent through Mary; our notice is attracted particularly to the name Panther in the list of ancestry. So, too, Andrew of Crete,[55] John of Damascus,[56] Epiphanius the Monk,[57] and the author of *Andronicus of Constantinople's Dialogue Against the Jews*,[58] name Panther as an ancestor of Jesus.

Mention in this type of literature, we must remember, is only of secondary value and is cited as such. However, use of the name Panther in respect to Jesus' lineage in both Christian and Jewish tradition strengthens this theory of the origin of Ben Pantera.

Finally, in answer to a possible objection that Jewish custom identifies a son by the name of his father but not his grandfather, it is to be observed that the Talmud concedes that the grandfather's name could be used in the same way as a father's name, for it teaches that grandchildren are like unto children.[59]

Thus in a realm of inquiry where we must deal with probabilities we arrive at the conclusion which seems most likely, namely, that Yeshu ben Pantera was given simply as a family name of Jesus in its earliest mention in the Talmud.

## 4. BARAITHA—B. ABODAH ZARAH 16b, 17a
### TOSEFTA—HULLIN II, 24

TEXT *(B. Abodah Zarah 16b, 17a)*:—Our rabbis teach (in a Baraitha): When R. Eliezer was arrested for *Minuth*, they brought him up to the tribunal for judgment. The court said to him, "Does an elder [1] such as you occupy himself with such useless [2] matters?" He answered: "I rely on the Judge." [3] The court thought he said it concerning him, whereas he said it with reference to his Father Who is in Heaven. He (the court) said to him, "Since you have faith in me—*dimissus*—you are released."

When he returned home, his disciples came in to comfort him, but he would not accept their solace. R. Akiba said to him, "Rabbi, will you permit me to say a word of what you have taught me?" He replied, "Say (it)." Said he [4] to him, "Rabbi, perhaps *Minuth* has come to hand and has pleased you; and on account of that, you were arrested." He replied, "Akiba, you reminded me! Once, I was walking on the upper street [5] of Sepphoris and found one of the disciples of Yeshu the Nazarene, by the name Jacob, a man of Kefar Sechanya. He said to me, 'It is written in your Torah: [6] "Thou shalt not bring the hire of a harlot, etc." How about making with it a privy for the high priest?' [7] But I did not answer him at all.[8] He told me, 'Thus did Yeshu the Nazarene teach me: "For of the hire of a harlot hath she gathered them, And unto the hire of a harlot shall they return"; [9] from the place of filth they come, and unto the place of filth they shall go.' And the utterance [10] pleased me. On account of this, I was arrested for *Minuth*. And I transgressed against what is written in the Torah: [11] 'Remove thy way far from her'—this is *Minuth*; 'and come not nigh the door of her house'—this is the government authority." [12]

TEXT *(T. Hullin II, 24):*—It happened that R. Eliezer was arrested for words of *Minuth* and they brought him to the tribunal for judgment. The court said to him, "Does an elder such as you occupy himself with such matters?" He answered: "I rely on the Judge." The court thought R. Eliezer said it only concerning him, whereas he meant it only in reference to his Father Who is in Heaven. He (the court) said to him, "Since you have faith in me, so I (regard you) too. I say, is it possible that these elders have gone astray through these words? [13] *Dimissus*—you are released." When he was released from the tribunal he was troubled that he had been arrested for the words of *Minuth*. His disciples came in to comfort him but he would not accept (it). R. Akiba entered and said to him, "Rabbi, may I say something to you? Perhaps you will not be distressed." He replied, "Say (it)." He said to him, "Perhaps one of the *Minin* said to you a word of *Minuth* and it pleased you." He replied, "By heaven, you reminded me! Once I was walking in a street of Sepphoris, found Jacob a man of Kefar Sichnin,[14] and he said to me a word of *Minuth* in the name Yeshu ben Pantiri, and it pleased me. And I was arrested for words of *Minuth*, because I transgressed words of Torah: [15] 'Remove thy way far from her, and come not nigh to the door of her house'; 'for she hath cast down many wounded.' " [16] It was a saying of R. Eliezer: "Ever let a man flee from what is hateful, and from what seems hateful."

DISCUSSION:—The story is repeated in Midrash Koheleth Rabbah on Ecclesiastes 1:8 and in Yalkut Shimeoni on Micah 1 and Proverbs 5:8, but inasmuch as these writings are of the post-Tannaitic period, they need not be considered here, nor do they add anything important.

In the two Tannaitic texts, translated above, there seem to be definite references to Jesus,[17] of fairly early date. R. Eliezer ben Hyrcanus, mentioned in the Mishnah some 320 times simply as R. Eliezer,[18] was a disciple of Yohanan ben Zakkai who was eminent at the time of the destruction of the Temple (70 C.E.).[19]

Beyond this one clear fact, we run into a number of problems in the interpretation of the incident. Is it a true happening or is it entirely fictitious? Edersheim [20] and M. Friedlander [21] do not regard it as historical, Zeitlin [22] disclaims it as Talmudic evidence of the historicity of Jesus; but Laible,[23] Herford,[24] Strack [25] and Klausner [26] do not think there is sufficient reason to doubt the historic validity of the passage. Is Jacob, the *Min* of Kefar Sechanya (or Sichnin), a disciple of Jesus, the same person as the previously mentioned [27] Jacob of Kefar Soma, who healed in the name of Jesus? Is the reference to an actual disciple of Jesus? Which one? Can we determine the year of the ill-fated conversation with Jacob?

This evidence of Jesus in the Talmud has been ingeniously reconstructed and interpreted by Joseph Klausner in *Jesus of Nazareth*.[26] Differing from others who have studied the passages and have believed that the two men named Jacob were the same, that the event took place at about 110 C.E., and that Jacob, therefore, was not an actual disciple of Jesus but rather an expounder of Jesus' teaching [27]—Klausner dates the incident at about 60 C.E., claiming that these two who were named Jacob came from two different cities and were two distinct persons, living at different times (for Jacob is a common Jewish name), and that the Jacob who talked with R. Eliezer was indeed a disciple of Jesus, none other than James (the Greek form for Jacob), called the "brother" of Jesus.[28]

The dating of this conversation between R. Eliezer and Jacob of Kefar Sechanya at about 60 c.e. establishes a Talmudic reference to Jesus that antedates the earliest Gospel record of the New Testament—which is placed by Klausner at 66 to 68 c.e.[29] and by a middle-of-the-road Christian authority at 70 to 85 c.e., with probability favoring the earlier date.[30] This Talmud passage would be, therefore, of tremendous significance were it not for the fact that serious flaws are to be discerned in Klausner's argument, flaws which are spotlighted in S. Zeitlin's analysis of "Jesus in the Early Tannaitic Literature." [31]

The criticism indicates that the Tosefta version (which is as early as the Baraitha, and could be earlier) reads "*in the name* of Jesus" and therefore does not connote a direct teaching from Jesus in person. It indicates further that Agrippa II was called "King" even after he lost the Jewish territories in 85 c.e. and that R. Eliezer could have discussed religious questions with King Agrippa, as reported in B. Sukkah 27a, as late as the year 95 or 96. Therefore Eliezer need not have been born as early as Klausner thinks.

Still further, Emperor Trajan persecuted the Christians in 109,[32] when R. Eliezer could have been arrested; that Jacob of Kefar Sechanya is the same as Jacob of Kefar Soma who sought to cure the nephew of Ishmael in 116 c.e., for the two incidents are related together in the Tosefta; and in the Babylonian Talmud version of the curing of Elazar ben Damah the deed is attributed to Jacob the Min of Kefar Sechanya (as a variant of Kefar Soma); [33] that R. Eliezer had to be reminded that a *teaching* of Jacob the *Min* had pleased him and not that he had *met* Jacob.

Therefore the meeting need not have been distant from the time of the arrest; and, especially, it shows that R. Eliezer need not have been a very old man at the time of his arrest, since the Hebrew word *zaken* is regularly used to mean "an elder," to signify a great scholar or leader, for in the story repeated in the Midrash the phrase employed reads, "a great man such as you." [34]

H. P. Chajes [35] suggests 95 c.e. as the probable date. On what grounds would one choose the year 95 in preference to 110? History relates that Domitian, second son of Vespasian, having become emperor in the year 79, was particularly unfriendly to scholars: he muzzled Juvenal, Pliny, Tacitus; he would not accept even diplomatic Josephus into his good graces. It was necessary for the Patriarch himself, Gamaliel II, and his leading scholars to travel to Rome to try to prevent the Roman emperor from persevering in a plan fraught with calamity; this was probably in the year 95.[36] But fate intervened. In September of 96 Domitian was succeeded by Nerva, a friendly emperor. His reign lasted only sixteen months; yet, in this brief period he brightened the outlook for the Jews in Palestine as well as in Rome.[37]

There is the possibility, therefore, that R. Eliezer may have been arrested by Domitian in 95 and set free the following year during the interlude of a friendly regime. His release may have come entirely on the merits of his case or through the intervention of his friends.

However, 109 (or 110) is the date most generally accepted. For several reasons it seems to be the probable one.

We read in history that Trajan, the Roman emperor of that time, promised to lend his support to rebuild the Temple. Word of this stirred joy in the hearts of the Jews. It produced consternation among the Jewish Christians who, having found their Messiah, required no Temple. The diametrically opposed reactions created the wedge between the Jews who still looked for the Messiah and those who believed Jesus to have been the Messiah. Heretofore, it had been difficult to distinguish between the two but now they moved apart,[37] even as some twenty-five years later the Bar Kochba attempt to throw off the yoke of Rome widened the cleavage.

Trajan, although he did not fulfill his promise to rebuild the Temple, was displeased with the attitude of the Jewish Christians and persecuted them in the year 109. Simeon, Bishop of Jerusalem, was put to death, according to the account given by Eusebius. Especially significant is the *Epistle* (X, 96) of Pliny the Younger (between the years 110 and 112) which preserves for us an actual, contemporary report wherein Pliny communicates to Trajan an official notice of the existence and conduct of the Christian community.

It is likely that in the Roman round-up of those suspected of being Jewish Christians, R. Eliezer, having been placed under the ban by R. Gamaliel II and deprived of the companionship of his colleagues and thus compelled by necessity to hold converse with sectarians, was arrested with the others. Then, found innocent, he was released. The Talmud relates that toward the close of his life his disciples and colleagues returned to him [38]—Rabbi Akiba among them. It was Akiba who helped Eliezer remember that it was the contact with Jacob the *Min* that had led him into humiliating trouble.

That the teaching, here quoted, is not found in the New Testament should not be disturbing, for we are informed by the ancient philosopher Celsus that there are, indeed, things about Jesus not mentioned there.[39] This rabbinic passage attests that not all of Jesus' teachings are included in the New Testament, but rather that certain ones, for certain reasons, were selected. There are those who believe that this one may be a quotation from the lost Gospel according to Hebrews.[40]

This text indicates, morever, the Pharisaic side of Jesus. It is not at all unlikely that Jesus would interpret Scripture like this, in the Pharisaic tradition,[41] nor is it unseemly that he would speak so plainly.[42] It sounds somewhat like a second century Uncanonical Gospel (found in 1905) teaching of Jesus: "The Saviour answered and said unto him, Woe ye blind, who see not. Thou hast washed in these running waters wherein dogs and swine have been cast night and day, and hast cleansed and wiped the outside skin which also the harlots and flute-girls anoint and wash and wipe and beautify for the lust of men; but within they are full of scorpions and all wickedness." [43]

The Tannaitic reference is not meant to be derogatory. On the contrary, it reports that the eminent and conservative leader in his generation, Rabbi Eliezer, had been pleased by this Scripture interpretation given in the name of Jesus.

Finally, the narration hints at the interference of the Roman government which may have had a good deal to do, more than we now know, with the division which developed between Judaism and Christianity.

As an addendum to this discussion, it is appropriate to identify the terms *Minim* and *Minuth,* used in the above text-quotations. These words seem to have some relationship to Christianity. Much has been written as to their exact meaning. R. Travers Herford and Hermann Strack assembled the rabbinic passages, about eighty, which mention the *Minim.*[44] They and many others have sought to give satisfactory explanations to these passages. There are conflicting opinions; a completely acceptable interpretation is still lacking. Without digressing too much from our main theme we shall summarize the several points of view regarding the *Minim* and attempt to reach a reasonable decision.

The term *Min,*[45] of which *Minim* is the plural, is found frequently in the Bible where it means "species," "variety," or "genus." [46] Thus, the word is used in the story of Creation (Genesis 1:11) which tells of the "fruit-tree bearing fruit *after its kind.*" It has the same meaning in rabbinic literature, as in M. Peah II:5, "one *kind* of seed"; or as in M. Bikkurim I:3, "the seven *varieties* of Palestine products." [47] However, in the rabbinic literature the term came to have a secondary meaning, namely, a *species* of Jewish belief and practice which is not true, a *variation* from the norm. There is the connotation of "going astray." Herford is sound in showing that another word, *zan,* which means "species," is related to *zanah,* "unfaithful," and that this would explain how by association the meaning of *Min* would be extended to apply to religious unfaithfulness, or apostasy.[48]

Other suggestions as to derivation appear less probable than this one. For instance, because of a similarity of sound the word *min* is related to the Arabic *man* which means "to tell a lie," or to the Syriac *mania* which means "madness." [49] Other theories hold that *min* is formed from initials of the three words which mean "believer in Jesus of Nazareth"; is an abbreviation of *ma'amin,* a "believer" in two deities; is taken from Manes and refers to a follower of the Manichaeans; is derived from *ma'an,* which means "one who denies." [50]

The connotation of unfaithfulness, which seems to be the more

probable view, is supported by the text-passage we have under
consideration, in which R. Eliezer, regretting his having been suspected as one of the *Minim*, quotes Proverbs 5:8 which tells of
the "strange woman"—"Remove thy way far from her, and come
not nigh the door of her house." Furthermore, the Tannaitic Midrash, Sifre #115, defines the *Minim* as follows: "that ye go not
about after your own heart," [51] this is *Minuth*, as it is said, "and I
find more bitter than death the woman, whose heart is snares and
nets, and her hands as bands," [52] and "the king shall rejoice in
God." [53]

In the Talmud and Midrash the *Minim* are Jewish heretics. But
who are these heretics? What is their heresy? There are those
who identify them as the early Jewish Christians. Others regard
them as Jewish Gnostics. There is considerable literature on both
sides of the debate.[54]

The problem arises because the term is used for *various* defec-
tions from Jewish practice. The majority of the scholars believe
that included among those who turned away from normative
Judaism and are called *Minim* were the Jews who became the
early Jewish Christians. This is the view of Graetz, Bacher, Herford, Strack, Kohler, Klausner, Büchler, H. Hirschberg, Levy's
*Dictionary*, Jastrow's *Dictionary*, the *Aruch Completum*.[55] Yet,
these conclusions are not without qualification.

Herford takes the position that a Gentile is never called a *Min*,
although one or two Talmudic instances do so in error.[56] He
proves conclusively that the term designates Jewish Christians,
yet he admits difficulties: the matters debated with the *Minim*
do not accord with Christian tradition; there is no reference to
Jesus as Messiah, which, after all, is the main point of difference
between the Jews and the Jewish Christians.[57]

Strack makes a necessary distinction between the connotation
of the term in the Amoraic period as against its simpler meaning
in the time of the Tannaim. Derived from the word, *min*, which
means *genus* or "kinds," it refers, he says, to varieties of Judaism
in contradistinction to the main, accepted pattern of Judaism.
Thus, he itemizes as existing in the Tannaitic period three kinds

of *Minim*: (1) Jewish, in the time before Jesus; (2) Jewish, in the time after Jesus; (3) Jewish Christians. One must be careful, always, in discriminating as to which *kind* of *Min* is meant in a Talmudic passage.

Knowing that comprehensive terms take on new meaning in the course of time, we realize the importance of making this distinction. Büchler demonstrated (soon after Strack) that while *Minim* originally alluded to Jewish heretics, it was used more frequently, by the time of the second and third centuries, to refer to non-Jewish sectarians in Galilee.[58] As a matter of fact, in the teenth century the Karaites were called *Minim*.[59] In his seventeenth-century disputation, Isaac Lupis maintained that the *Minim* of the Talmud were Sadducees who denied the Oral Law.[60]

The main modern exponents of the argument that *Minim* refers to Jewish Gnostics are Friedlander, Marmorstein and Grant. Friedlander takes up the problem in the second half of *Der vorchristliche jüdische Gnosticismus* and in Chapter IV of *Die religiösen Bewegungen innerhalb das Judentums im Zeitalter Jesu*. He points to similarities between Jewish Gnostic belief and practice and the rabbinic criticism of the *Minim*.

There also is the probability that the Gnostics created more trouble, and brought forth more hostility, in Judaism, than did the Jewish Christians. However, the known Jewish Gnostic, Elisha ben Abuyah, is not explicitly called a *Min*. Furthermore, how is one to explain the specific mention of Jesus in connection with *Minim*, as in this story of R. Eliezer? [61] Friedlander answers that the references to Jesus are late additions.[62]

A. Marmorstein states with definiteness that up to the third century the *Minim* were not Jewish nor Gentile Christians, but Jews imbued with Gnosticism.[63] Jewish Christians, he proceeds to prove, are *Poshay Yisroel*, the "sinners of Israel," the Jewish apostates.[64] Still, how are we to account for the mention of Jesus as taught by Jacob the *Min*?

Frederick C. Grant is the most recent authority to support the identification of the *Minim* as Jewish Gnostics.[65] His inter-

pretation, however, is disputed by Harris Hirschberg who maintains that in Talmudic literature *Minim* denotes adherents of
Pauline Christianity.[66] To defend his refutation, Hirschberg takes
the very passages used to support the theory of Jewish Gnosticism
and by them proves that Christians are meant; for example, that
the reference to the Two Powers in Heaven is a teaching of
Marcion, deduced from Paul; or, that the Mishnah forbids as
*Minuth* a particular method of wearing the Tefillin[67] because
it was thus done by Christians as a sign of Jesus as the
priest-Messiah,[68] for he is so regarded in the Epistle to the
Hebrews.

The controversy on the *Minim* is well summed up by Gershom
G. Scholem, Professor of Jewish Mysticism at the Hebrew University of Jerusalem. "Of the existence of a heretical Gnosis of a
dualistic and antinomian character on the outskirts of Judaism
there cannot be any doubt, to my mind. Surely these Gnostics
and not the Jewish-Christians are the target of some of the numerous references to 'Minim' in the older Rabbinical literature on
which, since the appearance of Graetz' *Gnosticismus und Judenthum* (1846), so many scholars have lavished a profusion of
thought. I do not propose to dwell on this controversy which,
like the voluminous literature on the subject of the Essenes, has
become the happy hunting-ground of those who delight in hypotheses." [69]

The *Minim* is not our primary subject of inquiry and therefore
we have no desire or space here to join in the "happy hunting-
ground" of the controversy. Yet there is some relationship to our
investigation of passages about Jesus. If Jacob the *Min* who healed
in the name of Jesus and who taught Eliezer an interpretation of
Scripture was a Jewish Gnostic, and not a Christian at all, it
makes a difference in our finding. We must come to some conclusion as to the meaning of *Min*.

It is possible that we can solve the problem by assuming that in
the earliest period of Christianity sharp lines were not drawn
between Jewish Christians and Jews, nor between Jewish Gnostics and Christian Gnostics. This point of view receives support

from James Parkes' account of the parting of the ways between Jews and Christians, when he writes that the Church and Synagogue of the second and third centuries were still in the process of absorbing or rejecting their intermediate groupings: "The interesting fact about this period is that from the two poles of Catholic and Rabbinic orthodoxy stretch an unbroken stream of intermediate sects. For there were some groups which had both Christian and Jewish representatives, such as the Gnostics and the Ebionites, and among the Jewish believers in Christ there appear to have been a number of different groups varying in their conception of the amount of the Law which should still be obeyed." [70]

The Talmud report of the necessity of introducing a liturgical device, the *Birchath Haminim*, whereby to detect Jewish sectarians participating in the worship of the synagogue is in itself evidence that clear-cut cleavages had not yet come into being.[71]

There is strong evidence that in this early period there was no marked differentiation between Jewish Gnosticism and Christian Gnosticism.

It is a generally acknowledged fact that elements of Jewish Gnosticism are contained in Christian Gnostic thought.[72] The blending of the two—Jewish and Christian Gnosticism—is seen particularly, as W. Bousset reminds us, in the Clementines.[73] In the transition stage, Jewish Gnosticism would be also Christian Gnosticism and it would be difficult to separate Jewish Gnostics from Jewish Christians.

If this be true, as it appears to be, we find that we are no longer faced with the alternative: the rabbinic passages on the *Minim* refer either to the Jewish Christians *or* to the Jewish Gnostics. We see now that they can encompass both. Kohler takes a position akin to this when in his chapter on Gnostic Sects he states that the Jewish Gnostics are called *Minim* in the Talmud and further in the chapter asserts that the Christian Gnostics are also called *Minim*.[74]

With this understanding of the term *Minim* we are not astounded that it should have so many shades of meaning in the rabbinic literature, for there were many doctrines and practices bubbling forth in the incipient stages of Christianity and post-exilic Judaism, and an undivided mingling of elements of both religions.

If some of the allusions to *Minim* are unrecognizable to us it may well be because these sectarian elements have not survived in the ultimate shaping of the religions. If we see in the *Minim*-passages strong measures taken against these sectaries we can now appreciate the fact that Judaism found it necessary to oppose Gnostic heresies as vigorously as did the Church. Gnostic sects spoke of "the accursed God of the Jews"; when their Gnosticism became a form of Christianity and as such continued to meet the disfavor of the rabbis we come to a point of fine judgment as to whether it was the Gnosticism or the Christian element which was opposed the more strongly.[75]

The fact that nothing is told of the *Minim* accepting Jesus as the Messiah but that the stress of the counter-argument is against their belief in Two Powers and against certain practices—this fact lends weight to the opinion that the rabbinic opposition was directed especially against the Gnostic element in the early Christianity.

Furthermore, there is general acceptance of the fact that Jewish Christians were completely separated from the Jews by 135 C.E., as a result of the Bar Kochba messianic revolt against Hadrian, and that they lost out also in the development of Christianity, surviving for several centuries as a remnant without telling influence on either religion.[76] If so, it is important that rabbinic references to Jewish Christians much after that date should not be regarded as references to Christianity proper. After the middle of the second century, whatever was said by Jews regarding Jewish Christians would relate to what was becoming an offshoot of historic Christianity and destined to wither away.

Christian Gnosticism, too, after achieving its greatest prominence in the second third of the second century receded thereafter until it was replaced in the second half of the third century by the Manichaean movement.[77] Late rabbinic allusions to Jewish Christians or Christian Gnosticism would, therefore, have no relevancy to the practical relations between Judaism and Christianity.

In future studies of the complete rabbinic record concerning Christianity it will be necessary to give full consideration to these limitations in the use of the term *Min*. Consideration will have to be given also to the Talmudic statement (B. Hullin 13b) that "there are no *Minim* among the nations," which connotes that only a Jew, but not a Gentile, would be called a *Min*.

Attention will have to be given to the origin and full meaning of the word *Notzrim*, as used in B. Taanith 27b, the name given to Christians, and used as part of the identification of Jesus (*Yeshu Hanotzri*). It will be necessary also to examine the possibility of other terminology as allusions to Christianity. Attention has already been called to the phrase *Poshay Yisroel*.

Despite oft-repeated assertions that *Goyim* in the Talmud and cognate literature does not mean Christians, there are instances where the word might have that meaning. Here are some examples: Midrash Tanhuma, *Ki Thissa*, 58b (Buber ed.), which tells that God did not write all of the Law for Moses because the *Goyim* will claim the Torah as theirs and therefore the Mishnah, Haggadah and Talmud were given orally to separate Israel from the *Goyim*; [78] Pesikta Rabbati 14b relates that God foresaw that the *Goyim* would translate the Torah and read it in Greek and claim to be the true Israel but the secret of the true Israel is in the possession of the Oral Law.[79] Utmost care must be exercised before identifying a *Goyim* passage as alluding to Christians; it almost always refers to non-Jewish peoples, without intending to allude to Christians.

Other phrases to be studied as possible references to Christianity in the later literature, in specific instances (in addition to *Notzrim*), are *nochrim*,[80] *Edomites*,[81] *umoth*,[82] *aralim*.[83]

For our present purpose it is sufficient to say that the wider subject—*Christianity* in Talmud and Midrash—is not exhausted with a study of only *Minim* passages.

Our immediate concern, however, was to demonstrate that Jacob the *Min* was a type of early Christian, teaching in the name of Jesus.

## 5. BABYLONIAN TALMUD—SHABBATH 116a, b

TEXT:—Rabbi Meir called it: [1] *aven gilyon*, the falsehood of blank paper. Rabbi Yohanan called it: *avon gilyon*, the sin of blank paper.

DISCUSSION:—The text is Gemara and would belong in Chapter III excepting for the fact that R. Meir, who is here quoted, is of the generation of Tannaim, dated 130 to 160 C.E.; [2] R. Yohanan bar Nappaha is, of course, of the second generation of Amoraim, he having lived a full life from about 180 to 290 C.E.[3] The text continues with a separate story which we shall now take up because it helps explain what is meant by *aven* (or *avon*) *gilyon*.

TEXT:—Imma Shalom was R. Eliezer's wife and R. Gamaliel's sister. There lived in her neighborhood a *philosoph* who had a reputation that he did not accept a bribe. They sought to expose him. She sent him a lamp of gold. They came before him. She said to him, "I desire that they give me a share of the family property." [4] He said to them, "Divide it." They said to him, "For us it is written, 'Where there is a son, a daughter does not inherit.'" He answered them: "From the day when you were exiled from your land, the Law of Moses has been taken away, and the law of *avon gilyon* [5] has been given, wherein it is written, 'A son and a daughter shall inherit equally.'" The next day he (R. Gamaliel) sent him a Libyan ass. He (the *philosoph*) said to them, "I looked at the end of the book, wherein it is written, 'I am not come to take away from the Law of Moses and I am not come to add to the Law of Moses,' [6] and it is written, 'where there is a son, a daughter does not inherit.'" She said to him, "Let your light shine forth as a lamp." R. Gamaliel said to her: "The ass came and kicked the lamp over."

DISCUSSION:—This passage also is Gemara and would belong properly to the Amoraic period but it is included here because the quoted characters in the episode belong to the time of the Tannaim.[7] Jesus is not mentioned specifically, but a supposed teaching of his is cited; therefore, it is given as the last reference in this section.

Now we come to the words: *aven* (or *avon*) *gilyon*. As Herford properly explains,[8] *gilyon* is the empty margin of ancient manuscripts where notations were often made. The Talmud is not definite in telling what is noted in the margins, and Herford does not think that *gilyon* by itself[9] ever means one of the Gospels. On this there is agreement, more or less. While M. Jost does take *gilyon* as referring to the evangelion,[10] M. Friedlander[11] argues that the allusion is to the Gnostic books of the magicians,[12] H. P. Chajes concludes that it means the Apocalyptic literature,[13] and Klausner expresses doubt that *gilyonim* denotes the Gospels.[14] *Gilyonim* could refer to a variety of unorthodox interpretations written into the margins of sacred books by individuals or followers of the many sectaries.[15]

Now we turn to the more difficult question: is *aven gilyon* a reference to the Gospels? Herford answers in the affirmative.[16] Part of his proof is the interpretation of the *Be Nitzraphi*[17] (associated with the *aven gilyon* which R. Meir calls the falsehood of blank paper) as "the house where Christians assemble"; but, according to Strack,[18] the evidence is entirely insufficient for such an inference. Little is known about the term. There is the suggestion that the word is in mutilated form and should read, with the change of one letter which may have become wrongly transcribed, *Be Nitzrene*, which might mean the "house of the Nazarenes" (Jewish Christians); and the companion-word, *Be Abidan*, which presents an equal problem, could be modified as *Be Ebion*, "the house of the Ebionites" (also Jewish Christians).[19] The suggestion is interesting but one hesitates to tamper with the text.

We must look further before reaching a conclusion. The decision depends in a measure on the previous discussion regarding the *Minim*. Thus, Friedlander[20] and Grant[21] would not allow that *gilyon* is a transliteration of "evangelion," but insist that the reference is to the worthlessness or sinfulness of the Gnostic scrolls. The combination, however, of two Hebrew words to make up the complete phonesis of *evangelion* is too striking to pass off as accidental, especially since two different Hebrew words are combined to *gilyon* to create *evangelion*. Therefore, while *gilyon* alone need not refer to the Gospels, there is strong likelihood that *aven gilyon* or *avon gilyon* do have that meaning.

Supporting this conclusion is the reference of Archbishop Amolo, in the ninth century, to the Jewish allusion to the Gospel as *havon-galion*.[22] As a probable origin of *evangelion*, Solomon Schechter mentions that the marginalia of the Nazarenes probably represented their annotations to Old Testament verses believed to be prophetic of Christ.[23] Klausner[24] and Jastrow[25] accept the statement of R. Meir and R. Yohanan as an allusion to the New Testament. The strongest confirmation, though, is given by the use of *avon gilyon* in the Talmud passage which follows, the one regarding the *philosoph*.

What is a *philosoph*? We are not too sure—possibly a public speaker; possibly a judge or arbitrator.[26] The intent of the story is not too difficult to perceive. Like many of the anecdotes of the Talmud it illustrates a point, with some humor added.

The judge of impeccable reputation is amenable to bribery. Upon the receipt of the gift of a golden lamp he decides, regarding inheritance, in favor of the woman, basing his decision on the *avon gilyon* which has replaced the Mosaic Law since the Exile. R. Gamaliel protests that, according to Biblical law, where there is a son, a daughter does not inherit.[27] When R. Gamaliel sends the judge a more expensive bribe, a Libyan ass,[28] the judge reverses his position, discovering further in the book that the Law of Moses cannot be changed (as expressed in Matthew 5:17). The story concludes with a saying that the ass kicked over the lamp, a clever way of emphasizing the moral that a more lavish bribe cancelled out the effectiveness of a lesser one.

This passage quotes in effect a verse from the Gospel of Matthew as the law of *avon gilyon*. *Avon gilyon*, therefore, must be the Gospel.

However, the viewpoint that this reference is to Christian teaching has been challenged. In a discerning analysis Solomon Zeitlin[29] points out that R. Gamaliel might have taken the case of dispute to a Jewish or Roman but not to a Christian judge (assuming that *philosoph* could mean a Christian judge); that inasmuch as Jewish law forbids the giving as well as the taking of bribes [30] it is unthinkable that one of the standing of Rabban Gamaliel would offer a bribe, even to test the wrongdoing of the *Minim*; that not to add to nor subtract from the Law of Moses is a well-known tradition in Judaism; that since R. Meir was the first to use the term *aven gilyon*, this story must be dated no earlier than the end of the second century; that the phrase, "The ass came and kicked the lamp over," is a popular expression of later times; [31] that the reference to "the ass" is not necessarily an allusion to the Messiah.[32]

Nevertheless, the preponderance of scholars on the theme [33] accept this as a passage relating to Christianity. In explanation of some of the difficulties cited it may be said that Gamaliel II was one who *would* go to extremes to win his point: because of a difference in interpretation he excommunicated his own brother-in-law and because of an unbending nature he alienated many of his best colleagues; it was in his time that the test-prayer to detect *Minim* was introduced into the liturgy. As for taking the case to the *philosoph*, he may have been, indeed, a Roman judge who, at the same time, was a Christian. The saying used in later litera-ture, that the ass kicked the lamp over, may have had its begin-ning in this story; "the ass" need not be regarded as an allusion to the Messiah to retain the validity of this reference.

There is no reason why one must adhere to the position that R. Meir was the first to refer to the Gospels as the evangelion. The *philosoph* episode could well give us our first instance. Dat-ing would be difficult. The Amoraic telling of the story is late, but if the incident actually took place it was after 70 c.e., when the Exile began, and before 110 c.e., when R. Gamaliel II died. Nicholson, Herford and Klausner prefer the approximate year 73 as the date of the episode, although it can be later.[34]

The absence in Matthew of any similar law about inheriting, as also the fact that the statement of the inviolability of the Law of Moses is rather at the beginning of Matthew than later on, can be explained by the theory that the evangelion to which the judge referred was the *Logia*,[35] from which Matthew obtained much of his material. There is also the theory that the quotation is from the Gospel according to the Hebrews.[36]

On the positive side is the more than haphazard connection of the verse in the story with the one retained in the New Testament. Deeper than the superficial meaning of the story is the satire on tampering with the Law of Moses, the subtle reminder that Jesus had advocated its validity and the argument against the Abrogation of the Law. J. Z. Lauterbach [37] adds the interesting suggestion that the entire question as to whether a daughter can inherit may be a veiled allusion to Jesus' Davidic descent through his *mother*, for he cannot claim Davidic Messiahship if a daughter does not inherit.

This completes the passages of the Tannaitic period, wherein the evidence is such as to tilt the scales in favor of these being authentic references to Jesus.

# REFERENCES INCORRECTLY IDENTIFIED
# WITH JESUS

On first impression it may seem odd to give references of the Tannaitic period incorrectly identified with Jesus. Why go to the trouble? Is it not entirely negative?

History, however, tells a tragic tale of bitterness and persecution predicated, in no small way, upon these mistakes—deliberate or unintentional—in the reading of the early portions of the Talmud. The record must be set straight! Moreover, even the modern scholars, who are friendly to the Talmud, fall into the same errors and quite innocently create false and harmful viewpoints. Thus, to correct error is to lead to truth.

## 1. THE BEN STADA REFERENCES

TEXT:—"He who cuts upon his flesh." It is a Baraitha tradition: Rabbi Eliezer said to the Sages, "Did not Ben Stada bring sorcery [1] from Egypt in a cut [2] upon his flesh?" They answered him, "He was a madman,[3] and we do not adduce proof from mad persons." * Ben Stada? He was Ben Pandera! [4] Rab Hisda said, "The husband was Stada; the lover, Pandera." Was not the husband Pappos ben Yehudah; his mother, Stada? His mother was Miriam, a women's hairdresser. As they say in Pumbeditha, "Stath da (this one strayed) from her husband." * [5] (B. Shabbath 104b)

DISCUSSION:—The portion within the asterisks, found also in B. Sanhedrin 67a, is Gemara—that is, of the Amoraic period. Its date is ascertained by the Aramaic of the original text and the participation of Rab Hisda, who died in 309 C.E. and is counted as belonging to the third generation of Amoraim in Babylonia.[6] It is included here to show how the confusion arose in those later centuries when it was believed by some that Ben Stada was another name for Jesus. Before continuing with the discussion, however, we shall translate the other pertinent texts.

TEXT:—"He that cuts marks on his flesh." R. Eliezer condemns, but the Sages acquit him. R. Eliezer said to them, "And did not Ben Stada learn [7] solely in this way?" They answered him, "Because of one madman are we to condemn [8] all clear-headed people?" (T. Shabbath XI, 15)

TEXT:—One who cuts an inscription on the skin is subject to punishment. However, if he only writes [9] an inscription on the skin, he is free of guilt. R. Eliezer said to them: "And did not Ben Stada bring magic from Egypt solely in this way?" They answered him, "Because of one fool are we to destroy many sensible people?" (P. Shabbath 13d or XII, 4)

TEXT:—All who are deserving of death, according to the Torah; they do not use hidden witnesses concerning them, except in the instance of an enticer.[10] How do they perform regarding him? They station two disciples of the Sages in an inner part of the house and he sits in an outer part of the house. They light the candle so that they can see him and hear his voice. Thus they did to Ben Stada in Lud. They concealed (as witnesses) two scholars of the Sages and stoned him. (T. Sanhedrin X, 11)

TEXT:—The enticer: this denotes an ordinary person. Not a Sage? No. Since he entices he is not a Sage? Since he is prevailed upon (to sin)[11] he is no longer a Sage. How do they perform to be subtle with him? They place two witnesses in hiding in an inner part of the house and have him sit in an outer part of the house and light a candle above him, that they may see him and hear his voice. Thus they did to Ben Stada in Lud: and they placed two scholars of the Sages as hidden witnesses, and they brought him to the Beth Din [12] and stoned him. (P. Sanhedrin 25c,d or VII, 16)

TEXT:—Thus they did to Ben Satra in Lud, they concealed witnesses, etc., and brought him to the Beth Din and stoned him. (P. Yebamoth 15d or XVI, 6)

TEXT:—For it is a (Baraitha) tradition: And the rest of all who are deserving of death, according to the Torah; they do not use hidden witnesses concerning them, except in this instance. How do they perform regarding him? They light a candle for him in the inner part of the house and place witnesses in the outer part of the house, so that they can see him and hear his voice while he cannot see them. Then one says to him, "Tell me what you said to me (when we were) alone." And he tells him. Then one says to him, "How shall we forsake our God Who is in Heaven and practice false worship?" If he returns (to God), it is well. But if he says, "Such (and such) is our obligation and such is appropriate for us," the witnesses who are listening outside bring him to the Beth Din and stone him. Thus they did to Ben Stada in Lud. °And they hanged him on the eve of Passover.° (B. Sanhedrin 67a)

DISCUSSION:—These excerpts tell of Ben Stada bringing magic from Egypt through a cut in his flesh. Although regarded as a fool or madman, he beguiled the people to sin against God and after standing trial, according to a particular procedure, he was brought to the courthouse and stoned in the city of Lud.

The latest of these Tannaitic passages, the last one here cited, reflects the confusion among the Babylonian Amoraim that Ben Stada refers to Jesus, for here some later hand tacked on the sentence (marked in the translation by circles), "And they hanged him on the eve of Passover," though there is not excluded the possibility that he, as well as Jesus, was hanged on a Passover Eve. It is necessary to realize that some of the Babylonian Amoraim could make mistakes—like any other mortal. They not only believed Ben Stada to be Jesus but, as shown in the first passage here quoted, mistook Mary Magdalene (the word for hairdresser is *Megaddela*) to be Mary the Mother,[13] and Pappos ben Yehudah (who really lived a century later in the time of Akiba)[14] to be the husband of Mary.

These errors continued for many centuries. Even Jastrow's usually reliable *Talmud Dictionary* states "Son of Stada, surname of Jesus of Nazareth."[15] He only follows the definitions given in the *Aruch* and in Levy's *Dictionary* and in the errors of others.[16] In a work of about one hundred pages explaining supposed Talmudic references to Jesus, Laible wastes one-tenth of these pages [17] arguing that Ben Stada is Jesus, and takes umbrage at the unfavorable reflections on the latter thus presented.

That Jesus, the founder of Christianity, is meant by Ben Stada, Herford says cannot be reasonably doubted.[18] With this wrong assumption he builds up to many conclusions which totter, once the foundation is proved unstable. We note, however, in the same volume, a saving suggestion that the premise may not be correct, that Ben Stada and Jesus may not have been identical.[19]

Despite similarities between incidents in the record of Ben Stada and that of Jesus, which could lead to the confusion, Rabbenu Tam—the twelfth-century Tosafist commentator on the Talmud—stated flatly that Ben Stada was not Jesus of Nazareth.[20] In 1240, R. Yehiel in his Paris disputation said the same.[21] In modern times, Derenbourg,[22] Joel,[23] Chajes,[24] Bacher,[25] Kohler,[26] Strack,[27] Klausner,[28] Ginzberg,[29] Lauterbach,[30] and the Soncino Talmud translators,[31] stress the necessity to differentiate between Ben Stada and Jesus.

The reasons for discarding the Ben Stada passages of the Tannaim as references to Jesus are mainly: we never find the full name, *Yeshu* ben Stada; the Toledoth Yeshu legends regarding Jesus speak of Ben Pandera, but not Ben Stada; Jesus was seized in Jerusalem and executed there, not in Lud; his acts were not those of Ben Stada; if R. Eliezer had Jesus in mind he would have named him as he did elsewhere in the rabbinic literature. There is wide agreement, in which we concur, that Ben Stada was not Jesus.

Who, then, was Ben Stada? Various suggestions are offered. One [32] is that he was James, the brother of Jesus,[33] who might have been called Ben Stada, he having had the same mother but not the same father as Jesus. However, his deeds were not those of Ben Stada; he is not known to have been in Lud; his death at the hands of the high priest, as reported by Josephus, would be much protested by the rabbis. Alternate possibilities are suggested by the same author: James named in Acts 12:2-4, and

James of Acts 1:13; [34] but there is no substantiating evidence for either one.[35]

J. Z. Lauterbach makes the interesting observation that in the Vilna edition of the passage in P. Sanhedrin 25d, and also in P. Yebamoth 15d, the name Ben Stada is printed Ben Sotra,[36] with other variations. He, therefore, emends the word to read *Sarata*[37] instead of *Stada*.[38] *Ben Sarata* would mean "an expert in tattooing." The very name thus refers to one who, adept at tattoo inscription, brought magic out of Egypt; a madman, he misled the people to worship falsity, threatened many with destruction, and was apprehended and executed at Lud. This theory recommends itself. Yet, one hesitates to indulge in such emendation of the text.

Another theory [39] is that which takes Ben Stada to refer to the pesudo-Messiah, Simon Magus, the magician mentioned in Acts 8:9–24. Further details are supplied by Justin Martyr, and in the Clementines which come from the Jewish-Christian-Gnostic group of the late second century. Simon Magus was born a Samaritan, went to Egypt as a young man and there acquired knowledge of magic. A former disciple of John the Baptist, he returned to Palestine with messianic pretensions, flourishing especially after the death of Dosthai who had assumed leadership of the group left by John the Baptist. With the harlot Helene as his consort, Simon Magus proclaimed himself the Christ—*Stadios*—The Standing (Eternal) One.[40] These facts and supplementary details in the *Recognitions* and *Homilies* bring about a close resemblance between Ben Stada and Simon Magus, although, it must be noted, there is no record that Magus was condemned and executed by the Jewish court at Lud. There is, however, a striking similarity between the name Ben Stada and Magus' self-designation, Stadios.

It was suggested by H. P. Chajes [41] and R. T. Herford [42] that Ben Stada might be the Egyptian "false prophet" described by Josephus. J. Z. Lauterbach accepts him as the tattoo expert. Simon Magus, likewise, must be meant by the "false prophet." Thus, several paths converge, leading to the identification of Ben Stada as this false prophet.

Concerning the false prophet—to whom Ben Stada must refer—

we read in Josephus: "Moreover, there came out of Egypt about this time to Jerusalem, one that said he was a prophet, and advised the multitude of the common people to go along with him to the Mount of Olives. . . . He said farther, that he would show them from hence, how, at his command, the walls of Jerusalem would fall down. . . . Now, when Felix was informed of these things, he . . . attacked the Egyptian and the people that were with him. He also slew four hundred of them, and took two hundred alive. But the Egyptian himself escaped out of the fight, and did not appear any more." [43] An incidental allusion is retained in the New Testament, wherein it is asked of Paul: "Art not thou the Egyptian, which before these days madest an uproar, and leddest out into the wilderness four thousand men that were murderers?" [44]

It is likely that the Egyptian false prophet and enticer (i.e., Ben Stada) was later captured by Jewish authorities in Lud (Lydda), near Jerusalem, tried, condemned and stoned, as described in the Talmud. The details of the rabbinic account apply to him, but not at all to Jesus. The date is set by the mention of Felix, who was Procurator of Judea from 52 to 60 C.E. It is thus probable that R. Eliezer would have heard something of his record and would have alluded to him.

It is not the primary assignment to discover who Ben Stada was. The main task is to present the evidence that he was not Jesus, as we have done. How deplorable that so much unfavorable comment has been heaped upon the Talmud and the Jews because of these references which we now know to have been interpreted erroneously!

Finally, a speculative thought comes to mind. Admitting that it is speculation, we ask: is it possible that, as passages in the literature of the Amoraim and of the Toledoth Yeshu erred in this item of mistaken identification,[45] and as the New Testament states how even Paul was thought to be the false Egyptian prophet—is it possible that portions of the Gospel account of Jesus attribute to him some of the trials and tribulations of Ben Stada, the disappointing savior of the middle of the first century?

## 2. THE BALAAM REFERENCES

TEXT:—Three kings and four commoners have no part in the world-to-come. Three kings are: Jereboam, Ahab and Manasseh. . . . Four commoners are: Balaam, Doeg, Ahitophel and Gehazi. (M. Sanhedrin X, 2)

TEXT:—The disciples of Balaam the wicked shall inherit Gehenna and go down to the pit of destruction, as it is said: "Men of blood and deceit shall not live out half their days." [1] (M. Aboth V, 19)

TEXT:—That *Min* said to R. Hanina: "Did you ever hear how old Balaam was?" He answered him: "It is not written in any record; excepting what is in Scripture: 'Men of blood and deceit shall not live out half their days' [1]—he must have been 33 or 34 years (old)." He (the *Min*) said to him: "You answered me properly. I have seen the memorandum concerning Balaam where it is inscribed: 'Thirty-three years (old) was Balaam the lame when Pinhas the Robber killed him.' " (B. Sanhedrin 106b)

DISCUSSION:—Rabbi Hanina, a disciple of Judah the Nasi, lived in Sepphoris and died 232 C.E. He is of the latest of the Tannaim and the earliest of the Amoraim.[2] If the *Min* was a Christian, would he ask of a rabbi the age of Jesus? Would he speak of Jesus in such terms? Either the *Min* was not a Christian or Balaam did not mean Jesus. The "memorandum" may have been an elaboration of the Biblical story of Balaam, possibly used by a Gnostic group.

TEXT:—"Balaam, also the son of Beor, the soothsayer" [3]—The soothsayer? He was a prophet. Said R. Yohanan, "At the beginning he was a prophet, but at the end he was a soothsayer." [4] (B. Sanhedrin 106a end)

TEXT:—Moses wrote his book and the portion about Balaam.[5] (B. B. Bathra 14b; P. Pesahim 3c; P. Sotah 20d)

DISCUSSION:—The Balaam passage is deliberately included in the Moses writings, according to Rashi, for a purpose. Herford finds in this an indirect allusion to Jesus.[6] Further, there is a theory that "the portion about Balaam" is not the Bible portion but a complete book on Balaam attributed to Moses.[7]

TEXT:—Rabbi Eleazar Hakappar says: God gave strength to his (Balaam's) voice, that it could rise from one end of the world to the other, because he looked and beheld the peoples who bow down to the sun and moon and stars, and to wood and stone, and he looked and beheld that there was a man, the son of a woman, who would rise up and seek to make himself God, and cause the entire world to err. Therefore, he (God) gave power to his (Balaam's) voice, that all peoples of the world might hear. And thus he did speak: Give heed, not to err after that man, as it is in Scripture: "God is not man that he should lie." [8] And if he says that he is God, he lies; and in the future he will cause to err—that he departs and returns in the end. He says, but will not do (it). See what is in Scripture: "And he took up his parable and said, Alas, who shall live when God doeth this." [9] Balaam said: Alas, who shall live of that people that listens to that man who makes himself God? (Yalkut Shimeoni §766, to Nu. 23:7)

DISCUSSION:—Many pages were written, when it was the vogue, on the discovery in rabbinic literature of a number of hidden allusions to Jesus by use of the Biblical name of Balaam.

According to Strack,[10] this trend was initiated by mention of the thought in a letter written by S. J. L. Rapaport in 1833. Abraham Geiger gave impetus to the suggestion in 1868 with the publication of *Bileam und Jesus*.[11] Without going too far afield, it but need be said that Laible took with a vengeance as applying to Jesus the horrible things stated about Balaam in the early as well as later rabbinic writings.[12] In the *Jewish Encyclopedia*, the usually reliable S. Krauss wrote: "As Balaam the magician and, according to the derivation of his name, 'destroyer of the people,' was from both of these points of view a good prototype of Jesus, the latter was also called Balaam." [13]

Accepting Balaam as a type-reference to Jesus—"what Balaam was, such also was Jesus" [14]—Herford builds up quite a picture of the "violence of the hatred" [15] of the Talmudic Jews against Jesus. The danger of letting fancy run riot is especially demonstrated in his attempt, as others have done, to find in the names (in M. Sanhedrin X, 2) associated with Balaam some secret reference to others in the drama of Jesus who would be shut out from the world-to-come. The three Apostles, he submits, who would be most closely associated with Jesus are Peter, Judas Iscariot, and Paul; these three, therefore, he believed are meant by Ahitophel, Doeg, and Gehazi.[16] Klausner speaks of such hypotheses as "mountains hung on a hair." [17]

Misleading items encouraged erroneous conclusions. These are: the mention of Balaam as dying at the age of thirty-three at the hands of Pinhas the Robber who *could* be Pontius Pilate,[18] the mention of a prophet ending up as a soothsayer, that "Balaam" means Jesus because the word in Hebrew can be divided to mean "without the people" or "no share with the people," [19] that the "portion of Balaam" refers to the Gospels, that Luke 4:29 speaks of Jesus being led to the brow of a hill as in the Balaam story, etc.

What helped scholars to discover that this pursuit was following a false lead is the fact that, in certain passages, Balaam and Jesus are mentioned as separate persons. Such is the text quoted last in this grouping, the one from the Yalkut Shimeoni collection of Midrashim. Only the first portion—"God gave strength to Balaam's voice, that it could rise from one end of the world to the other"—is Tannaitic,[20] spoken by R. Eleazar Hakappar, who died in 260 c.e.[21] The remainder of the excerpt properly belongs to the treatment of the Amoraic period; however, if we identify the thought as pertaining to Jesus, we have Jesus and Balaam here as two separate entities. Even clearer is the differentiation between the two in the Amoraic selection from B. Gitin 56b, 57a—to be discussed in Chapter III.

In 1905, Bacher recognized the almost universal acceptance of the hypothesis making Balaam typical of Jesus and he argued that it was going too far to assume this even in the passages concerning the Biblical sections dealing with Balaam.[22] It is significant that Geiger,[23] who helped set the trend, did place restrictions upon identifying Balaam with Jesus, and that Herford in his later work changed considerably his viewpoint in regard to the Balaam quotations.[24]

The attempt to make Balaam mean Jesus gives the definite impression of being forced. The few points of similarity are trivial. Unlike Balaam, Jesus was not regarded as a prophet nor a soothsayer, and was not haughty. He was not lame. He was not slain by Pinhas the Robber. Most telling is the fact that in two instances Balaam and Jesus are separately named within the text.

One could build as good a case identifying Balaam with Simon Magus, a better case perhaps,[25] or one could do the same with Nicolaitans in connection with which the New Testament specifically alludes to Jesus.[26] However, there is no reason why we cannot regard the Balaam passages as actually denoting Balaam.[27] He became the "horrible example" in Jewish tradition even as he did in Christian tradition.[28]

Definitely severing the connection between Jesus and Balaam— in the Tannaitic period—the Talmud scholar Louis Ginzberg wrote: "One may therefore state with absolute certainty that the entire Talmudic-Midrashic literature does not know of any nicknames for Jesus or his disciples. . . . Jesus is never named in old sources otherwise than Yehoshua, Yeshu, Yeshua or Jesus the son of Pantera." [29]

This also would rule out, and properly so, the possible reference to Jesus in the following:

TEXT:—After those occurrences, King Ahasueros elevated the Aggagite, Haman, son of Hamedatha. His ancestors were . . . Diosos (or, Josos). (Tractate Soferim 13:6)[30]

DISCUSSION:—The possibility, presented by Strack,[31] is given because Josos has at times been taken to mean Jesus.[32] The period of persecution of Jews gave rise to the thought of a point of connection between Haman and Jesus. However, it is remote to claim Josos as a variant spelling of Yeshu. Furthermore, most of the names given in the passage are identifiable as those of oppressive political rulers; and the role of Jesus would not fit into such a category.

### 3. REFERENCES TO A CERTAIN PERSON

TEXT:—Rabbi Shimeon ben Azzai said: I found a scroll of genealogical record in Jerusalem and in it is written, "A certain person was illegitimately born of a married woman." * To support the words of Rabbi Yehoshua. * (M. Yebamoth IV, 13; [1] B. Yebamoth 49a)

DISCUSSION:—The words between the asterisks are found as an addition in present editions of the Mishnah. R. Shimeon ben Azzai, a contemporary of Akiba, was a Tanna who lived at the end of the first, and in the first third of the second, century c.e.— possibly killed after the Bar Kochba rebellion.[2] This establishes the quotation as of fairly early date. R. Yehoshua (ben Hananiah), alluded to, was a disciple of R. Yohanan ben Zakkai, and in his youth sang in the Jerusalem Temple.[3]

The use of the word *peloni* ("a certain person") gave rise to the belief that this was a veiled and cautious reference to Jesus.[4] Thus, approving Derenbourg's conclusion to this effect,[5] S. Krauss in *The Jewish Encyclopedia* designates the above text as "the earliest authenticated passage ascribing illegitimate birth to Jesus."[6] Laible gives bitter assent that this is a Tannaitic reflection on Jesus' birth, although he modifies a strictly polemic position by commenting that, other than in the time of Akiba, the use of the phrase "that man" or "a certain person" to tell scandalous things of Jesus came mostly in the post-Talmudic period "as a consequence of the oppression on the part of the Christians."[7] As is often the case, Herford follows Laible, but with more sympathy,[8] and, surprisingly, Klausner teaches that undoubtedly the reference here is to Jesus.[9]

What are the reasons for these conclusions? They are: that there would be the need to veil the reference to Jesus; that a prominent person must have been meant; that there was sufficient cause for a hostile expression at this time; that Origen in *Contra Celsum* speaks of accusations ascribing to Jesus a spurious birth; [10] that the words of R. Yehoshua, which are supported, deal with the penalty of death by decision of the Beth Din.

The answer to these supposed reasons is not too difficult to perceive. The death-penalty item has no relevancy to Jesus; it applies only to explain a spurious birth as one which condemns the adulterous parents to punishment by death. Further, the Celsus mention is of a *betrothed*, not married, woman having a child. Moreover, the assumption of strong anti-Jesus sentiment in the time of Akiba is based upon the interpretation of passages which, as will soon become evident, does not hold up.[11] Finally, if a prominent person is necessarily meant, why point to Jesus as the prominent person, when practically every authority who has given study to our theme explains the scarcity of Talmudic references to Jesus by the fact that he had made scarcely any impression on the rabbinical teachers of his day and of subsequent generations, that they were virtually unaware of his existence? [12]

There were other prominent names concerning whom genealogical records were kept. To give but one example, Josephus tells a story of the birth of Samson [13] which bears a resemblance to the account of the birth of Jesus as given in the Gospel according to Matthew; in Jewish tradition Samson was a prominent person, one of the *Judges*.

We must bear in mind the admonition of the ancient rabbis, that "if one exposes his fellowmen to humiliation publicly he has no portion in the world-to-come" [14]—and as S. Zeitlin properly observes [15] in his study of our present passage, this word of warning would be sufficient reason for the Tanna to avoid naming the one he had in mind, the illegitimately-born person of Jerusalem (not of Galilee) of high social standing (not of the people, as was Jesus).

The validity of these arguments will be realized more clearly when we now consider the next text-quotation.

TEXT:—They asked R. Eliezer: "What of a certain person (*peloni*) regarding the world-to-come?" He said to them, "Have you not asked me only about a certain person?" "What about the shepherd rescuing the sheep from the lion?" He said to them, "Have you not asked me only about the sheep?" "What about rescuing the shepherd from the lion?" He said to them, "Have you not

asked me only about the shepherd? What of an illegitimately-
born person as to inheriting? What, as to the levirate duties?
What, as to whitewashing his house? [16] What, as to whitewashing
his grave?" [17]—(he asked these questions) not that he put them off
with words [18] but that he never said anything which he had not
heard from his teacher. (B. Yoma 66b) [19]

DISCUSSION:—The text is a Baraitha and is partly repeated in the
Tosefta. Rabbi Eliezer, as we have observed, is of the second
generation of Tannaim. The passage is both confusing and ambiguous. A similar one is the following Tosefta.

TEXT:—They asked R. Eliezer: "What (is the rule) as to an illegitimately born person performing the levirate duty (to his
brother's wife)?" He said to them, "What as to his inheriting?"
(They responded) "And what as to his inheriting?" He countered, "What as to his performing the levirate duty?" (They
asked) "What as to whitewashing his house?" He said to them,
"And what as to whitewashing his grave?" (They asked) "What
as to whitewashing his grave?" He countered, "What as to
whitewashing his house?" (They asked) "What as to his raising
dogs (in Palestine)?" He said to them, "What as to his raising
swine?" (They asked) "What as to his raising swine?" He countered, "What as to his raising dogs?" (They asked) "What as to his
raising chickens?" He said to them, "What as to his raising small
cattle?" (They asked) "What as to his raising small cattle?" He
countered, "What as to his raising chickens?" (They asked)
"What as to his rescuing a shepherd from a wolf?" He said to
them, "Do you not mean to ask me about a lamb?" (They asked)
"What about his rescuing a lamb?" He countered, "Do you not
mean to ask as to whether he ought to save the shepherd?" (They
asked) "What as to a certain person (*peloni*) (having a share)
in the world-to-come?" He said to them, "It seems that you
mean to ask about a certain person (*peloni*)." (He evaded the
questions) not because R. Eliezer wished to confuse them but because he did not make a statement which he had not derived
from his teachers. (T. Yebamoth III, 3, 4)

Although Klausner [20] and others whom he quotes see in this exchange of questions in both passages a probable allusion to Jesus the evidence is far too flimsy. On the basis of a corrected translation it seems that the question regarding the world-to-come could have been asked concerning any prominent person in disfavor.

It might have been a Sadducee, perhaps of spurious birth, who denied immortality and who took a particular position on the prohibition, as a remembrance of the destruction of the Temple, of whitening the walls of the home and of the grave. The razing of the Temple made a deeper impression on the generation of R. Eliezer than did the recollection of Jesus. Assuredly, in the half century after the Exile of 70 C.E. there must have been chaotic internal conflicts—many revolving about the Sadducees.

Their leaders, like John Hyrcanus (135–104 B.C.E.) and Alexander Jannaeus (103–76 B.C.E.), had shady genealogies.[21] While it is true that by the time the Temple was destroyed the Sadducees had gone downhill and had lost their importance, nevertheless Josephus still boasts of the strict genealogical records of the priests kept in Jerusalem.[22] This, at least, would bear some relation to the birth-record mentioned in M. Yebamoth IV, 13. However, this is not to insist that a Sadducee is meant. All that is needed is to demonstrate that the reference need not be, and cannot be, to Jesus.

As support for this viewpoint, it may be added that on the above Mishnah-text Dalman[23] disputes the likelihood of a reference to Jesus. Of these several passages Bacher writes that the allusion, in all probability, is to a member of some distinguished Jerusalem family, whose illegitimate birth is recorded, the purpose being to warn others to preserve their family registry free from stain.[24] He takes the position that "a certain person" need not necessarily mean Jesus.

Moreover, in the Soncino Talmud translation[25] there is the observation that *peloni* ("a certain person") may be regarded as the equivalent of "John Doe," as in presenting a legal situation.[26] These passages may possibly refer (as Rashi claims) to Solomon's, or (according to the Tosafoth) to Absalom's family tree, and the anonymous expression used in deference to the Davidic Dynasty.

In this connection it is worth noticing a theory of Louis Fin-kelstein.[27] Recognizing the absurdity from both the Jewish and Christian viewpoint of asking whether Jesus had a share in the world-to-come, he agrees with the improbability of this being a reference to Jesus. He indicates the traditional explanation that the first *peloni* is identified with Solomon and the second *peloni* with Absalom: the sentence would, therefore, mean, "What of Solomon's right to the world-to-come?' He answered, 'Do you not ask me rather concerning Absalom?' " Then Finkelstein sug-gests the possibility that the first *peloni* is the Hebrew word for Philo and that the second *peloni* alludes to Philo's renegade nephew, Tiberius Alexander, Procurator of Judea (c. 46–48 c.e.) —and that this is expressive of R. Eliezer's low estimate of the Philo family. Whatever merit may reside in this theory, *peloni* in Tannaitic times does not refer to Jesus.

Let us examine still one more Tannaitic text.

TEXT:—"An impudent one." R. Eliezer says: (it means) an illegiti-mate child. R. Yehoshua says: a son of a *niddah*:[28] R. Akiba says: an illegitimate child (who is also) a son of a *niddah*. Once, when the elders were sitting at the gate,[29] two children passed in front of them. One (of them) covered his head and the other uncov-ered his head.[30] Him who uncovered his head R. Eliezer desig-nated "an illegitimate child"; R. Yehoshua said, "a son of a *niddah*"; R. Akiba said, "an illegitimate child *and* a son of a *niddah*." They said to R. Akiba: "How have you the audacity to contradict the words of your colleagues!" He answered them: "This I shall prove." He went to the mother of the child and saw her sitting in the market, selling peas. He said to her, "My daughter, if you tell me this which I inquire of you I shall bring you to the life of the world-to-come." She replied, "Swear it to me." R. Akiba vowed with his lips but disavowed in his heart. Said he to her: "This your son, what is the fact concerning him?" She answered, "When I entered the bridal chamber I was a *niddah* and my husband remained apart from me; but my para-nymph came to me, and by him I had this son—it resulted that this child is illegitimate *and* a son of a *niddah*." They said: Great was R. Akiba, for he put his teachers to shame. * In that hour they said: Blessed be the Lord God of Israel who hath revealed his secret to R. Akiba ben Joseph. * (Tractate Kallah 51a in ed. Ram.; Tractate Kallah, ed. Koronel p. 18b, or 41d; pp. 191–192 in ed. Higger)[31]

DISCUSSION:—The tractate which contains this passage is of later composition than most of the Talmud, but it is considered here because the persons of the story are Tannaim of the end of the first and the early part of the second century. The sentence marked by asterisks is obviously a still later addition, the narrative already having a conclusion.

On the face of it, this story has not the remotest relation to our theme. It is introduced only because some who have studied it imagined an allusion to Jesus.[32] That it cannot be so regarded is quite clear. There is no mention of Jesus or Mary; the use of the Tannaitic names is entirely apocryphal; these Sages are portrayed out of character; Akiba and his colleagues here represented lived a century after Jesus and certainly could not have spoken to him in his boyhood.

The erroneous notion as to this text arose much later, after Miriam *Megaddela* was wrongly thought to be the mother Mary, and Pappos ben Yehudah to be her husband.[33] Practically every scholar of standing in the twentieth century who has studied our theme has come to the conclusion that there is no authenticity in this passage.[34]

It is amazing, though, with what tenacity error persists. In his book *From Jesus to Paul*,[35] Klausner refers to the fact that Talmudic literature considered Jesus "impudent"; as evidence, the footnote refers us to the above text. This, despite the fact that in *Jesus of Nazareth* Klausner introduces for study this passage concerning "an impudent one" with his finding: "It is questionable whether this following *Talmudic* story is primarily concerned with Jesus." [36]

It cannot be emphasized too strongly: the Talmud record must be given clearly; distortions must be removed, once for all!

## 4. JESUS A CENTURY EARLIER

TEXT:—Our rabbis taught (in a Baraitha): Always let the left hand push away and the right hand bring near: not like Elisha who repulsed Gehazi with both hands, and not like R. Yehoshua ben Perahyah who repulsed Yeshu [1] with both hands. . . .* What of Rabbi Yehoshua ben Perahya? When King Jannaeus slew our rabbis, R. Yehoshua ben Perahya and Yeshu went to Alexandria of Egypt. When there was peace,[2] Shimeon ben Shetah sent to him: "From me, Jerusalem the Holy City, to you, Alexandria of Egypt, my sister. My husband dwells in your midst and I sit desolate." He [3] came by chance to a certain inn, where they accorded him much honor. He (R. Yehoshua) said: "How lovely is the inn." The other (Yeshu) said to him: "Rabbi, she [4] has defective eyes." [5] He (Yehoshua ben Perahya) said to him: "Wicked one, do you occupy yourself with such things!" He sounded four hundred trumpets [6] and anathematized him. He (Yeshu) came before him many times and said to him, "Receive me." But he paid no attention to him. One day he (R. Yehoshua) was reciting the *Shema*,[7] he (Yeshu) came before him. He was minded to receive him. He made a sign to him with his hand (to wait).[8] He (Yeshu) thought he had repulsed him. He went and set up a brick and worshipped it. He (R. Yehoshua) said to him, "Repent!" He replied: "Thus did I receive instruction from you, that every one who sins and causes many to sin, they give him no chance to repent." And a teacher has said: Yeshu practiced sorcery and enticed and led Israel astray. * (B. Sanhedrin 107b; repeated in B. Sotah 47a, without the final sentence).

TEXT:—He who says that Judah ben Tabbai was a Nasi; for him the happening in Alexandria is support for this. The people of Jerusalem wanted to install Judah ben Tabbai as Nasi in Jerusalem. He, however, fled and went to Alexandria. Then the people of Jerusalem wrote: "From Jerusalem the great to Alexandria the small. How long will my betrothed live with you while I am sitting here in sorrow because of him?" He left to board a ship. He said, "Deborah the hostess who has received us, was she lacking in any way?" One of his disciples answered him, "Rabbi, her eye blinks." He said to him, "Two things are against you: one, that you suspected me;[9] another, that you looked upon her.[10] Did I say in any way, beautiful in appearance? I talked only about her actions." And he was angry with him. Then he departed.[11] He who says that Shimeon ben Shetah was Nasi; for him the happening in Ashkelon is a support. (P. Hagigah 77d; compare with P. Sanhedrin 23c).

DISCUSSION:—The second text is really Gemara but is quoted here because it relates to the first text; but even in the first passage the part bounded by asterisks is Gemara and is beyond the Tannaitic period.

The question is as to whether the Yeshu named in the Baraitha portion is Jesus of Nazareth. The Gemara excerpts are added above to assist us in reaching the truth.

Alexander Jannaeus, here mentioned, reigned from 103–76 B.C.E. His slaying of the rabbis is dated at about 87 B.C.E.[12] If Jesus of Nazareth is truly meant in this passage, then it would seem that he lived about a hundred and fifteen years earlier than is generally accepted. Epiphanius reflects some knowledge of such a belief,[13] though it is possible that his information is no more than this Talmud text. Around 937 C.E., Kirkisani, who wrote a history of Jewish sects, followed the same trend of speculation and designated R. Yehoshua ben Perahyah as an uncle of Jesus.[14] The Toledoth Yeshu related Jesus to R. Yehoshua ben Perahyah and Shimeon ben Shetah, but it probably based itself on what had already become an unfounded tradition.[15]

Those who find in these passages a definite reference to Jesus of Nazareth [16] resort to the argument that the Talmudic teachers were simply mistaken in their chronology. They make much of the flight to Egypt, the argument with the rabbis, the setting up of a new method of worship, the accusation of causing a multitude to sin. They place value upon the frequency with which this identification is repeated in Jewish tradition.

However, the weight of evidence is conclusive that the passages cannot refer to Jesus of Nazareth.

First, the error in chronology cannot be so lightly dismissed. Yehoshua ben Perahya is supposed to have flourished in the latter half of the second century, prior to the reign of Alexander Jannaeus, and he is one of the so-called "Pairs" of Sages who preceded the Pair, Judah ben Tabbai and Shimeon ben Shetah. Among those who seek to accept this early date are the people who desire to prove the non-historicity of Jesus; they say that Jesus *was* a disciple of Yehoshua ben Perahya and that a hundred years or so after his lifetime there lived a false prophet whose deeds and fate were attributed to Jesus and written into the New Testament.[17] Such a theory would set a solitary Talmud text against so much else that argues the other way—and refusal to accept such a theory leaves us with a discrepancy of date which places great doubt upon the validity of this Talmud story.

Second, the entire account—as agreed by Bacher,[18] Strack [19] and Klausner,[20] Zeitlin [21] and others [22]—sounds historically unreal, just an invention.

Third, the reason given in this episode assuredly would be an odd one for starting a new religion. It certainly does not accord with the recorded character of Jesus.

Fourth, is it likely that there were two rabbis of two different generations to whom exactly the same thing happened? The Palestine version tells the story of Judah ben Tabbai, not of Yehoshua ben Perahya and does not name Jesus at all. The Babylonian version gives the impression of having tacked on the concluding sentence with mention of Jesus the Nazarene leading the people astray,[23] and gives every indication of being the less authentic version. Laible and Klausner think that even the Baraitha mention of Jesus in the Babylonian Talmud text is a late addition, that the genuinely original reading was simply, "Always let the left hand push away and the right hand bring near." [24]

Fifth, if Ben Stada is taken to be Jesus it becomes easier to connect this story with Jesus' (Ben Stada's) flight to Egypt. But we have seen that Ben Stada could not have been Jesus.

Sixth, it would be most difficult to establish the fact that in the Tannaitic period the imposition of the ban took place as here indicated. It is only in later Amoraic times that the Shofar was used to excommunicate in a similar way.[25] Furthermore, the worship of a brick is known only in the Hermes cult; it is not Christian.[26] In the disputation in 1240, R. Yehiel was forced to deal with these passages and, in so doing, added that the brick was fashioned as a cross;[27] however, the Talmud gives no indication whatever that this was so. Anyway, it was the death of Jesus that gave meaning to the cross; how, then, could Jesus have worshipped it?

Seventh, although there is a Jewish tradition connecting Jesus with Yehoshua ben Perahyah there is also a tradition which greatly doubts it. In addition to Yehiel and Nahmanides,[28] David Gans in *Zemah David*,[29] Isaac Abravanel in *Maayene Hayeshuah*,[30] Zalmon Zevi in *Jüdische Theriak*,[31] and Abraham Perissol in *Maggen Abraham*,[32] argue that the Jesus mentioned in the Talmud as of a century earlier is not the Jesus of Christianity. It is interesting to observe that even in the "Book of Tradition" (*Sefer Hakabbalah*),[33] Abraham ibn Daud of the twelfth century records the tradition that Yehoshua ben Perahyah was the teacher of Jesus but then adds the "true tradition"[34] that Jesus was born in the fourth year of the reign of Alexander (Jannai) and died, at the age of thirty-six, in the reign of Aristobulus, the son of Jannai; this latter tradition would denote a date for Jesus as a contemporary of Judah ben Tabbai rather than of the earlier Yehoshua ben Perahya, but still would not agree with the date given in the Christian tradition.

Eighth, while the Munich, Florence and Karlsruhe manuscripts and the early printed editions of the Talmud mention Yeshu, only the Munich text adds "the Nazarene." We are therefore led to the conclusion that this solitary reading is incorrect, that some other Jesus was meant—for Jesus was a common name, as Jesus ben Sirach, Jesus (Justus) the historian, a Jesus other than Jesus of Nazareth, named in the New Testament,[35] still others named by Josephus.[36] The fact that this rejected disciple came to Egypt, where Greek was spoken, makes it quite understandable that he should have a form of his Hebrew name

Yehoshua which would approximate the Greek, Jesu: namely, Yeshu.

An intriguing suggestion is offered by J. Z. Lauterbach [37] as to the Jesus who might have been intended. The allusion may possibly be to Jesus ben Sirach, grandson of Jesus ben Sirach. The latter was the author of the apocryphal work we know as Ecclesiasticus, which was regarded by the rabbis with disfavor as one of the "external books." [38] The younger Jesus ben Sirach, who translated Ecclesiasticus into Greek, came from Egypt around 132 B.C.E., which corresponds to the generation of Yehoshua ben Parahya. There were particular legends regarding Jesus, the author of the apocryphal work, not unlike those which later became associated with Jesus.[39] Thus, with the additional tie-in with regard to Egypt—for Jesus of Nazareth is also supposed to have been there [40]—a confusion developed in the course of three or four centuries, in which the three named Jesus were merged: Jesus ben Sirach the elder, Jesus ben Sirach the grandson, and Jesus of Nazareth.

For our present purposes it is sufficient to show that the passage under discussion is not an authentic allusion to Jesus. In all likelihood it was Judah ben Tabbai who fled to Egypt at a time of persecution (as reported in the Palestinian Talmud), for he was a contemporary of Shimeon ben Shetah and he lived in 87 B.C.E. during the persecution of the Pharisees by Alexander Jannaeus. Jesus is not mentioned in the account of the incident which is told of Judah ben Tabbai. But the Babylonian Talmud redactors who lived at a distance from the scene of the event described the story erroneously as though it had happened to Yehoshua [41] ben Perahya and, through confusion or deliberately, in the Amoraic centuries the name Yeshu crept in.

## 5. MISCELLANEOUS ITEMS

TEXT:—R. Meir used to say: What is the meaning of the saying, "For he that is hanged is a reproach unto God?" [1] Like two brothers, twins, resembling each other: One ruled over the whole world and the other went for robbery. After a while, this one who went for robbery was caught and they hanged him on the gallows, and all passersby say: "It seems that the ruler is hanged." Thus, it is said, "For he that is hanged is a reproach unto God." (Tosefta, Sanhedrin IX, 7)

DISCUSSION:—R. Meir, a disciple of both Ishmael and Akiba, was a leading Tanna in the second third of the second century.[2] Herford writes that one can hardly doubt that the above passage refers to Jesus.[3] The evidence submitted comprises the following: the New Testament verse, "He that hath seen me hath seen the father"; the reference to hanging, which may be regarded as the crucifixion; the gibes of bystanders at Jesus' crucifixion;[4] and the relationship (as brothers) between the Ruler of the World and Jesus.

These items of evidence, however, quickly vanish upon closer inquiry. For one thing, the Hebrew term *tzalub* in the original text need not necessarily mean crucifixion, though it is used in that sense too; it is used equally to denote hanging on a gallows, as in the case of Haman (the discussion of which in Midrash Rabbah to Esther 9:2 is therefore untenable as a possible allusion to Jesus).[5] Furthermore, how explain the accusation that Jesus took to robbery?[6]

The meaning of the passage is obvious, requiring no forced interpretation. The point is: if a human being, created in the image of God, is hanged for a crime such as robbery, those who see him hanging see a reproach unto God, whose creation had so deteriorated. This plain understanding of the passage is supported by Bacher[7] and Strack.[8]

TEXT:—Two who walk on a journey; one has a pitcher of water in his hand. If they both drink of it they both die. If (only) one drinks, he can reach civilization. Ben Patura expounded: it is better that they both drink and die than that one look on and see his companion die. However, when R. Akiba came he taught: "that thy brother may live with thee"[9]—your living takes precedence. (B. Baba Metzia 62a)

DISCUSSION:—This is a Baraitha. M. S. Rens [10] proposes that the name, Ben Patura, means Jesus. He supports his theory by holding that use of the term *darash* ("expound") instead of the usual *limed* ("teach"), without its being connected with the interpretation of a verse, is extraordinary and would be used by one who taught on his own authority—as did Jesus. He says, further, that Jesus referred to himself as *filius patri* ("son of the Father") [11] which would be in Hebrew *Ben Patri*, corrupted into Ben Patura.

This theory is proved untenable by several authorities, especially by J. Z. Lauterbach, [12] who cites many passages where *darash* is used in this way [13] and, for good measure, shows where this text (and Ben Paturi's *darash*) is found in the Sifra [14] *with* the Scriptural verse at the opening. He points out the oddity of having one part of the name (Ben) in Hebrew and the other part (Patri) in Latin; that Patura or Paturi, if a contemporary of Akiba of the early part of the second century C.E., could not be Jesus; also, that the fuller form of the name is given as Yehuda ben Patiri, who, Lauterbach believes, could well be Yehuda ben Betera. [15]

TEXT:—"The servant shall bow down to the anointed one." (B. Sanhedrin 61b)

DISCUSSION:—This is said in connection with idol-worship. It might be considered a guarded allusion to Jesus. S. Funk [16] does indeed see in this a reference to the Christian acceptance of Jesus as the Messiah-servant. However, the context of the passage makes it clear that this is but a symbolic catchword or mnemonic. [17]

TEXT:—The witnesses are examined by use of a substitute for the Divine Name—so—"May Yose smite Yose." (M. Sanhedrin VII, 5)

DISCUSSION:—The author of this saying is R. Yehoshua ben Karha, of the third generation of Tannaim, of the period from 140 to 160 C.E. [18] The suggestion is made that the first Yose [19] represents Jesus, the Son, and the second Yose represents the Father, God.

Thus interpreted, the witnesses would be questioned in order to ascertain whether the one occused of blasphemy placed Jesus above God.[20]

There is not much to the suggestion, however. It is unlikely that even for illustrative purposes the rabbis would allude to Jesus as a divinity. "Yose" is given as a substitute for the Divine Name because the name of God was too sacred to speak when defining the nature of blasphemous speech; another, unmistakable, yet commonly used name was substituted.[21] Rashi, of the eleventh century, in his comment on the passage [22] stated simply that this particular substitute was used because it had four letters even as there are four letters in the Tetragrammaton.

There is incidental interest in one or two further guesses as to the choice of the name Yose. One is that it is the deity Jovis, spelled in Hebrew with the letters jumbled.[23] Because some of the rabbinic textual variations [24] in giving this item spell the word *Yoseh* [25]—which Nathan ben Yehiel considers the correct variant since it has three of the four letters of the Tetragrammaton—A. Kohut mentions the possibility of this form of the word alluding to Zeus.[26] There is, though, the suggestion that *Yose* is the correct form, since its letters have the numerical value (*gematria*) of *Elohim*, which means God—each adding up to eighty-six. Despite its recent reappearance,[27] Kohut long ago rejected the *gematria* theory in this matter on the grounds that the working out of numerical equivalents belongs to later Haggadic exegesis.[28]

TEXT:—And these have no share in the world-to-come. . . . R. Akiba says: Also he who reads heretical books, or who whispers charms over a wound, and says: "I will put none of the diseases upon thee, which I have put upon the Egyptians; for I am the Lord that healeth thee." [29] (M. Sanhedrin X, 1)

DISCUSSION:—This passage is introduced here for consideration because, as brought out in B. Shebuoth 15b and P. Shabbath 8b, the Talmud does not oppose healing, so long as a Bible verse is not used as part of the formula.[30] The forbidden part of the charm is the use of the verse which has the name of God; yet

Leviticus 1:1 and Leviticus 13:9 are forbidden, although God's name is not included.

The item to consider is the fact that the significant verse-formula for healing is: "I am the Lord thy God that healeth thee." Those three Hebrew words [31] have the numerical value 388; by adding 3 for the number of words we get 391, and 391 is exactly the numerical value of *Yehoshua*,[32] which is the fuller form of the name Yeshu.

In Jewish tradition, Hebrew words or phrases of numerical equivalence are regarded as having a special relationship. Therefore, Louis Ginzberg [33] suggested the likelihood that the crypto-Christians made use of this verse with these three words to perform healing in the name of Jesus, without openly naming Jesus but letting the numerical correspondence serve as the agent of reference. It is this secret practice which Akiba may well have opposed.

As indicated in our analysis of the previous passage, it is hazardous to apply *gematria* to this early period.[34] Its use has been mainly homiletic and mystical. Furthermore, there is practically unlimited license in the connections one can make in playing this game of numbers. Hebrew words easily lend themselves to it. We are aware, for instance, of the harm inflicted by those who suddenly discovered that in the *alenu* prayer the word "of nothingness" may be seen the *gematria* of "Jesus," [35] and that *akum* ("worshippers of the stars and zodiac") could have the numerical value of "worshippers of Christ and Mary." [36] The suggestion regarding this text-quotation from the Mishnah is an ingenious one, in any case.

We now have completed the section given over to an inspection of most Tannaitic passages erroneously believed to refer to Jesus. An effort was made to include all possibilities which have been offered but guesses can be exceedingly speculative, so that we can never be sure that we are aware of them all. The ones given, however, represent a fairly complete survey of the field. We must now examine yet one more aspect of this subject.

## SECTION C

## INDIRECT ALLUSIONS

The work done heretofore on Jesus in Talmud and Midrash has been mainly the assembling of passages in the rabbinic literature which name Jesus, or employ a name which, correctly or erroneously, is believed to have meant Jesus. This procedure establishes arbitrary boundaries to the field of inquiry. Is it not within the realm of plausibility that he could have been alluded to without specific mention of his name?

Guided by the attitudes to Jesus revealed in those texts which do name him, and by means of other evidences, should we not be able to discern allusions to him made indirectly?

It is true that some of those who have written on this theme have presented the passages wherein dualism and trinitarianism are opposed. Why, however, stop with these? Inasmuch as early Christianity accepted Jesus as the Messiah, should we not pay attention to the Messiah references? If Jesus was regarded as one greater than Moses, should we not attempt to gain added knowledge of the Jewish viewpoint through a study of what is told of Moses in the rabbinic record?

An essential in the belief in Jesus is that he is God incarnate, bringing divinity closer to man; should we not investigate further in this direction? The Talmud and cognate literature regard Jesus, in instances where his name is mentioned, as one who performed healing and other acts which believers designate as miracles; should we not seek further information on the rabbinic opinion of miracles?

In examining the record for this further light we must exercise the utmost caution, for the reason that the rabbinic statements on these subjects are primarily and essentially the natural unfolding of the religion, a continuation of the basic principles of the Bible and some of the non-Biblical Jewish literature of the earlier period, and the attitudes evolved and expressed may have resulted quite independently of the person of Jesus or of the rise of Christianity.

Furthermore, conceding the influence of external factors, how can we differentiate between the influence of Christianity and that of other theological and philosophical teachings akin to those of Christianity which flourished during the Tannaitic centuries? At best we can deal only with probabilities and, even so, it is imperative to refrain from extravagant guesswork.

Yet, there are indications of some Christian influence upon Judaism. "The rise of Christianity," Herford wrote,[1] "instead of being fatal to Judaism, gave it new life; all the latent energy of the old religion was roused to combat the opposition of the new." One need not agree entirely with so strong a statement but it is significant that Herford, who gave so much study to the subject, should have reached such a conclusion.

In his *Introduction to the Talmud*, Strack holds that the first attempts to put the Oral Law into written form are traceable to the first half of the second century C.E. and he advances the conjecture that the codification and the writing down of the Jewish tradition, culminating in the Mishnah and similar productions, resulted in some degree from the formation of the New Testament canon then in process.[2]

James Parkes relates the influences of Christianity on Judaism in the second century[3] and A. Marmorstein deals with the third century.[4] Samuel S. Cohon presents a study of the Fall of Man, Original Sin, Mediation and Redemption, and discloses that, while these things became central in Paulinian Christianity, they remained on the periphery of Judaism; yet in Judaism the rabbis "often voice a polemical note, aiming to controvert heterodox teaching within the Synagogue and of other faiths."[5]

In the *Story of Bible Translations*, Max Margolis tells how Aquila, the proselyte to Judaism who came from Pontus, worked under R. Eliezer ben Hyrcanus and R. Yehoshua ben Hananiah to produce a word-for-word translation of Hebrew Scripture into Greek, for the Septuagint translation had become disfigured and had become a tool for the furtherance of Christianity, whereas Aquila's strictly literal translation served as "the Synagogue's weapon of defence against the nascent Church." [6]

Through these several instances and numerous others which could be added we see that there *was* Christian influence on Judaism; yet the name of Jesus is not necessarily specified.

An all-embracing study of the relationship between Judaism and Christianity would demand attention to such matters as: Abrogation of the Law, Validity of the Oral Law, Who Is the True Israel, Antinomianism, Fall of Man, Original Sin, Power of Mediation, Atonement, Repentance, Salvation, Redemption, Divine Grace, Asceticism, Monasticism, Church and State, Liturgy, Logos, Holy Spirit, Virgin Mother, Saints, Relics, Sacraments, Hierarchy, Celibacy, Codes of Conduct, Diaspora, Survival of the Jew, Mission of the Jew—and much else. These, however, are themes which are beyond the dimensions of this book.

We shall remain within the limits of what the Talmudic mention of Jesus suggests, namely: Jesus as Messiah, as Son of God and as worker of miracles. Even within this scope, it will be necessary to restrict the quotations to a number sufficient to indicate the trend of thinking. This limitation is prompted by two reasons: the rabbinic material is vast; also, not being censored, as in the case of specific passages about Jesus, it is available in the usual collections of rabbinic literature.

## 1. UNITY OF GOD

TEXT:—Therefore, man was created singular . . . that the *Minim* might not say: there are many Powers in Heaven. (Mishnah, Sanhedrin IV, 5)

TEXT:—Man was created last. And why was he created last? That the *Minim* might not say: there was a partner with Him in the work (of creation). (Tosefta, Sanhedrin VIII, 17)

DISCUSSION:—The *Minim* designate, as we have observed, non-Christian heretics no less than Jewish Christians. The mention of *many* Powers, in the first text, is sufficient to classify this as a general statement of the unity of God in opposition to those who believed in several Powers. It cannot be regarded with any definiteness as alluding to Jesus.[1]

The second text brings a more probably reference.[2] The passage alludes to man sharing in the work of God: Jesus, in Christian tradition, is the Man-God. Still, we know that the battle against the concept of two deities is an ancient one in Judaism, antedating Jesus. It is reflected in the opposition to the dualism of the Persian system and remained prominently in Judaism, finding expression in the prayer book, too, in such phrases as, "Thou formest light and darkness, good out of evil." What may be regarded as the earliest equivalent of a "confession of faith" in Judaism is the recital of the *Shema* declaration of God's unity. The *Shema* is the very first subject discussed in the Mishnah. Why is it first? Why is it followed in the liturgy by the affirmation: "True and firm belief is this for us"? [3]

Certainly the positive assertion of God's unity antedates the rise of Christianity but the *formulation* of Jewish *doctrines* appeared necessary, according to K. Kohler, "particularly in opposition to the Christian and Mohammedan creeds." [4] Moreover, it is of interest to observe that Philo, although his place in the unfolding of Judaism is a disputed one, expressed the opinion that the Unity of God is a higher concept than the Trinity.[5]

TEXT:—That *Min* said to Rabbi, "He who formed mountains did not create wind and he who created wind did not form mountains, as it is in Scripture: 'For, lo, He that formeth the mountains, and createth the wind.' " [6] He (Rabbi) said to him, "Fool, look at the end of the verse, 'The God of hosts is His name.' " He (the *Min*) said to him, "Give me three days' time and I will refute you." Rabbi sat in a fast for three days. When he was about to eat they said to him, "The *Min* is at the gate." He said, " 'They put poison into my food.' " [7] He said to him, "Rabbi, I bring you good news. Your enemy found no answer and fell from the roof and died." (B. Hullin 87a)

DISCUSSION:—"Rabbi" is Judah the Nasi, the compiler of the Mishnah. Therefore, although the passage is Gemara, the incident deals with the most prominent Tanna. The point of the odd story is the Jewish denial that there were two creative Powers.

TEXT:—It says: "I beheld, till thrones were placed," [8] and it says, "A fiery stream issued and came forth from before him"; [9] not to give an opening for the peoples of the world to say that these are two Powers, but "I am the Lord thy God." [10] . . . R. Nathan says, thence is an answer to the *Minim* who say there are two Powers, for when the Holy One, blessed be He, stood and said, "I am the Lord thy God," who stood up and protested? (Mechilta, *Yithro*, #5, p. 66b ed. Friedmann)

DISCUSSION:—Mechilta is Midrash of the Tannaitic period, on the Book of Exodus. The full text describes God as the Lord of all time and of all that has been done in the world.

TEXT:—"See now that I, even I, am He." [11] This is an answer to those who say there is no Power in Heaven. He who says there are two Powers in Heaven is answered by: "And there is no god with Me." [12] (Sifre, *Haazinu*, #329, p. 139b)

DISCUSSION:—Sifre is Midrash of the Tannaitic period, on the Book of Deuteronomy. A similar comment, combining use of the two texts above, is given in Mechilta, *Beshallah*, #4, p. 38a.

If we are to accord to these passages the possibility of being allusions to Jesus we are confronted with the problem that they speak of two gods, not of the Trinity such as we know it in Christianity. To this the answer would be that although the idea of Trinity is hinted at in the New Testament,[13] and was in the thinking of some of the Christians of the early period, nevertheless it did not become a dogma of Christianity until the fourth century, and even from that time on there were Christian groups who opposed trinitarianism.[14]

On the periphery of Judaism there were occasional tendencies toward conceiving duality in the divinity: for example, mention of the spirit of arch-Adam.[15] Gnosticism and the religion of Persia taught dualism—but the second Power was regarded as being opposed to God, not a co-worker. In Christianity the Father and the Son and (with the final formulation of the Trinity) the Holy

Spirit blend in a harmonious, not conflicting, Godhead. There-fore, these rabbinic passages may be best explained as references to Christian belief. So they are understood by others, too, who have studied these texts.[16]

This view is strengthened by the verse in the Epistle to the Hebrews which tells that "God . . . hath in these last days spoken unto us by his Son . . . by whom also he made the worlds." [17] This Epistle, known among the ancient Jewish Chris-tians, presents Jesus in the role of co-creator with God—pre-cisely the two Powers opposed by the rabbis.[18]

Furthermore, we find in the Tannaitic record several battles on the interpretation of Old Testament verses, as to whether they mean One God or more than one; for example, the debate be-tween the *Min* and R. Ishmael ben Yose [19] (B. Sanhedrin 38b), and the position against the *Minim* taken by Shimeon ben Azzai (Sifre Nu. #143, p. 54a and B. Menah. 110a) [20] that the name of God is not really plural. This kind of thing, discussion as to whether the Scripture verse connotes more than One God, is a characteristic of Christian-Jewish polemics.[21]

## 2. INCARNATION OF GOD

TEXT:—"The sons of God saw." [1] R. Shimeon ben Yohai called them: the sons of judges. R. Shimeon ben Yohai execrated all who call them: the sons of god.[2] (Midrash, Genesis Rabbah, 26:8)

DISCUSSION:—R. Shimeon ben Yohai was of the third generation of Tannaim. He vigorously denied that God could become in-carnate in a son.

TEXT:—"Behold I will stand before thee there upon the rock in Horeb." [3] God said to Moses: In every place where you find a trace of the feet of man, there am I before you. (Mechilta, *Vayassa*, Beshallah, #6, p. 52b)

DISCUSSION:—It is implied here that God resides in every human being, not exclusively in a special one.

TEXT:—"Thou in Thy love hast led the people." [4] Thou hast wrought grace [5] for us, for we had no works, as it is in Scripture, "I will mention the lovingkindness of the Lord"; [6] also, "I will sing of the mercies of the Lord for ever." [7] And from the beginning the world was built only upon grace, as it is in Scripture, "I declare the world is built upon grace." [8] (Mechilta, *Shiratha*, Beshallah, #9, p. 42b)

DISCUSSION:—Linking together these three sample texts we see that the Tannaim believed that God is present in all human beings. It is not necessary for Him to come to earth as Man-God. Forever He is close to all and His grace is, as it has been, with the world for all time.

### 3. THE MESSIAH HAS NOT COME

There are hundreds of passages in rabbinic literature telling of the Messiah and his coming. There is no direct proof that these texts have any relation to the appearance of Jesus and the acceptance by Christians of him as the promised Messiah. This is to say that, other than through *interpretation* of the authentic references which name Jesus in the Talmud and cognate literature, there is no out-and-out statement in this literature which says: Jesus is not the expected Messiah. Such a thought, however, is implied in the references to the Messiah. If the rabbinic Sages knew of Jesus and of the religion based on him as the Messiah, and yet taught that the Messiah has not come, we may infer that this constitutes a denial of Jesus as the Messiah.

The alternatives would be that they never heard of the Christian acclaim of Jesus as the Messiah or that, in teaching men to expect the Messiah in the future, the Sages did so entirely uninfluenced by what they knew of the Christian doctrine regarding Jesus.

A reasonable view would be that many of the Jewish leaders, certainly those living in areas where Christianity flourished, did hear that Jesus was believed to be the Messiah. Nevertheless, they spoke forth the hope that the Messiah was yet to come. They expressed a principle of Judaism. They brought comfort and hope to their own people. In the main, these statements had no polemic purpose, but there is the likelihood that secondarily and indirectly they could have served as a denial that Jesus was the awaited Messiah.

The Messianic passages are far too numerous to quote. A cross-section of them is given in *Everyman's Talmud.*[1] Those of the Tannaim, not nearly as numerous as those of the Amoraim, are described in G. F. Moore's *Judaism in the First Centuries of the Christian Era,*[2] Joseph Klausner's *Die messianischen Vorstellungen im Zeitalter der Tannaiten* and in Isaac Abravanel's *Mashmia Yeshuah.*[3] Here are several of specific interest:

TEXT:—R. Shimeon ben Yohai said: My teacher Akiba used to expound Numbers 24:17 [4] to mean "Koziba shall come forth out of Jacob." When Akiba saw Bar Koziba he said, "This is King Messiah." R. Yohanan ben Torta said, "Akiba, grass will sprout through your cheeks [5] ere the son of David comes." (P. Taanit IV, 8 or 68d)

DISCUSSION:—Although this is Gemara it deals with Akiba, a Tanna. There is every reason to believe that Akiba knew of the Christian belief in Jesus as the Messiah. Yet, approximately a century after the Crucifixion, he placed his confidence in Bar Koziba as the hoped-for Messiah. It was misplaced confidence, as the other rabbi told him in definite terms. Both these Tannaim agreed, impliedly, that Jesus was not the Messiah. Historically this passage is significant, inasmuch as the wide adherence gained by Bar Koziba's claim to Messiahship is regarded as an important factor in the final separation of the Jewish Christians from the Jewish community.[6]

TEXT:—Prepare a seat for Hezekiah, king of Judah, who is coming. (B. Berachoth 28b)

DISCUSSION:—Although it is Gemara, this tells a saying of the distinguished Tanna, Yohanan ben Zakkai, on his death-bed. If this be a reference to the Messiah, as it is believed to be, it identifies Hezekiah as the Messiah and represents in Jewish literature something of the idea of "a second coming."

TEXT:—R. Eliezer the Great says . . . in the period preceding the Messiah impudence will abound . . . and the kingdom will be turned to *Minuth*. (M. Sotah IX, 15)

DISCUSSION:—W. Bacher holds that this is a late addition, tacked on the Mishnah text,[7] and is not really the statement of R. Eliezer. Lauterbach, accepting this position, then translates: "as a result of the (would-be) Messiah the kingdom turned to *Minuth*." He suggests the possibility that this could be an allusion to Emperor Constantine's conversion to Christianity.[8]

Accepting this as a later insertion, Herford observes that it is appended to a section of the Talmud which tells of the difficulties of Judaism subsequent to the destruction of the Temple and that it would be natural to consider the woes which lie ahead, before the coming of the Messiah.[9] He argues that it could not refer to the conversion of Constantine because not only Eliezer but also Nehemiah, to whom the statement is attributed in other places,[10] lived before the time of Constantine; even R. Isaac,[11] into whose mouth the saying is placed in one instance, who lived within the period of Constantine, makes no specific reference to the conversion.

The interpretation is a difficult one. The all-important word [12] in the text *could* mean either "future" (Herford: is at hand) or "consequence" (Lauterbach: as a result). The fact that several persons are given the credit creates doubt that any of these is the true author. The date, therefore, could be sufficiently after Constantine's conversion. The mention of the destruction of the Temple by Rome may well have been regarded a suitable place at which to attach the report of the conversion of Rome to Christianity. There remains, though, the difficulty of believing that the rabbis would refer to Jesus as *Meshiha*, Messiah. Would they not have used a term which means *would-be Messiah*, messianic pretender or Christian Messiah?

Moreover, the Babylonian Talmud (Sanhedrin 97a) supports a Tannaitic date for the statement by quoting R. Nehemiah and giving it as a Baraitha. The Soncino translation, in an attempt to explain the reference as an allusion to Christianity, comments that it is a remarkable forecast in 150 c.e. by Rabbi Nehemiah that Rome would officially accept Christianity in 313 under Constantine.

TEXT:—How long will the days of the Messiah last? R. Akiba said: forty years. . . . R. Eliezer [13] said: a hundred years. R. Berechia said in the name of R. Dosa: six hundred years. R. Judah the Nasi said: four hundred years. . . . R. Eliezer said: a thousand years. (Tanhuma, *Ekeb* #7)

DISCUSSION:—This is a later Midrash which quotes opinions of the Tannaim. Other passages have them specify other durations.[14] This reference is included here as but a sample of the considerable speculation in the attempt to ascertain by textual hint combined with arithmetic how soon the Messiah would come,[15] how long the period of trials would be and how magnificent would be the happier days-to-come.

## 4. MIRACLES: MOSES

TEXT:—It has been taught: On that day R. Eliezer used all possible arguments to (confirm his opinion) but they did not accept them. He said to them, "If the Law agrees with me, may this carob-tree prove it." Then, the carob-tree was torn a hundred cubits from its place or, as some say, four hundred cubits. They said to him, "From a carob-tree no proof can be brought." Again he said to them: "If the Law agrees with me, may this water-channel prove it." The water flowed backward. They said to him, "From a water-channel no proof can be brought." Then he said, "May the walls of this House of Study prove it." The walls buckled and were about to fall. R. Joshua rebuked the walls, saying, "If students of the Torah dispute about the Law, what has it to do with you?" Out of deference to R. Joshua the walls did not fall but out of deference to R. Eliezer they did not become straight but remained buckled. Then R. Eliezer said, "If the Law agrees with me, let it be proved from Heaven." A *Bath Kol* [1] issued forth and said, "What have you against R. Eliezer? The decision of the Law is always according to him." [2] R. Joshua

stood up and said, "It is not in Heaven." [3] What does this mean?
R. Jeremiah said, "The Torah was given us from Sinai; we pay
no attention to a *Bath Kol.* For already from Sinai the Torah
said, 'By a majority you are to decide.' " [4] (B. Baba Metzia 59b;
similarly, in greater detail, in P. Moed Katan III, 1 or 81c, d)

DISCUSSION:—The incident given in a Baraitha has to do with important Tannaim. It is reminiscent of the saying, "The voice of
the people is the voice of God." Its significance in relation to our
theme is the fact that the Tannaim refused to heed signs and
miracles in seeking to comprehend the will of God expressed in
the Torah and to crystallize it in religious practice laid down in
rabbinic law.

The Talmud record regarding miracles is at first sight somewhat puzzling. A good summation, though, is given in *A Rabbinic Anthology* [5] and in *Judaism in the First Centuries of the
Christian Era.* [6] Of interest to us is the fact that while saintly
Sages were regarded as having performed wondrous deeds, re-
course was never had to miracles to prove the truth of a religious doctrine. The attempt by R. Eliezer was the single exception, and he was squelched by R. Joshua. The decision against
R. Eliezer in this incident—and let us remember that R. Eliezer
lived in the latter part of the first and the early part of the second
century C.E—is a contradiction of I Corinthians 1:22, "For the
Jews require a sign, and the Greeks seek after wisdom," [7] and
of Matthew 12:39, "An evil and adulterous generation that seeks
after a sign." [8]

The miracles of the Old Testament stood in a class by themselves. Other than these, miracles were regarded in the light of
Deuteronomy 13:2-6, namely, that a false prophet could mislead
the people to "serve other gods" by signs and wonders. Thus,
we already have seen that the Tannaim looked upon Jesus as one
who practiced sorcery and led the people astray. Moreover, as
Christianity emphasized more and more the miracles of the Birth
and Resurrection of Jesus and his wondrous acts, rabbinic Judaism correspondingly placed miracles into a subsidiary category,
minimizing their place, after Old Testament times, in the reve-

lation of religious truth.[9] From this we may infer definitely an indirect allusion to Jesus.

TEXT:—R. Alexandri said in the name of R. Hiyya bar Abba: "Greater is the miracle wrought for the sick than for Hananiah, Michael and Azariah." (B. Nedarim 41a)

DISCUSSION:—Hiyya bar Abba, named in the Gemara here, was of the fifth and last generation of Tannaim. This and other passages are quoted by Alexander Guttmann to show the trend toward believing that, although miracles were regarded as the foundation of belief, "overemphasis of Biblical miracles and simultaneous depreciation of Talmudic miracles had an apologetic-theological angle. It was largely aimed at the miracles of rising Christianity. The decline of the miracles as regards influencing law and practice goes parallel with the growth of Christianity." [10]

Conversely, as the miracles of later times were depreciated and as the new revelation from Heaven (to Jesus) was rejected, the role of Moses was heightened. This is shown in some of the Tannaitic passages but especially in the later Midrashic literature [11] which we shall examine in Chapter III.[12]

# SUMMARY

Here now is the record concerning Jesus in the rabbinic Judaism of the Tannaitic period, that is, for the first two and a quarter centuries of the Christian Era.

The findings in the vast realm of this literature are amazingly scant and restricted. There are remarkably few passages proved genuine. A temptation in this kind of study, which might mislead into unwarranted conclusions, has been carefully avoided. This temptation is the tendency to end an analysis of a potential allusion to Jesus by stating that nothing authentic is proved, that it is only a *hint*, but subsequently, in the analysis of other passages, to use the *hint* as a base upon which to build further conclusions. Thus after several repetitions, the *hint* becomes a solid foundation —but an incorrect one.[1]

The greater part of this chapter was given over to demonstrating the unreliability of what, at some time or other, were considered probable or even unquestionable references to Jesus. The evidence was compiled, the arguments were evaluated and that viewpoint was accepted which was the more probable one. Thus we arrived at the untenability of identifying Jesus with what is recorded of Ben Stada, of Balaam, of "a certain person," of a lad who lived in the time of Akiba a century later than the New Testament date of Jesus, of a disciple of Yehoshua ben Perahya who lived more than a century earlier than the New Testament date of Jesus, and of miscellaneous items. We found some of the reasons for these mistaken identifications: the misleading clues contained in the Gospel story, the similarities of one or more details in these Tannaitic passages with the Christian tradition of Jesus, the straining, because of the intense interest in a theme where the record is so meagre, to find more than is there, the prompting of a polemic or apologetic or even irenic motivation, the reading back into an early record of what later developed in literature (as in the Toledoth Yeshu) as a misconstruction, the honest mistakes of scholarship and the irresponsible theories of guesswork.

Why was it necessary to give so much space to proving the improbability of these references? Is it not a negative pursuit, the mere making of an erasure? No, it was necessary not only for the sake of setting the record straight but also because of the deplorable damage done by these untruths—damage measured in terms of theological misinterpretation, historical misunderstanding, the burning of books, the fostering of animosity which is a negation of the very idea of religion, and the persecution and slaying of the Jewish inheritors of the Talmud.

It is particularly depressing to discover that even professedly friendly writers on this theme allow personal prejudices to interfere—so that Laible, for instance, takes the position that the Jews said these execrable things but we must understand that they, poor people, could not say otherwise, for they did not have the light properly to see. "A thorough study of these passages must," Laible thinks, in one of his milder moods, "shake the belief of the Jews in the authority of the Talmud . . . and must further induce the Jews to read the New Testament." [2] In the writer's opinion, greater evil than good has been done by Laible's study of the theme—the twofold evil of untruth coupled with calumny.

In the swamps of error the germs of disease are bred. The swamps must be drained and the germs of disease destroyed in the bright sunlight of truth.

We found five authentic references in the Tannaitic era. With regard to these, too, we deal with probabilities. This should not be discouraging. The same limitation is encountered in reconstructing the life of Jesus from the Christian record or when dealing generally in the sphere of ancient history, as Maurice Goguel explains so ably in his discussion of "the historical and the religious problem of Jesus." [3]

We have assumed the position that where Jesus is not named, the burden of proof is upon him who seeks to identify the passage as a reference to Jesus; where Jesus is named, the burden of proof is upon him who seeks to disprove it as an authentic reference. Further, we have taken the stand that because there are discrepancies in some of the references this does not mean that all of the record is invalid. Gerald Friedlander does not appear to be sound when, finding that one Talmud passage places Jesus in 87 B.C.E. and another places him in 120 C.E., he argues that both these dates could not be correct and therefore concludes that all the references to Jesus in rabbinic literature are entirely legendary.[4]

In the seemingly authentic passages of the Tannaitic period we find that there was a person called Yeshua, Yeshu, Yeshu Hanotzri or Yeshu ben Pandera [5] who practiced magic and who healed people, that this was regarded as sorcery, that for enticing and leading the people astray he was hanged on the eve of Passover —but that prior thereto the public announcement went out for forty days inviting testimony in his behalf, with allowance of ample time for it to appear.[6] He had five disciples: Mattai, Nakkai, Netzer, Buni, Todah.[7] From Jacob who taught in the name of Jesus, Rabbi Eliezer ben Hyrcanus (about 95 or 109 C.E.) learned an agreeable interpretation of Scripture, given by Jesus in the method of the Pharisees; but Eliezer subsequently regretted getting into difficulties with the secular powers by reason of heeding the words of those who veered from the established norm.[8]

At some time between 70 and 110 C.E., R. Eliezer's wife, Imma Shalom, and brother-in-law, R. Gamaliel II, consulted a judge (*philosoph*) who quoted from *avon gilyon* a teaching like that given by Jesus in Matthew 5:17 and which may well have been taken from the Logia, or Testimonia, or Christian Gospel; and Rabbi Meir, who flourished in the second third of the second century, made mention of *aven gilyon*.[9] Almost a century after the crucifixion, in the family of Rabbi Ishmael, a staunch supporter of Judaism, his nephew sought from Jacob of Kefar Soma healing in the name of Jesus, but the uncle strenuously objected that this would be a violation of Judaism.[10]

While these are authentic instances of specific mention of Jesus, these five are not of equal value or reliability. The passage which tells of the charge against Jesus and of the death penalty is in some respects the most significant, yet it presents the greatest number of difficulties. It reflects either confusion or deliberate construction; it appears to be an unhistoric tradition. The same may be said, however, of certain portions of the Gospels, especially those dealing with the trial and crucifixion.[11] The story of the *philosoph* may not be factual, it may not relate to a Christian judge nor to a saying of Jesus but by the test of probability it is to be regarded as a true allusion to the teaching of Jesus. The naming of the five disciples is valuable in that disciples are acknowledged to have taught the new doctrine, though the number named may raise questions and the names may not all be indentifiable. The two accounts relating to Jacob, who healed in the name of Jesus, give the impression of being the most factual.

We had occasion to inquire into the appellations of Jesus, especially the meaning of Ben Pandera. Especial attention was called to the fact that, with a careful and unbiased analysis of the potential passages of reference, there was in the Tannaitic period no slur on the birth or parenthood of Jesus. While it is true that Origen, around 248 c.e., quotes in *Contra Celsum* the word of a heathen opponent of Christianity that he had heard such a report from a Jew,[12] the Talmudic literature of his day has nothing of this nature. Are we then to take this second-hand rumor of one who was engaged belligerently in polemics against the Jews, and who probably himself, seeking an explanation for the name Panthera, put his theory into the mouth of an invented character— or are we to be instructed by the lack of such mention in the Talmudic document which goes back to the lifetime of Jesus and in which hundreds of authors would have had an opportunity to express such a view? In fact, the New Testament has no such accusation against the Jews, though there is much else. We must bear in mind that if scholars admit the necessity of subjecting the Bible to historical and literary criticism, how much more important it is to do the same with regard to the Patristic writings, such as the work of Origen.

It further is to be observed that there is no particular animus shown toward Jesus. There is the resistance which would be expected in a religion that would not accept him as the Christ or Son of God. Whatever is recorded is given in an almost matter-of-fact way—an incidental mention of a matter not of primary concern. And, in truth, Jesus was not of primary concern to

Judaism in the first two centuries. But the very fact that the mention is so casual is the best argument for its historic validity.[13] The more emotion and coloration there is in any record the less reliable it is.

Because of Justin Martyr's accusation of persecution of Christians by Bar Kochba in the third decade of the second century [14] —and the acceptance of this statement by many historians—it is appropriate to point out that in the portion of the Talmud which covers the second century there is nothing of his or Rabbi Akiba's persecution of followers of Jesus or of the reviling of the name of Jesus. On the contrary, according to the Tannaitic record there were Jews of rabbinic families who were willing to be healed in the name of Jesus.

Two questions now come to mind. One is: why is there so little in the Talmud, close to the lifetime of Jesus? The other is: why is there *what* there is?

Toward answering the first question we have the plausible suggestions of Klausner [15] to the effect that in the Talmud very little is told of the times of the Second Temple, not even mention of the name of Judas Maccabeus; [16] also that the chaotic events of the first century of the Christian Era—ultimately leading up to the destruction of the Temple in Jerusalem and the sovereignty of Judea—overshadowed the appearance of Jesus. Moreover, there is not one quotation from the now extant apocalyptic writings, as Louis Ginzberg asserts, in the vast rabbinic literature of the first six centuries.[17] Why then be amazed that there are so few allusions to Jesus?

To these two reasons may be added the thought that possibly the Talmud did contain more information but that it was lost either in the natural loss of old documents or by reason of Christian censorship of the later centuries whereby items could not be restored even through the older manuscripts extant, helpful though they have been.[18]

There is yet another reason to contemplate. Viewed from the standpoint of Judaism, perhaps there was relatively little to record. It is generally acknowledged that, in all but several respects, the ethical teachings of Jesus and the preachment and conduct of Jesus were in keeping with Jewish tradition—there was nothing unusual to report. The Christian scholar of the life of Jesus, Julius Wellhausen,[19] declared pointedly, "Jesus was not a Christian, he was a Jew"; therefore, if he spoke and lived as a Jew, there would be nothing startling to record. For this reason, perhaps, Philo Judaeus, the historian Josephus (of whom more is to be said below) and the historian Justus—all Jewish contemporaries of Jesus, who might also have been expected to tell *something* of him, are silent. "There is no indication in Jewish literature that the appearance of Jesus, either as a teacher or as a social or political leader," K. Kohler writes in confirmation of this thought, "made at the time a deep or a lasting impression on the Jewish people in general." [20]

Having given these explanations it may now be said, though, that the five authentic references of the Tannaim are not insignificant when compared with what is to be found in other non-Christian sources of that time.

There are, it is true, two passages in the works of Flavius Josephus which mention Jesus. One (*Antiquities* XVIII.III.3, ¶¶ 63, 64) reads: "Now, there was about this time Jesus, a wise man, [if it be lawful to call him a man], for he was a doer of wonderful works, a teacher of such men as receive the truth with pleasure. He drew over to him both many of the Jews, and many of the Gentiles. [He was the Christ.] And when Pilate, at the suggestion of the principal men amongst us, had condemned him to the cross, those that loved him at the first did not forsake him; [for, he appeared to them alive again at the third day; as the divine prophets had foretold these and ten thousand other wonderful things concerning him.] And the tribe of Christians, so named from him, are not extinct at this day." [21] The second (*Antiquities* XX.IX.1, ¶ 200) reads: "He (Ananus) assembled the Sanhedrim of judges, and brought before them the brother of Jesus, who was called Christ, whose name was James, and some others . . . and delivered them to be stoned."

Considerable controversy has raged about these two references. Scholars of repute hold both passages *in toto* to be later Christian interpolations.[22] Not many in our day would regard them as authentic in their entirety.[23] There are those who maintain that the short second passage is entirely authentic and that the longer first quotation is authentic only in part, that portions above indicated in brackets are a later Christian interpolation.[24]

If we agree with those who regard as interpolation everything in the writings of Josephus concerning Jesus, the Talmud becomes the more significant. If we accept the reduced amount as authentic, there would still be cause to wonder why Josephus, who wrote at great length and in considerable detail, who lived in Galilee, which is the scene of much of Jesus' activity, and who was the author of *Antiquities* in the year 93 C.E., should have made such scant mention of Jesus. The reason generally given is that he did not care to offend the Romans.

In this connection attention should be called to *Yosippon*, which is said by some to be a Slavonic version of Josephus' *Jewish War*.[25] It tells Jewish history from 539 B.C.E. to 70 C.E. in popular fashion and contains folklore allusions to Jesus. There are those who date it as early as the fifth or sixth century and those who date it as late as the twelfth century. Some believe that the author was a Christian; more believe that he was a Jew. The greatest degree of agreement is in the opinion that Josephus was not the author. Therefore, it need not concern us any further at this point.[26]

What are the other non-Christian early sources concerning Jesus?

There are the pagan sources. Tacitus, between 115 and 117 C.E., wrote that Nero tried to place responsibility for the burning of Rome on people called "Christians": "This name comes to them from Christ, whom the Procurator Pontius Pilate, under the rule of Tiberius had handed over to the torture; repressed for the moment, this detestable superstition broke out anew, not only in Judea, where the evil arose, but at Rome . . . and finds many people to support it." [27] Pliny the Younger, between 110 and 112 C.E., wrote to Trajan that the Christians of his province Bithynia sing a hymn "to Christ as to a God." [28] Suetonius (65–135) somewhere around 125 wrote: "He (Claudius, probably in 49 C.E.) expelled from Rome the Jews who, under the influence of Chrestos, did not cease to agitate." [29] Celsus, quoted by Origen, brings us to the late date of 178.

These non-Christian sources before the time of Celsus are astonishingly meagre. Only one of the pagan writers actually names Jesus. How striking—and important—when contrasted with these is the record of the Tannaim!

What, now, is the value of the Jewish record in the effort to find early documentation which would help establish the historicity of Jesus? The answer is seen when we compare its dates with those of the other early sources. The two texts found in B. Sanhedrin 43a cannot be fixed at a definite date within the Tannaitic time-area. It should be noted, however, that undated traditions of the Talmud are often traceable to early origins.[30] The incident of R. Ishmael might have occurred in 116 c.e., possibly earlier; that of R. Eliezer, in 109 or 95, preferably the former; that of Imma Shalom and R. Gamaliel, some time after 70, with a likelihood indicated for the year 73. Thus, while the evidence for historicity is not conclusive, it is at least as telling as any from non-Christian sources.[31]

It compares favorably, as to date, even with the Christian evidence. The extra-Canonical Gospels are not considered reliable data.[32] As for the Canonical Gospels and Acts, there is considerable difference of opinion in setting the probable dates of composition. Klausner places Mark at about 66–68, Matthew at beyond 70 and near the end of the century, Luke (who is given as the author also of Acts) at the beginning of the second century, John at the middle of the second century.[33] Goguel believes Mark to have been written in 70 to 72, with a revision ten years later; Luke, between 72 and 90 (Acts, around 85); Matthew, in 90 at the earliest; John, a collection of independent incidents, gathered over a wide period.[34] Enslin specifies 70 to 85, probably nearer 70, for Mark; just before 100, for Matthew; just about 100, for Luke; 105 to 110, for Acts; the first three or four decades of the second century, for John.[35] On the basis of this sampling of dates assigned to the writing down of the early Christian tradition we notice how closely it parallels the time-range of the early passages of the Jewish tradition.

In this problem of validating the historicity of Jesus, it is interesting to take note that the Jewish literature of the first two centuries of the Christian Era does not introduce the question as to whether Jesus actually lived or was merely a myth.[35a] As we have seen, other points were raised, but not this. In those early generations, had there been a doubt that Jesus was ever a real person we would expect the Jewish teachers to make mention of it in their advocacy of Judaism. But they did not, either directly or indirectly.

However, we must be careful not to make too much of this argument. It is not conclusive. Can we attribute to ancient peoples our modern concept of myth, or historicity? Furthermore, this manner of logic lends itself to fallacious extension whereby one could attempt to prove that whatever the early Jewish tradition does not specifically mention in contradiction to the Christian tradition must have taken place. Yet, within limits, the observation is an intriguing one.

Now for the second question—why is there in the Tannaitic record *what* there is?

From what was learned in answer to the first question we can see that what is likely to be recorded would be what is startling, dramatic, not customary. Thus, the impression remained that here was one who performed unusual acts—regarded by some as miracles, by others as mere sorcery.[36] A brilliant turning of a phrase of Scripture would be recalled by a rabbi. Confirmation of the non-abrogation of Mosaic Law would be cited. It was remembered that Jesus was executed, but the event was interpreted in the light of Judaism. He left disciples to carry on his work; certainly this is of importance, otherwise there would be no Christianity. Healing was performed in his name; this is always noteworthy and unforgettable.

With considerable insight the Jewish historian, H. Graetz, writes: "It was not to be expected, however, that through his teaching alone Jesus could attract devoted followers, or achieve great results; something more was required, something strange and wonderful to startle and inflame. . . . The Christian chronicles abound in extraordinary events and descriptions of miraculous cures performed by Jesus. Though these stories may in part be due to an inclination to exaggerate and idealize, they must doubtless have had some foundation in fact.

"Miraculous cures—such, for example, as the exorcism of those possessed by demons—belonged so completely to the personality of Jesus that his followers boasted more of the exercise of that power than of the purity and holiness of their conduct." [37] This made the greatest impression and found a place in the Talmud.

That there is no criticism of the moral principles enunciated by Jesus but of his sorcery and enticement to false worship tends to support a view such as that expressed by G. F. Moore that more than the antinomianism, it was the soteriology of Christianity that rendered it in Jewish opinion of those times a religion which was in error.[38]

If our interpretation of the *Minim* be correct, the Tannaitic literature discloses, further, the various shades of Jewish-Christian-Gnostic thought in the early centuries of Christianity, making it difficult to differentiate between one and the other. It conveys an impression of the importance of Jewish Christians as being greater than that indicated in the Christian tradition. This may have been true, however, only within Jewish circles. In this regard it is illuminating to discover that from Jewish Christians has come to modern scholarship the oldest archeological record of Christianity in the form of inscriptions on stone ossuaries recently found near Jerusalem and, assuming the interpretation as a correct one, believed to date from the year 70 and to contain lamentations by Jewish disciples on the crucifixion of Jesus.[39] It must be stated, however, that this interpretation of the inscriptions is challenged for want of sufficient proof.[40]

Furthermore, if it was difficult for Jews to differentiate between Jews and Jewish Christians, making necessary the introduction of test formulae into the liturgy, it probably was equally difficult for Christians to tell the difference. Therefore, one is led to wonder to what degree the hostility, expressed by Paul, John and others of the New Testament, was directed against the Jewish Christians rather than against the Jews.[41]

Finally, in this chapter we learned the principal Tannaitic

instruction regarding the Unity of God, who does not become incarnate. We learned the prevailing belief that the Messiah had not come, that Moses and his Law are still supreme, that miracles do not necessarily prove a new truth. We found that these points of emphasis may have alluded indirectly to Jesus and, if so, are more important than any reference which names him.

Judaism, in its unfolding during the first centuries of the Christian Era, had its own problems of survival and its own evolving message for guiding and enriching the life of the Jewish people. Its teachers, therefore, engaged in a very minimum of discussion concerning Jesus. The positive side seems to have been emphasized, not the negative. The rabbis, in the main, did not set out to demonstrate what was wrong in the teaching, claims or acts of Jesus and his disciples but rather to stress what was good in the Jewish tradition. They may, indeed, have been conditioned, one way or another, by Christian doctrine in the environment in which they lived, but their paramount aim was to provide nourishment to sustain the soul of their people.

CHAPTER III

# AMORAIC PERIOD

# III

THE research into the Amoraic period takes cognizance of the Amoraim, who are the Gemara authorities of the third, fourth, fifth and—including the Saboraim—the sixth centuries. Their work was continued by the Responsa of the Geonim to the middle of the eleventh century and, because of the similarity of the literature, it can be included in this section; but no references to Jesus have been brought to light in the writings of the Geonim, excepting in Saadia Gaon, who was really a philosopher as well as a Talmudist and whose views, therefore, must be reserved for a later chapter.

The commentators on the Talmud add little of significance. Their value is in mirroring the attitudes of their own generations. But inasmuch as their thoughts are printed as part of the Talmud, they are included in this chapter, although they will be noticed again when we deal in Chapter IV with the later centuries in which they lived.

The post-Tannaitic Midrashim also belong in this chapter. Even though the date of composition of a number of the Midrashic collections extends into the later centuries, the final assembling of material not coming to an end until the termination of the Gaonate in 1040, nevertheless the actual *creating* of Midrashim was not carried on much beyond the completion of the Babylonian Talmud,[1] which is roughly the *terminus ad quem* of this chapter.

Whereas Laible and Herford did not sufficiently divide the Talmudic material so as to make a clear distinction between the early and the late before entering upon interpretation, Strack did make the differentiation. But his pamphlet is scarcely more than a presentation of the text with a translation, and whatever discussion there may be is limited to footnotes, so that no extensive interpretations are given and no clear conclusions or findings can

be learned; he dismisses the Amoraim with the opening observation that they knew nothing of the life and works of Jesus. Klausner distinguishes between what is early and late and gives his
interpretation but, because of the limitations of brevity imposed
by the allotment of but a single chapter to this subject, he
virtually dismisses the statements of the Amoraim.[2]

Therefore, there never has been an adequate presentation of
the Amoraic period. It should not be overlooked. It has its importance, not only because of what it tells regarding the third to
the sixth centuries but also because it provides the connecting
link with the Toledoth Yeshu, the polemics of the Middle Ages
and much else which will be of concern in the next chapter. To
skip the Amoraic period is like trying to build a three-story
house with the second story missing.

It cannot be gainsaid that whatever we shall find recorded in
the Gemara is less important in reconstructing the history of
Jesus than in revealing later Jewish attitudes to Jesus, and incidentally in reflecting the relations between Jews and Christians.

Life is continuous. Divisions of time, therefore, are arbitrary.
As was stated before, the division we have adopted for the study
of the record of Jesus in rabbinic Judaism is the one which recommends itself as most suitable because the Talmud itself can be
separated into the earlier Mishnah and the later Gemara. Still, we
realize that in the previous chapter we touched here and there
upon what really belongs to the time-area of this chapter. But it
had to be done to clarify the points discussed. It would be waste-
ful to repeat. Therefore, let it be noted here that what is reported
in Chapter II concerning the Amoraim is to be considered as part
of this section also.

Now, as before, we list first those passages which are considered authentic; then those which are incorrectly identified
with Jesus.

## SECTION A

## AUTHENTIC REFERENCES TO JESUS

We shall begin with those texts which relate to the ones partially treated in Chapter II.

### 1. THE DEATH OF JESUS AND HIS DISCIPLES

TEXT:—Ulla says: Would you suppose that he (Yeshu the Nazarene) [1] was eligible for a defence? Was he not an enticer? And the Merciful hath said: "Thou shalt not spare, neither shalt thou conceal him." [2] But it was different with Yeshu, for he was near to the government. (B. Sanhedrin 43a)

DISCUSSION:—This follows the Baraitha which tells of the execution of Jesus on the eve of the Passover.[3] Ulla, who thus expressed his opinion, lived at the end of the third and the beginning of the fourth century.[4] Those writers on our theme who identified Jesus with Ben Stada and concurrently built up a strong position that Akiba was exceedingly hostile to Christians, have wondered why this text does not mention Lud as the place of execution. Now that we have seen that Jesus and Ben Stada are to be considered as separate and apart, we need not be troubled over Lud nor the conditions in the time of Akiba as they might have affected Jesus.

Two of the Hebrew phrases have raised problems in translating them. In one instance, Herford separated *zechuth hu* from *bar hafuchi* and the translation read: "Would it be supposed that Yeshu the Nazarene, a revolutionary, had aught in his favor?" [5] This error led to the further one, by him and others who based themselves on this translation, that of expatiating on the rabbinic attitude as one which considered Jesus a revolutionary. Bacher, in his review of Herford's book,[6] immediately recognized the error; years later, in his article in the *Universal Jewish Encyclopedia*,[7] Herford corrected the translation.

The second phrase, where there is some doubt as to the mean-

ing, is the final one in the text. Laible argues that this is to be
taken as a reference to the reluctance of Pontius Pilate to have
Jesus put to death, as shown in the New Testament; he resorts to
this interpretation to pour out his venom: "While the doctors of
the Law panted for the blood of Jesus, the Roman governor,
overcome by his sublimity and purity, could only with difficulty
bring himself to confirm the capital sentence." [8] That such was
not at all the nature of Pontius Pilate has been demonstrated by
Philo's report of his cruelty, told in the letter of Agrippa to
Gaius,[9] and by Josephus' recital of the tumult and slaughter
Pontius Pilate caused among the Jews and also among the Samaritans, and of his final recall from his post.[10] This is one of the main
items where historical analysis of the New Testament has proven
helpful. Incidentally, the New Testament in one place does confirm what Josephus and Philo tell of Pilate, for we read in Luke
13:1, "There were present at that season some that told him of
the Galilaeans, whose blood Pilate had mingled with their sacrifices."

Herford recognizes that Laible's theory may be regarded as
"somewhat far-fetched" and translates the Hebrew phrase to
mean "near to the kingdom," explaining that this alludes to Jesus'
frequent reference to "the kingdom." [11] Strack disagrees with this
explanation and also with the one of S. Krauss that "near to the
kingdom" is an intimation of Jesus' supposed Davidic descent; [12]
what relevancy would that have to the outcome of the trial?

While the intent of the phrase is not too clear, the interpretation which recommends itself to the writer is the suggestion [13]
that Ulla was thinking of the delay occasioned by Pilate's trans-
ferring of the hearing to Herod when he learned that Jesus "belonged unto Herod's jurisdiction." In the Gospel of Mark we
read, "At that time Herod the tetrarch heard of the fame of
Jesus," [14] and in Luke we read further, "And when Herod saw
Jesus, he was exceedingly glad: for he was desirous to see him
of a long season, because he had heard many things of him; and
he hoped to have seen some miracle done by him." [15] Jesus, in
other words, was near to the government in the sense that Herod,
who held jurisdiction over him, took a particular interest in

Jesus.[16] Therefore, in deference to Herod, the punishment of Jesus was held off forty days so that some defence might make its appearance.

TEXT:—When Haman saw that his words were not heeded he started wailing and weeping in the garden of the palace and said, "Hear me, you trees and all plants which I have planted since the days of Creation—the son of Hammedatha is about to ascend to the mast of the son of Pandera." (II Targum to Esther 7:9)

DISCUSSION:—This is quite late in composition. It is entirely imaginary—and is an indirect reference to the hanging of Jesus.[17]

TEXT:—They brought Mattai (to be sentenced). He said to them, "Shall Mattai be killed? It is in Scripture: 'When (*Mathai*) shall I come and appear before God?'" [18] They said to him, "Yes, Mattai shall be killed; for it is in Scripture: 'When (*Mathai*) shall he die and his name perish?'" [19] They brought Nakkai. He said to them, "Shall Nakkai be killed? It is in Scripture: 'The innocent (*Naki*) and righteous slay thou not.'" [20] They said to him: "Yes, Nakkai must be killed; for it is in Scripture, 'In secret places doth he slay the innocent (*Naki*).'" [21] They brought Netzer. He said to them, "Shall Netzer be killed? It is in Scripture: 'A twig (*Netzer*) shall grow forth out of his roots.'" [22] They said to him, "Yes, Netzer shall be killed; for it is in Scripture: 'But thou art cast forth away from thy grave like an abhorred offshoot (*Netzer*).'" [23] They brought Buni. He said to them, "Shall Buni be killed? It is in Scripture: 'Israel is my son (*Beni*), my first born.'" [24] They said to him, "Yes, Buni shall be killed; for it is in Scripture: 'Behold I will slay thy son (*Bincha*), thy first born.'" [25] They brought Todah. He said to them, "Shall Todah be killed? It is in Scripture: 'A psalm of thanksgiving (*Todah*).'" [26] They said to him: "Yes, Todah shall be killed; for it is in Scripture: 'Whoso offereth the sacrifice of thanksgiving (*Todah*) honoreth me.'" [27] (B. Sanhedrin 43a; repeated in Yalkut Makiri to Is. XI, p. 84, with variations)

DISCUSSION:—The Amoraic text follows the Baraitha [28] which names the five disciples of Jesus. This later addition is patently unreal and unhistorical, an entirely homiletical invention. There is general agreement on this point.

Beyond this point, there are differences in interpretation. Once we discover that Ben Stada is not Jesus and that Lud has no connection with the death of Jesus we remove the ground from under the argument of Laible,[29] Herford [30] and Strack [31] that this passage reflects the persecution of Christians by Jews in Bar Kochba's time. As Klausner [32] properly reminds us, even the hostile statement of Justin Martyr tells of Jews scourging Christians but not of putting them to death; also, the entire addition is mere *pilpul* dialectics.

The attempt to find in these five names five different references to the death of but one person—Jesus—collapses when we take the position that the first sentence of the passage is Baraitha, a position well established.[33] The play on the meanings of the names is, thus, only an after-thought—possibly a century or two after the names themselves were first recorded.

If we agree that the play on the Scriptural meanings of the names is a later addition, then Bacher [34] would be wrong in his assertion that these five names particularly were chosen as the names of Jesus' disciples because they happen to be names lending themselves to word-play.

Finally, it is to be pointed out that, if the intention *were* word-play, three of the names would have to be *Beni* instead of *Buni*, *Mathai* instead of *Mattai*, and *Naki* instead of *Nakkai*.[35] Obviously, these were five actual names of disciples. We already have touched upon the various attempts to identify these names with those of known disciples of Jesus. Some we seem to be able to recognize. Others may be nicknames of disciples. What adds to the difficulty in establishing identification is the fact that the New Testament names of disciples are given in Greek; these are in Hebrew; between the pronunciations in the two languages there can be considerable deviations.

This post-Tannaitic elaboration, then, on the names of Jesus' disciples is pure fancy, arising possibly at a time of the oppression of the Jews, and employing considerable homiletical license.

There are two additional items of interest relative to these names.

It is suggested that these five names represent five groups of Christian doctrine, that the texts and counter-texts here given possess messianic connotations and that this, therefore, is a trial of Christian *testimonia*.[36] Attention is directed, according to this theory, to a *Testimony Book* in early Christian literature, the five sections beginning with terms which the sponsor of the theory seeks to identify with the five names of this Talmud passage. Still, this theory, too, falls if it be true that the texts and counter-texts are only later additions.

The other item is the enumeration in one of the versions of the Toledoth Yeshu [37] of Simeon, Matthia, Elikum, Mordecai, Thoda and Johannos as disciples: these would correspond, perhaps, to Simon Peter, Matthew, Luke, Mark, Thaddaeus, John—the four evangelists with Peter and Thaddaeus added. Now, in the repetition of the B. Sanhedrin 43a story of the disciples, the Yalkut Makiri fails to name the disciple Netzer (interpreted to mean Jesus or Christian), and we have four remaining who might be Matthew (Mattai), Luke (Nakkai), John (Buni) and, if there were a way to get Mark out of Todah, we would have the names representing the four Gospels. Until a suitable explanation is found to forge the last link transforming Todah into Mark this item must remain unproved.

## 2. HEALING IN THE NAME OF JESUS

TEXT:—The grandson (of R. Joshua ben Levi) had a choking fit.[1] A certain man came and whispered to him, of the name of Yeshu Pandera. And when he came out, he (R. Joshua) said to him: "What did you whisper to him?" He answered him, "A certain word." He said, "It might have been better for him to have died, than this." And it was like this to him: "Like an error which proceedeth from a ruler." [2] (P. Shabbath end of X or 14d)

DISCUSSION:—The same story is found also in P. Abodah Zarah 40d, 41a and Midrash Koheleth Rabbah I.8 on Ecclesiastes 10:5.

R. Joshua ben Levi, an outstanding Haggadist, lived in Palestine
in the first half of the third century.[3] An incident reported concerning his grandson would thus come definitely in the period of
the Amoraim, as the Aramaic language of the passage likewise
indicates.

The thought is clear. Even at this late date there were Jews
who resorted to healing in the name of Jesus. This tends to bear
out the conclusion that it was the healing aspect of Jesus that
made the deepest impression. However, whereas it was debatable
in the Tannaitic period whether it is proper thus to be healed,[4] at
this later date the opposition was much more pronounced.

It is interesting to observe that in the Aramaic text it is stated
that the healer whispered *of* [5] the name of Jesus. It might mean
that he told a good deal concerning Jesus or Christianity, and did
not simply utter a formula for healing. This could be implied
because in the earlier passages the expression is "on behalf of," or
"in the name of" [6] Jesus.

### 3. JESUS DISTORTED JEWISH TEACHING

TEXT:—Onkelos bar Kalonikos, son of Titus' sister, sought to become a proselyte. He had Titus brought up out of his grave by
necromancy. He asked him, "Who is respected in the other [1]
world?" He (Titus) replied: "Israel." "How about joining their
ranks?" He replied: "Their commandments are many and you
cannot fulfil them. Go, oppose them [2] in that world and become
head, as in Scripture: 'Her adversaries are become the head.' [3]
Every troubler of Israel is made a head." He said to him, "What
is the sentence for a man such as you?" He answered, "What he
decreed for himself. Every day they collect his ashes and sentence
him and burn him and scatter him over the seven seas." He
(Onkelos) called up Balaam by necromancy. He asked him,
"Who is respected in the other world?" He replied: "Israel."
"How about joining their ranks?" He replied: "Thou shalt not
seek their peace nor their prosperity all thy days forever." [4] He
said to him: "What is the sentence for a man such as you?" "Boiling semen." He (Onkelos) called up Yeshu by necromancy. He
asked him, "Who is respected in the other world?" He replied:

"Israel." "What about joining with them?" He said to him, "Seek their good and seek not their harm; every one who injures them, it is as if he injured the apple of his eye." He asked him, "What is the sentence for a man such as you?" He answered him, "Boiling filth." For a teacher has said, Everyone who mocks at the words of the wise is sentenced to boiling filth. Come, see what there is between the transgressors of Israel and the prophets of the peoples of the world. (B. Gittin 56b–57a)

DISCUSSION:—In this bizarre quotation, the thought is that Titus burned the Temple, therefore he should burn; Balaam led the Israelites to serve Baal Peor, idolatry involving abnormal sex acts, therefore his punishment relates to sex.[5] Jesus was regarded as having befouled his instruction, therefore his punishment corresponds to that. The last sentence makes the point that this was the usual punishment for mocking at the words of the wise: it was not created just for Jesus.

The passage is late,[6] of the Amoraic period, as indicated by the original language, even though Titus' nephew is the presumed subject of the story. But it is only a story, expressed in a manner in keeping with that age and environment but entirely fictitious—even if the Tosafists of the twelfth century did believe it true. If Onkelos was a heathen desiring to become a Jew, how would he, a non-Jew, be named in Jewish fashion as *bar*, "son of, etc."? Strack reminds us that when Haggadah is meant to convey even a bit of historic fact it makes it clear by quoting some substantiating evidence,[7] which the text above fails to do.

Two thoughts are conveyed by this passage. One is that Jesus and Balaam are two separate entities. Klausner, discussing the text, goes so far as to assert that there is not a single passage in Talmud or Midrash wherein Balaam would mean Jesus and none other.[8]

There is, further, the testimony of Louis Ginzberg that it is decidedly wrong for authors, Jewish as well as Christian, to regard the name Balaam as alias for Jesus in the legendary literature of the Jews.[9] The evidence is cogent that not only for the Tannaim but for the Amoraim also, Balaam was not Jesus. We can go no further than to say that their being mentioned together in a passage indicates that some relationship was thought to exist between one and the other; even so, a clear distinction is made between the character of Jesus and that of Balaam.

The second thought is that even at this late period Jesus is regarded as a Jew. Unlike Titus and Balaam who would want to injure the Jews, Jesus advises seeking their welfare, for "he who injures them is like one who would injure the apple of his eye." This appears to be the major emphasis of the entire account, with other ideas given as minor points. Along these lines, Zeitlin goes one step further and asserts the purpose of the story to be a recommendation by Jesus to Christians not to persecute the Jews.[10] This is an opinion which receives support in the fact that the Toledoth Yeshu, which was assuming definite form in the later period of the Amoraim, represents a man named Elijah as cautioning Christians not to injure Jews, and Simon Peter counselling them to be concerned with the welfare of the Jews.[11]

Whatever criticism there was of Jesus was that he was a transgressor,[12] that he distorted the teachings of his Judaism. This viewpoint is further represented in the following texts.

TEXT:—When the rabbis left the house of Rab Hisda—some say, the house of Rab Samuel bar Nahmani—they said to him thus: Our heads are burdened. Rab and Samuel—others say, R. Yohanan and R. Elazar (ben Pedath). He (the former) says: Our heads in Torah and burdened with commandments. He (the latter) says: Our heads in Torah and in commandments are burdened with vituperation. "No breach"[13]—our society be not like the society of Saul whence came the Edomite, Doeg. "And no going forth"—our society be not like the society of David whence came Ahitofel. "And no outcry"—our society be not like the society of Elisha whence came Gehazi. "In our broad places"—that we may not have a son or disciple who burns his food in public like the Nazarene. (B. Berachoth 17a, b)

TEXT:—And Rab Hisda said that Rab Jeremiah bar Abba said: What is (the meaning) of Scripture: "There shall no evil befall thee, neither shall any plague come nigh thy tent"[14] . . . Another explanation: "there shall no evil befall thee"—that evil dreams and thoughts may not tempt you; "neither shall any plague come nigh thy tent"—that you should not have a son or disciple who burns his food in public, like Yeshu the Nazarene. (B. Sandehrin 103a)

DISCUSSION:—First it is important to understand what is meant by the phrase, "burns his food in public." One could take it literally or figuratively. Laible, accepting the literal meaning, claims that it denotes the public offering of sacrifice to idols, namely, that the Talmud accused Jesus of idolatry, and, for good measure, Laible adds the egregious statements that Jews of old, as well as many today, firmly believed that Christians in their assemblies offered sacrifices to idols.[15] This explanation Herford properly calls absurd.[16] If we adhere to the literal expression, the most we can see in it is a reference to the burning of incense or candles in Christian worship.[17]

This phrase, however, has a figurative sense, too. As used in B. Berachoth 34a it connotes heresy.[18] There the discussion states that he who, praying before the Ark, makes a mistake rendering him suspect of heresy shall be replaced by someone else; the latter should refuse, for if he does not he is like food without salt; but he should not refuse too much, else he is like food burned by salt. In this Gemara there is a specific connection established between burned food and heresy. Jastrow's *Dictionary* advocates the figurative interpretation, giving rabbinic quotations where the phrase is used in the sense of "spoiling a dish"; however, in B. Sanhedrin 103a it implies more than "disgraces his education in public," which he suggests,[19] for we have noticed here the association with heresy.

We favor the figurative meaning because Jesus is alluded to as a *disciple*—and misapplication of learning would be a logical inference. Jesus the Jew exaggerated certain of the Jewish teachings he learned, and the result is burned food—heresy—which led many astray.

The mention of R. Hisda and R. Samuel bar Nahmani informs us that we are dealing with the views of the third generation of Amoraim, whose date is the end of the third and the opening of the fourth century.[20]

# REFERENCES INCORRECTLY IDENTIFIED WITH JESUS

## 1. THE MOTHER OF JESUS

TEXT:—When Rab Joseph came to the verse [1]—he wept: "There is that is swept away by want of righteousness." [2] He said: Who is there that has passed away before his time? Indeed, as in this (coming from) Rab Bibi bar Abaye, who was constantly with the angel of death. The angel said to his messenger: "Go, bring me Miriam the women's hairdresser (*meggadela*)." He went and brought him Miriam the governess of children (*megaddela*). He (the angel) said to him: "I told you, Miriam the women's hairdresser." He answered, "If so, I will take her back." He (the angel) said to him: "Inasmuch as you have brought her, let her be counted (among the dead)." (B. Hagigah 4b)

DISCUSSION:—In itself this passage of the latter part of the third or the beginning of the fourth century has no relationship to our theme. It is given here because the Tosafoth commentary on this Talmud text says: "He was with the angel of death. He told what already had happened, for this of Miriam the women's hairdresser was at the time of the Second Temple, for she was the mother of a certain person, as it is in Shabbath, page 104."

TEXT:—Ben Stada? He was Ben Pandira. Rab Hisda said, "The husband was Stada; the lover, Pandira." Was not the husband Pappos ben Yehudah; his mother, Stada? His mother was Miriam, a women's hairdresser. As they say in Pumbeditha, "*Stath da* (this one strayed) from her husband." (B. Shabbath 104b)

DISCUSSION:—This is the passage meant (in the Tosafoth interpretation of the previous text) and was considered by us in Chapter II, Section B. This is the Amoraic portion of the passage. It reflects the confusion of the Amoraim resulting from their blending of Ben Stada, whoever he was, with Jesus. We learned, in the previous chapter, that Ben Stada might have been Simon Magus, the Samaritan-born, Egyptian-trained, false prophet. Something of this confusion is seen in the report of Tertullian that Jesus was libelled, among other things, as "a Samaritan possessed of the devil." [3]

Rab Hisda (who died in 309 c.e.) [4] wondered how Ben Stada could be Ben Pandira. He sought an explanation. He could have been wrong in his solution to the problem. He *was* wrong, for the Gemara itself offers a substitute solution. But this, too, reveals the same mistake in identification. There are, in fact, several mistakes. Pappos ben Yehudah could not have been the father of Jesus for the simple reason that he lived a century after Jesus. [5]

They heard that the mother was, according to Christian tradition, Mary (Miriam, in Hebrew). But why Mary Megaddela? Lauterbach presents an interesting theory which suggests a triple confusion: that *megaddela* alludes to the long hair possessed by Mary, sister of Martha, wherewith she wiped the feet of Jesus, according to John 11:2; that these Amoraim took Mary Magdalene to mean Mary with the long hair, rather than Mary of Magdela; that Mary Magdalene was then misunderstood to be Mary the mother. [6] This theory merits attention. Another theory offers the thought that there was in those days a reflection upon the character of a woman who was a hairdresser; still another, that the morals of the town of Magdala were in disrepute. [7]

The next step is to make *Stath da* (*Stada*) an epithet for Miriam. It means "this one strayed" and is supposed to allude to Miriam's infidelity. Why should *this* be said of Miriam?

A possible explanation is that if Simon Magus is conceded to be Ben Stada, his consort Helene, reported to have been immoral, [8] could have been merged indiscriminately with Mary. Other than this suggestion, it may be that the problem arising from the theology of the Virgin Birth may have led to such a conclusion; or that Mary Magdalene was regarded unfavorably, for she had to be healed of evil spirits. [9] The last step in the mixup made Pappos the husband, since he was known to have had a faithless wife. [10]

Now we can understand that, as the author of B. Shabbath 104b was misled by the Aramaic word *megaddela* into imagining that the person referred to was Mary Magdalene, the mother of Jesus, so the Tosafists of the twelfth century made the same double mistake in explaining the Hagigah passage which really has no relation to Jesus.[11] If a note of levity be permitted, it seems that (in this text) even the angels were confused by *megaddela*.

It is interesting to speculate why Mary Magdalene was remembered more than Mary the mother and was erroneously taken to be the mother of Jesus. A likely explanation is suggested by Klausner's emphasis on the importance of Mary Magdalene in keeping alive the memory of the crucified Jesus, so that he was not forgotten as were the unsuccessful Messiahs in the days of the Second Temple. To this effect he quotes Renan: "The glory of the Resurrection is accordingly due to Mary Magdalen. Next after Jesus, hers was the most essential part in the founding of Christianity." [12] It is understandable that she who was the chief witness of the risen Christ and testified that he *was* the Messiah should be closely identified with Jesus.

One other observation on this comment of the Tosafists, namely, the use of *peloni* ("a certain person") to refer to Jesus: it will be recalled, in the previous chapter it was demonstrated that this phrase could not mean Jesus. Why now, in the twelfth and thirteenth centuries, does it allude to Jesus?

The simple answer is that it is a well-known fact that words in a language take on different meanings over a period of years and centuries. For example, in the time of Shakespeare, *villain* meant a "country gentleman"; now it connotes a "wicked person." Thus, *a certain person* conveyed no added connotation until the time when Christianity had gained in temporal power and it was not safe to engage in free speech when discussing Jesus; therefore, perforce a substitute allusion was introduced. Alas, how necessary this was during the time of the Tosafists—the time of the Crusades.

TEXT:—R. Yohanan said (concerning Balaam): At first he was a prophet, at the end a soothsayer. Rab Papa said: This is what people say, "From princes and rulers, she became a chaser after ship-draggers." (B. Sanhedrin 106a)

DISCUSSION:—We have here a good illustration of forcing an interpretation where it does not exist. By translating this passage as "She was the descendant of princes and rulers, she played the harlot with carpenters," it is argued that *she* refers to the mother of Jesus who was of Davidic descent, who was married to a carpenter and who was said to have given birth to Jesus out of wedlock—and to clinch the argument the connection is made between Balaam and Jesus.[13]

But we have established that Balaam does not mean Jesus. Thus far no Talmudic statement of the illegitimate birth of Jesus has been substantiated. Further, if the husband was a carpenter, why should the text say "carpenters," in the plural form? The exact translation of the text shows no word for *descendant* and the word translated *carpenters* means also *ship-draggers*.[14] The meaning of the passage calls for the latter definition, for the phrase is like the modern saying, "she chases after waterfront characters."

Rab Papa died in 375. He is known as one who quoted sayings of the people [15]—and this is one of them. We agree with Bacher,[16] namely, that this passage could not possibly refer to the mother of Jesus.

TEXT:—R. Hiyya bar Abba said: When a strayed son says to you, "There are two gods," say unto him "I am He of the Sea; I am He of Sinai." . . . R. Hiyya bar Abba said: If a strayed son says to you, "There are two gods," say unto him: "The Lord spoke with you face to face" [17]—it is not written "gods" but "God" spoke with you. (Pesikta Rabbati 100b, 101a, ed. Friedmann)

DISCUSSION:—Here, too, the statement attributed to an Amora of the second half of the third and the beginning of the fourth century [18] can be twisted "to refer to none other than Jesus," if the crucial words are translated "son of the harlot" and it is assumed that Mary's reputation has been besmirched in the Talmud.[19]

However, nothing derogatory regarding Mary is established, as far as the Talmud is concerned. The expression, "son of a harlot" [20] may be used to refer to anyone who challenges the unity of God—like saying "son of a dog." This is unlikely. As we have discovered in the discussion of the *Minim*,[21] the probable meaning of the Aramaic original is, "one who strayed from the faith"—a possibility which Friedmann,[22] who edited the passage, calls to our attention.

## 2. THE BALAAM REFERENCES

TEXT:—And he (Balaam) took up his parable, and said: "Alas, who shall live after God hath appointed him?" [1] Resh Lakish said: Alas for him who makes himself to live by the name of God. (B. Sanhedrin 106a)

DISCUSSION:—The homily by Resh Lakish, who died somewhat before 279,[2] is regarded as a reference to Jesus.[3] But, as Rashi explains, "Balaam, who made himself to live by the name of God, made himself God." It must be remembered that in homiletical exposition there is a good deal of fanciful speculation and "poetic license." Therefore, if the acts of Balaam are thus exaggerated it may be understood as characteristic of Haggadah—we do not weigh every word as in a legal document. There is no requirement for a theory that this applies to Jesus. At this date, Jesus' name could still be mentioned with impunity; [4] if he was meant, why such concealment?

TEXT:—Rab Mathnah and Rab Samuel bar Nahman both say: It would be in order to read the Ten Commandments every day. Why do we not read them? Because of the claim of the *Minim*; that they should not say, "These alone were given to Moses on Sinai." R. Samuel bar Nahman in the name of Rabbi Yehudah ben Zebuda says: It would be in order to read the Section of Balak and Balaam every day. But why is it not read? In order not to tire the congregation. (P. Berachoth I, 8, or 3c)

DISCUSSION:—R. Samuel bar Nahman, of the third generation of Amoraim, was a famous homilist.[5] His statements, together, are taken merely as evidence of a special connection between Balaam and Jesus.[6] That is, if we assume that the *Minim* here means Jewish Christians, but is there evidence that they claimed what is described in the text? *Minim*, unless more definitely indicated by the context, means "heretics." [7]

We have seen that Balaam is not an *alias* for Jesus.[8] What may have germinated the thought is the picture of Balaam as a prophet to the Gentiles, given in the Midrash Sifre comment on Deuteronomy 34:10, "There arose not in Israel a prophet like Moses." [9] This passage, which is regarded as an Amoraic addition to the Tannaitic Sifre,[10] continues with a recital of the ways in which Balaam was superior to Moses. This is elaborated in a later Midrash [11] which places Balaam on the level of Moses, that Gentiles may have no reason to protest. "Had we but had a prophet like Moses, we would have served God." To Christians, Jesus *is* greater than Moses: he gave the New Testament in *fulfilment* of the Old. How natural, then, that there should be those who would see in Balaam a substitute name for Jesus. Nevertheless, the evidence is convincing that the Talmud and Midrash do not equate Jesus with Balaam, as we have already observed.

### 3. MISCELLANEOUS ITEMS

TEXT:—As to Ben Netzer, could he be called there king, and here robber? (B. Kethuboth 51b)

DISCUSSION:—This is mentioned because of the similarity between Ben Netzer and Nazarene. Isaac Abravanel (1437–1508) happened to comment on Daniel 7:8, "See, do see how they interpret the other 'little horn' as Ben Netzer, who is Yeshu the Nazarene." This false lead is followed by Levy, Keim and Edersheim.[1] But Herford properly indicates that none of the rabbinic passages which mention Ben Netzer [2] are such as to suggest Jesus. Perhaps the Talmudic name of one of Jesus' disciples stimulated the thought.[3] In any event, Graetz correctly identifies Ben Netzer as Odenathus, who set up the quickly ended kingdom of Palmyra, about 260 C.E.[4] Ben Netzer is not Jesus.

TEXT:—(Nebuchadnezzar placed Joshua into the furnace.) Joshua emerged unhurt, only his garments were seared, but the false prophets were consumed. Joshua explained the singeing of his garments by the fact that he was directly exposed to the full fury of the flames. Now why was he (thus) punished? R. Papa said: Because his sons married wives unworthy of the priesthood; and he did not protest, as it is said, "Now Joshua was clothed with filthy garments." Now, surely, it was not his custom to wear filthy garments. But this suggests that his sons married wives unworthy of the priesthood. (B. Sanhedrin 93a) [5]

DISCUSSION:—This passage is not contained in any other collection of references to Jesus. It is included here only because the Church Fathers explain this story as allegorically alluding to Jesus—since Jesus and Joshua are cognate names. This is suggested by Ginzberg as a possible reason for the rabbinic finding of a fault in Joshua, according to the Haggadah.[6] But, of course, the similarity in names is purely coincidental.

TEXT:—Rab said, The first Man (Adam) spoke Aramaic, as it is in Scripture: "How weighty also are Thy thoughts unto me, O God." [7] (B. Sanhedrin 38a)

DISCUSSION:—This has been proposed as a pertinent allusion [8] because Jesus is sometimes designated as the Primordial Man, Adam,[9] and because he spoke Aramaic.[10] It is immediately apparent that there is not much to this proposal. Another Midrash passage tells that the language at Creation was Hebrew.[11] The New Testament refers to Jesus as "the last Adam," not "the first Man." [12] It would not be likely that the Jewish teachers would refer to Jesus as Primordial Man, without some qualifying comment.

TEXT:—He who reads in the external books, such as the books of Ben Laana and the books of the *Minim*.[13] (P. Sanhedrin X, 1 or 28a)

DISCUSSION:—These are among the prohibited books. G. F. Moore interprets "the books of Ben Laana" as "the Gospels." [14] Elsewhere, the word *Laana* is spelled *laaga*;[15] in the Midrash the word used in the same connection is Tagla.[16] Louis Ginzberg argues against Moore's opinion. It has been suggested, also, that Tagla would refer to the Book of Revelation, and that the word was purposely distorted to Laanah, which means "wormwood." [17] The text is too much corrupted for us to reach a positive conclusion. There is the belief that Laanah refers to Apollonius of Tyana, a pagan philosopher; Tagla is Empedocles; that both words mean "foxes," alluding to fables of Bidpai; that *Homers* is the correct reading, not *haminim,* and alludes to the Books of Homer or of Hermes.[18]

# INDIRECT ALLUSIONS

We continue now, on the basis of the position stated in the introductory pages of Section C of Chapter II, to look for indirect allusions to Jesus which do not mention his name or substitute name but which contain reasonable indications that they refer to him. We consider now the statements of the Amoraic period.

## 1. UNITY OF GOD

TEXT:—The *Minim* asked R. Simlai how many gods created the world. He said to them, "Of me you inquire? Go and ask the first man, as it is in Scripture: [1] 'For ask now of the days past, which were before thee, since the day that God [2] created man upon the earth.' It is not written here 'they created' but 'He created.' " They said to him, "It is in Scripture: 'In the beginning God created.' " He said to them, "Is it written 'they created'? Rather is it written 'He created.' " R. Simlai said: "Wherever (in a Biblical passage) the *Minim* find (support for their) heresy [3] the refutation is alongside."

They (the *Minim*) returned and asked him, "What of that which is written: 'Let us make man in our image, after our likeness'?" [4] He said to them: " 'And they created man in their image,' it is not written here but 'And God created man in His image.' " [5] His disciples said to him (after the others left): "Rabbi, you have thrust them aside with a broken reed.[6] What do you answer to us?" He said to them, "In the past Adam was created out of the dust and Eve was created out of Adam. From Adam onward it is 'in our image, according to our likeness.' It is impossible for a man without the woman, and it is impossible for woman without the man, and it is impossible for both of them without the *Shechinah* (Divine Presence)."

They returned and asked him, "What is that which is written: '*El, Elohim, Yahweh; El, Elohim, Yahweh;* [7] He knoweth'?" [8] He said to them, "It is not written here 'they know,' but it is written 'He knoweth.' " His disciples said to him, "Rabbi, you have thrust them aside with a broken reed. What do you answer to us?" He said to them, "It is not written here 'they know,' but it is written speaks (of a king) as Basileus, Caesar, Augustus."

They returned and asked him, "What is that which is written, '*El, Elohim, Yahweh* hath spoken and called the earth?' " [9] He said to them, "Is it written here 'they have spoken and they called?' Rather is it written, 'He hath spoken and called the earth.' " His disciples said to him, "Rabbi, you have thrust them aside with a broken reed. What do you answer to us?" He said to them, "The three of them are one name, just as a person who says (of a worker at construction): workman, builder, architect."

They returned and asked him, "What is that which is written, 'For He is a holy God'?" ("God" and "holy" are plural.) [10] He said to them, " 'They are holy' is not written there but 'He'— 'He is a jealous God.' " [11] His disciples said to him, "Rabbi, you have thrust them aside with a broken reed. What do you answer to us?" R. Isaac said, "Holy in every kind of holiness." (The text here elaborates on holiness in its multiplicity.)

They returned and asked him, "What is that which is written, 'For what great nation is there that hath God so nigh (plural) unto them as the Lord our God is whensoever we call upon Him?' " [12] He said to them, " 'Call upon them' is not written here but 'call upon Him.' " His disciples said to him, "Rabbi, you have thrust them aside with a broken reed. What do you answer to us?" He said to them, "He is near in every kind of nearness." (P. Berachoth 12d, 13a)

DISCUSSION:—This passage is repeated practically the same in Midrash, Genesis Rabbah VIII.9. The Midrash Psalms on Psalm 50:1 (p. 139b #1, Buber ed.) repeats the essential portion of the passage—but here, R. Simlai explains to his disciples the three names of God as follows: "To teach you that God created the world with three names, equivalent to the three good attributes by which the world was created: wisdom, understanding and knowledge, as indicated in Proverbs 3:19, 20."

A list of textual refutations to Scripture quotations of the *Minim*, including several of those given above, is found in B. Sanhedrin 38b, spoken by R. Yohanan. R. Simlai and R. Yohanan were both of the second generation of Palestinian Amoraim, dated in the second half of the third century.

The language of the text quoted above sounds very much like an actual disputation, perhaps of several sessions: "The *Minim* returned and asked." We have seen that the *Minim* could be, but need not be, Jewish Christians. Of this type of passage, Montefiore and Loewe write: "Heretics, or unbelievers, or perhaps Christians, seem often to have worried the rabbis about these plural forms, as if they proved that the Scriptures taught that there was more than one God, or that God was not one." [13]

There always is the possibility that the discussion was not with Christians, that Jesus was not meant. However, the fact that some of these very same texts are used by Christian writers of the second, third and fourth centuries to prove the divinity of Jesus, and that the Jewish answer represented by them resembles what we have in this passage,[14] offers strong support for the belief that these are, indeed, indirect allusions to Jesus.

TEXT:—He created in the beginning one man only, so that the *Minim* should not say: "There are several Powers in Heaven." (B. Sanhedrin 38a)

TEXT:—"Meddle not with them that are given to change." [15] Meddle not with those who say there is a second god. R. Yehudah bar Simon said, "And it shall come to pass, that in all the land, saith the Lord, two parts therein shall be cut off and die." [16] The mouths that say, "There are two Powers," they shall be cut off and die. And who will endure in the future? "But the third part shall be left therein." [17] These are Israel, who are called thirds, for they are in threes: Priests, Levites, Israelites; from three Patriarchs: Abraham, Isaac, and Jacob. . . . There is One and there is no second; He hath neither son nor brother. He hath neither brother nor son, but: "Hear, O Israel, the Lord our God, the Lord is One." [18] (Midrash, Deuteronomy Rabbah II.33; similarly Numbers Rabbah XVI.14)

DISCUSSION:—R. Yehudah bar Simon was a Palestinian Amora of the fourth century. His strong language may have been stirred up by the bitterness of anti-Jewish polemics and the restrictive legislation of that century.

To these texts may be added two already quoted in another connection: Pesikta Rabbati 100b, 101a, which answers the strayed son who says there are two gods; B. Sanhedrin 106b, in which R. Shimeon ben Lakish says, "Woe unto him who makes himself to live in the name of God" and which Rashi interprets "makes himself God." [19] There are other texts too. The evidence is there: Judaism strongly opposed dualistic or trinitarian conceptions and could have meant the Christian doctrine regarding Jesus.[20]

## 2. INCARNATION OF GOD

TEXT:—R. Abahu said: If a man says to you, "I am God," he is a liar. "I am the son of man," in the end he will regret it. "I will go up to Heaven"—he that says it will not perform it. (P. Taanith 65b)

DISCUSSION:—This is said in interpretation of the verse of Scripture: "God is not a man, that He should lie; neither the son of man, that He should repent: when He hath said, will He not do it? When He hath spoken, will he not make it good?" [1] This thought is expressed in Yalkut Shimeoni §766, previously mentioned,[2] wherein Balaam predicts that a man will come with a false claim to be God.

R. Abahu lived in Palestine during the second half of the third century and is counted among the third generation of Amoraim.[3] His statement is regarded by Herford as a definite reference to Jesus.[4] Strack is equally positive and supports his stand with parallel references to the New Testament,[5] holding, also, that "son of man" means "the Messiah." [6]

The passage *could* refer to Jesus, for it expresses a fundamental attitude of Judaism which makes difficult the acceptance of the divinity of Jesus. However, it must be borne in mind that this attitude is so entrenched in Judaism, so many times reiterated *before* the time of Jesus, that it need not *necessarily* refer to him. After all, every time the teachers of a religion emphasize a basic truth in the religion it is not to be assumed that they are arguing against someone else's religion. If that were so, we would become suspicious of every declaration of faith, lest an oblique criticism were being made of some other faith. The reasonable opinion, therefore, is but to hold that this text could allude indirectly to Jesus as the incarnation of God.

TEXT:—"Like a son of the gods," [7] Reuben said: At that hour an angel descended and struck that wicked one (Nebuchadnezzar) on his mouth. He said to him: "Correct your words. Has He a son?" He retracted (his statement) and said: "Blessed be the God of Shadrach, Meshach, and Abednego who hath sent"—it is not written here "his son" but—"who hath sent his angel and delivered his servants who trusted in him." (P. Shabbath VI, 9 or 8d)

DISCUSSION:—The item here is the mention of a son of God. The speaker, Reuben, is not easily placed. Strack is probably correct in designating him as a Palestinian Haggadist of the second generation of Amoraim, a contemporary of R. Yohanan bar Nappaha.[8]

TEXT:—Another explanation of "I am the Lord thy God." [9] R. Abahu said: A parable of a king of flesh and blood—he reigns and he has a father or a brother or a son.[10] The Holy One, Blessed be He, says: I am not so. "I am the first" [11]—that I have no father. "And I am the last"—that I have no son. "And beside me there is no God"—that I have no brother. (Midrash, Exodus Rabbah XXIX.5; to Ex. 20:2)

TEXT:—"There is One that is alone, and He hath not a second; yea, He hath neither son nor brother" [12]—but——"Hear O Israel, the Lord our God, the Lord is One." (Midrash, Deuteronomy Rabbah II.33; to Dt. 6:4)

DISCUSSION:—R. Abahu has already been described. The second text is attributed to R. Aha, a contemporary of R. Judah ben Simon, of the fourth generation of Amoraim.[13] The actual composition of the Midrashim, as was stated in the opening of this chapter, is of quite late date.

Both of these texts are considered to be statements pointed at the sonship of Jesus. Yet, who is the "brother"? The reference to "brother" weakens the argument that these are allusions to Jesus. Reread the Scriptural quotation from Ecclesiastes: it could definitely have reference to Jesus—excepting that it was written long before Jesus appeared on the scene of human events. At the same time, it is to be recognized that wherever Jews came in contact with Christian teaching and then expressed disbelief in the incarnation of God in a son it is a possible reference to Jesus.

As was done in examining the opinions of the Tannaim, we could adduce many passages of the Amoraim which tell that God can be as close as possible to all mankind without having to become incarnate in a Man-God. One text brings comforting assurance that *whenever* we importune God, He receives us; [14] another, that though we have no merit or good works, God extends His grace to us: [15] ever so many passages reiterate the Biblical teaching that God is the Father of every human son and daughter.

### 3. THE MESSIAH HAS NOT COME

TEXT:—This is what a certain *Min* said to R. Abahu: "When will the Messiah come?" He said to him: "When darkness has covered you." He said, "You are cursing me." He said, "The passage is written, 'For, behold, darkness shall cover the earth, and gross darkness the peoples; but upon thee the Lord will arise, and His glory shall be seen upon thee.'" [1] (B. Sanhedrin 99a)

DISCUSSION:—The interest in this text is the conversation with one of the *Minim* concerning the Messiah. If the *Minim* were Jewish Christians we would have reason to expect many such, but the strange fact is that this is the only instance, so far as we know, in all of the Tannaitic and Amoraic literature. Stranger still, if Herford's opinion be accepted, this one saving instance hardly seems to put the *Min* in the light of being a Jewish Christian. [2] Why would he inquire of a rabbi as to when the Messiah will come?

However, the *Min* could be, in fact, a Jew who accepted Jesus as the Messiah. First, R. Abahu conducted several discussions with men of this category and the naming of Abahu here as one of the disputants is significant. Secondly, his opponent may have made a vigorous affirmation that the Messiah has come in the person of Jesus, following it up with ridicule on the folly of waiting for a Messiah who has already come, asking with scorn, "When will the Messiah (whom you vainly expect) come?" R. Abahu answered, measure for measure, with some acrimony. This type of spirited debate, with insult added, is not unusual in the documented polemics of the Middle Ages [3] and gives the clue as to what this debate might have been. The Talmud would not be likely to quote the abusive remarks of the *Min* but only his concluding statement, which gives Abahu the opening to say what he did.

TEXT:—Israel has no Messiah (to come), since they already enjoyed him in the days of Hezekiah. (B. Sanhedrin 98b)

DISCUSSION:—This is another exceptional passage. The spokesman is R. Hillel II, Patriarch from 330 to 365, a lineal descendant of *the* Hillel. What is remarkable here is the fact that, while hundreds of texts in the Jewish tradition could be cited that the Messiah is yet to come, this one takes the position that the Messiah *has* come. So Christianity argued. But Hillel named Hezekiah, not Jesus, as the Messiah. His statement gains in interest when we recall that in the Christian-Jewish polemics of the Middle Ages, texts which the Christian side argued as promises of Jesus' coming were argued by the Jewish side as referring to Hezekiah. Of significance, too, is the fact that the eminent Tanna, Yohanan ben Zakkai, looked forward to the second advent of Hezekiah.[4]

What prompted R. Hillel to make his observation? We can only guess. Had he despaired of the future,[5] when, as a religious leader of his people, there were placed upon his shoulders the heavy responsibilities of the critical fourth century when Christianity was elevated as the religion of the Roman Empire? Or, on the contrary, did he believe in a future for Israel but place his faith in a Messianic Era rather than in a personal Messiah?

Did he intend his words as opposition to the fervid calculations of his contemporaries as to the date for the Messiah to come, with subsequent disappointment when the date arrived but no Messiah? This is the opinion of Kohler.[6] It might be supported by these Talmudic comments: "May the curse of Heaven come upon those who calculate the date of the coming of the Messiah and thus create political and social unrest with the people";[7] "the Messiah will come when nobody expects him."[8]

Were his words directed against the Christian teaching of Jesus as the Christ, by saying, in effect, that in Judaism the belief in the Messiah is not a fundamental doctrine—which others in Jewish history, such as Joseph Albo[9] and Moses Sofer,[10] said many centuries later?

Did Hillel really intend this passage, as Rashi later interpreted it, to mean that the redemption of Israel in the future would be not by a Messiah but by God? Schechter regards this explanation as plausible,[11] pointing to rabbinic support such as: "They are the redeemed of the Lord (as in Isaiah 35:10), and not the redeemed of Elijah, nor the redeemed of the King Messiah";[12] "We desire a king no longer. We want again our first King, God; as it is said, 'The Lord is our King; He will save us' (Isaiah 33:22)."[13] It is not impossible, Schechter believes, that such texts were prompted by polemics with Christians.

Thus we see that there are several possible interpretations of Hillel's saying, each of which could point to an indirect allusion to Jesus. In elaborating the thought we have observed additional Amoraic references to the Messiah. Of the extensive Amoraic literature on the subject we have space for only one or two more illustrations.

TEXT:—Isaac bar Nappaha said, "The son of David will not come until the whole world is converted to the belief in *Minuth*." Rabbah said: "What verse (proves it)?" "It is all turned to white; he is clean." (B. Sanhedrin 97a)

DISCUSSION:—The author of this remark lived in the fourth century in Tiberias, in Caesarea and in Babylonia. He may have had in mind the trend of the Roman Empire toward Christianity—as we noticed in a similar statement attributed to the Tanna, R. Eliezer.[14] A Baraitha preceding the present passage quotes R. Nehemiah (150 c.e.). R. Isaac was an outstanding Haggadist and, therefore, this expression may be but an imaginative statement that the world would deteriorate into heresy before the Messiah comes.

His saying is made more meaningful by the comment of Rabbah who makes use of Leviticus 13:13 which speaks of leprosy turning to white, but which may be transformed homiletically into saying, in effect: "The Messiah will not come until the whole world is converted to the belief in heresy, that is, turned *to the Son.*"

Those who, like the Soncino English translation of the Talmud, do not agree with this interpretation explain that the Bible verse is not quoted in order to play upon the word which could mean "to white" or "to the son" but rather in order to convey the figurative meaning of the text: in the signs of leprosy, a white swelling is uncleanliness, but if all the skin turns white it is declared clean; so, when all the world has turned to heresy, the world is then about to be purified.[15]

A plausible explanation of this passage is that when the Tannaim, R. Eliezer and R. Nehemiah, made the statement they meant that the pre-messianic travail of humanity would entail world-wide heresy, and that they did not prophesy the conversion of Constantine to Christianity. But when R. Isaac repeated the statement he could have applied it to the conditions of his own day, namely the official adoption of Christianity by the Roman Empire, beginning with Constantine.

The statements which have been quoted thus far are those of unusual interest. The main trend in Jewish rabbinic tradition is to hope for the Messiah,[16] who is sometimes regarded simply as one who will redeem Israel from foreign subjugation,[17] sometimes as one who will bring about a world upheaval;[18] a Messiah ben Joseph will be the forerunner of the Messiah ben David;[19] in the final time of the Messiah there will be blessings manifold.[20] This grouping of items as to the Messiah is, in a way, most important because the Jewish tradition of the Amoraic period as well as of later times, when confronted with the presentation of Jesus as the Messiah, compared the current conditions with those predicted for the post-messianic days and decided that the Messiah had *not* come.

## 4. MIRACLES: MOSES

TEXT:—More precious to God is the proselyte who comes of his own will than all the multitude of Israel who stood before Mount Sinai, for had Israel not witnessed the thunder, the lightning, the quaking mountain and the sounding trumpets, they would not have accepted the Torah; but the proselyte, who did not see one of these, came and gave himself to the Holy One, blessed be He, and took upon himself the yoke of Heaven. Can anyone be more precious to God than this person? (Tanhuma, Lech Lecha #6; p. 32a, Buber ed.)

TEXT:—"I will bless Thy name for ever and ever." [1] Not as now will it be then. Now, if God has performed for them a miracle, they sing a song unto Him; if not, they are silent. But in the time-to-come, they will never cease but will keep on continually to utter songs and blessings, for they will say, "We have no duty other than to bless Thee with ever new blessings." (Midrash Psalms on Ps. 145:1; p. 267b, #1, Buber ed.)

TEXT:—(Joshua ben Levi quoted a teaching of Hillel) The giving to man of his daily bread is as wonderful a marvel as the dividing of the Red Sea. [2] (Pesikta Rabbati, p. 152a)

TEXT:—What was the difference between Moses and the other prophets? They looked through nine window-panes [3] and he looked through only one. They looked through a cloudy window-pane but Moses, through a clear one. (Midrash, Leviticus Rabbah, I.14)

TEXT:—"For this commandment . . . is not in Heaven." [4] Moses said (to Israel), "That you should not say, 'Another Moses is to arise, and bring us another Law from Heaven,' therefore I have made it known to you that it is not in Heaven, that nothing is left of it in Heaven." (Midrash, Deuteronomy Rabbah, VIII.6)

DISCUSSION:—These texts added together convey a fair impression of the rabbinic lessening of emphasis on the necessity of basing faith on signs and miracles. That the motivation of this attitude was a part of the evolution of Judaism is certain, but it may be assumed that it was indirectly, in some degree, a position taken against the Christian emphasis upon the miraculous nature of Jesus.[5]

The later period of the Talmud and Midrash continued to disallow a new dispensation given through Jesus. It would not countenance the abrogation of the Law. It consequently stressed all the more the eternal role of Moses.[6]

# SUMMARY

The Jewish tradition of the time-area of the Amoraim yields little of a startling nature. Being removed from the days of Jesus by at least two centuries, the teachers of this period had no direct or even second-hand or third-hand contact with Jesus or his disciples.[1] Thus, what is related regarding the death of Jesus or of his disciples is speculative or outright homiletic interpretation of Scripture, regardless of external fact.[2]

Rab Hisda, who lived until 309 C.E., erroneously believed Ben Stada to be another name for Jesus,[3] so dim had the actual events become. As a matter of fact, Hisda thought Jesus was called Ben Stada for the reason that the husband of Mary was named Stada. But someone else, a teacher probably of the fourth or fifth century, thought Stada was the mother of Jesus, known also as Mary Magdalene.

This does not mean that all the Amoraim made the same mistake of confusing these two persons.[4] It is common fault to accept an opinion or statement of one of the teachers of the hundreds named in the Talmud and from this to generalize with the conclusion: "The Talmud teaches . . ." A good criterion whereby to judge is the one given by the Talmudist, J. Z. Lauterbach: "Only such teachings which have been formulated by representative and responsible Jewish teachers and indorsed by the majority of the people, as represented by their teachers, throughout the various periods of Jewish history, can be considered as the true authoritative Jewish teachings."[5]

We learn that in the time of the Amoraim healing was still performed by the followers of the Nazarene, who whispered something of Jesus.[6] This is added evidence that the curative powers of Jesus had made a lasting impression—much more than his teaching. Yet, we now find reference to his teaching, too.[7] He is pictured as a Jew who taught Jewish doctrine and observance, but who "burned the food"—enticing many to heresy.

As in the study of the Tannaitic period it was necessary here, too, to discard the references incorrectly identified with Jesus: the legend about Mary Magdalene and the reflection upon the

137

mother of Jesus; [8] the allusions to Balaam; [9] references to Ben Netzer, Joshua the High Priest, Adam, Ben Laana.[10] We came to realize that the Amoraim could make mistakes when dealing with events separated from them by hundreds of years, as is done even by scholars of modern times. We found that traditions could be in error, too, especially traditions about Jesus which developed in the environment of the Babylonian Amoraim where Christianity was scarcely known first-hand. Of particular interest was the endeavor to discern what led to the mistaken identifications, for we gain thereby an insight into the whole matter of motivation.

Again, the question may be asked: why is the record so meagre? Jews were in contact with Christians. They must have heard about Jesus. The answer, as before, must be that the Jews were primarily concerned with their Judaism. Judaism and Christianity separated by the middle of the second century. Christians went their way; Jews, theirs. Those who desired to live the Christian life, did so. Jews continued as Jews. The Talmud was created to enrich, intensify and detail the fullness of a Jewish life; it was not interested in Christianity; it had its own work to do.

Ernest Jacob has clearly summarized the answer: "The teachers retired into their schools after the destruction of Jerusalem and devoted themselves entirely to the development of the Law, which was to ensure the continued existence of Judaism, and did not concern themselves with movements outside of their own sphere." [11]

When we realize that there is not even a word in rabbinic literature concerning the Apostle Paul,[12] we come to appreciate what there *is* recorded regarding Jesus.

The Sages of the Talmud of the third, fourth and fifth centuries give us quite a few allusions to Christianity, by use of one term or another. This fact, combined with the diminishing mention of Jesus, leads to the conclusion that as Christianity gained in numbers and in political power *it*, not Jesus, became the immediate concern of the Jewish leaders. Anti-Jewish legislation, preachment and acts of violence made it necessary to deny the rejection of Israel, the abrogation of the Law, the inferiority of Judaism, a future without promise or hope. This was done, not so much as out-and-out denial but by newer and greater and more elaborate emphasis upon the validity of the Law of Moses, the Unity of God, God having no Son, a religion that increasingly requires no miracles for proof, the ultimate fulfilment of God's love and promise to Israel with the coming of the Messiah.

Thus, in the Amoraic period, as the direct references to Jesus become less numerous and less significant, the indirect allusions, as a possible reply to Christian doctrine and conduct, become more abundant and more vital in rabbinic Judaism.[13]

Now we must travel beyond the Talmud into the many centuries during which Jewish life was patterned on the normative Judaism of the Talmud.

CHAPTER IV

POST-TALMUDIC PERIOD

# IV

AFTER the completion of the Talmud the Jewish communities, wherever they happened to be in Palestine or Babylonia or in the far-flung lands of the Diaspora, lived and taught Judaism in strict accordance with the Talmud. The Responsa of the Geonim, the Commentaries on the Talmud, the Codes of Rabbinic Law, the folklore of the Midrash, the expanding liturgy of the Synagogue, the excursion into philosophy, and the developing customs and ceremonies—these were all built upon the foundation of the Talmud. Internally there was the triple challenge of Karaism, mysticism and rationalism. Externally, the world with one hand held forth the counter-attractions of Christianity and Mohammedanism and with the other hand seized Judaism by the throat to choke out its life. But the Jewish way of life—rabbinic Judaism—went on, as established by the Talmud, through many centuries, into the eighteenth century when several unprecedented forces combined to create a new era in Judaism.[1]

Inasmuch as Jewish life was thus conditioned by the rabbinic literature, it is now appropriate to our theme to inquire as to the Jewish record concerning Jesus in the post-Talmudic period.

The important factor in this period is the growth in numbers and power of the adherents of the religion founded on Jesus the Christ. Christianity, at first a persecuted religion struggling for survival, became in 311 a tolerated religion in the Roman Empire. Followers of the various faiths were on the same level, the rights of each equally respected, in the early decrees of the Emperor Constantine. Then, his Edict of 315, issued at the behest of the Church Fathers, denied the Jews the right to receive proselytes. Severe penalties were to be meted out to the "illegal" proselyte and also to the Jews accepting him into Judaism. The Council of Nicea, at which Constantine presided, decided in 325 that Easter should always come on the Sunday after the full moon of the spring month; in so fixing the date, it was agreed, it would no longer be necessary to depend upon the Jewish calendar. Thus, an important link between Jews and Christians was severed. Earlier, there had been the Council of Elvira, Spain (c. 300); later in the same fourth century there were decisions adverse to Judaism in the Church Councils of Antioch (341) and Laodicea (360).[2]

"The Middle Ages, for the Jew at least, begin with the advent to power of Constantine the Great (306–337)," Jacob R. Marcus epitomizes in *The Jew in the Medieval World*.[3] "He was the first Roman emperor to issue laws which radically limited the rights of Jews as citizens of the Roman Empire, a right conferred upon them by Caracalla in 212. As Christianity grew in power in the Roman Empire it influenced the emperors to limit further the civil and political rights of the Jews."

During the reign of Emperor Constantius II (337–361) devices of harassment, discrimination and persecution were invoked to subjugate Judaism and to give every advantage to Christianity— this with the slogan, "My will is the Church law."[4] There followed a temporary respite. But in 379 Gratian issued an edict for the Roman territory of the west which he ruled and Theodosius I issued an edict in 380 for his territory of the east—whereby Christianity became the state religion.

From now on we read in history the story of a dismal tragedy. Conrad Moehlmann has called it *The Christian-Jewish Tragedy*. While the roots are embedded in the very process of a daughter religion growing out of, and away from, the mother religion, it was in the fourth century that the bitter results came to fruition.

Now it was no longer a matter of argument over the interpretation of Bible verses or of disputation as to whether the Messiah had or had not come. Now there was legislation, severe legislation! It may be studied in the *Codex Theodosianus*,[5] compiled in the middle of the fifth century. There, where the date of each law is given, we can trace the deterioration of the political, professional, economic and social status of the Jewish communities. Restriction after restriction was imposed by law until the very legality of Judaism was abolished by Emperor Justinian (527–565),[6] subjecting the Jew to the mere whim and mercy of the sovereign. The pattern was thus set for the loss of rights which characterized Jewish history in so many countries during the greater part of the Middle Ages.

Denunciatory preaching by men like Cyril of Jerusalem, Ambrose of Milan and Chrysostom of Antioch led to acts of violence in which synagogues occasionally were destroyed and, if destroyed, were hardly ever restored. This too set a pattern, the pattern for medieval destruction of property, confiscation of property—and slaughter.[7]

Justinian, in the extension of his Empire, created an absolute autocracy of one church, one state, one law, controlled by one man—the Emperor. He brought an end to the Samaritans.[8] He interfered seriously with the internal affairs of the Jewish religion. He issued an order—Novella 146—defining synagogue procedure. He gladly would have witnessed the demise of Judaism. Yet, unlike the Samaritans, the Jews have persevered and have withstood every attack.

What was Novella 146 of Justinian? It was permission granted to read Holy Scripture in the synagogue in Greek, Latin or any other tongue, and not exclusively in Hebrew, if the congregation so desired; and it recommended especially the use of the Septuagint, the Greek translation—as the Novella states—by men who were illuminated by prophetic grace to sense the coming of the Lord and Savior Jesus Christ. It prohibited entirely the *deuterosis* or, as it is called, the second tradition. "For it is not part of the sacred books, nor is it handed down by divine inspiration through the prophets, but the handiwork of man, speaking only of earthly things, and having nothing of the divine in it. But let them read the holy words themselves, rejecting the commentaries, and not concealing what is said in the sacred writings, and disregarding the vain writings which do not form a part of them, which have been devised by them themselves for the destruction of the simple." [9] It threatened with death any of the Jewish people who denied the resurrection or the judgment, or the work of God, or that angels are part of creation. It warned against the "depravity of the interpreters" who do not cling to the literal words of Scripture.

This sovereign command is quite to the point. There is, however, one uncertainty for us as we examine it. What is meant by *deuterosis*? [10] The church writers took it to mean the Oral Law (Talmud); but the decree of prohibition referred to its use in the *synagogue service*, and the Talmud is not part of the liturgy. Some take it to mean the *Targum*, the Aramaic translation of Scripture; but *any* language was permitted. S. Krauss believes it to be the study of the Talmud in the rabbinic schools; but the prohibition related to the synagogue.

The probable explanation is that of H. Graetz, namely, that *deuterosis* consisted of sermons given by the rabbis in the synagogue, whose theme generally insisted that the Messiah was yet to come and whose primary intention was to fortify the people against their persecutors. When these sermons were outlawed the same results were obtained by deftly inserting the message of comfort and hope, in somewhat veiled fashion, in the liturgical poems, or *piyyutim*; as a writer in the twelfth century recorded: "The *piyyutim* were instituted at a time of persecution." [11]

It was crucial that the sorely oppressed people find the morale that would make them willing to cling to their Jewishness despite all manner of pain. They found it mainly in the virtues of rabbinic Judaism, particularly in the faith that Scripture and the interpretation derived therefrom were divine revelation, and in the hope of God's redemption in days to come.

When deprived of the right of free speech, as in the law of Justinian, they gave the message of the pulpit in the guise of a poetic prayer rather than as a sermon.

Under persistent conditions of oppression they found some measure of escape from tyranny, also, in the underground folklore which accumulated concerning him in whose name they were persecuted—the legends known as Toledoth Yeshu.

## SECTION A

## TOLEDOTH YESHU

*Sefer Toledoth Yeshu*[1] is a booklet, not commonly found nowadays, which pretends to narrate the story of Jesus. The title means "Life of Jesus." Alternate titles are *Maaseh Talui*,[2] or *Maaseh de'otho ve'eth beno*,[3] or *Maaseh Yeshu*.[4]

Earliest specific mention of elements of Toledoth Yeshu was made by Agobard, Archbishop of Lyons, in the approximate year 826, in his *Epistola de Judaicis superstitionibus*.[5] His successor, Amulo, also called attention in 846 to such a document in his *Amulonis Epistola, seu Liber contra Judaeos, ad Carolum Regem*.[6]

The earliest extant text in the Jewish literature are the six Aramaic fragments found in the Genizah of the old Ezra Synagogue in Cairo, Egypt—built in the seventh century and in which valuable documents had accumulated during the course of a thousand years—discovered some fifty years ago by Solomon Schechter.[7]

The Karaites, a dissident sect of Judaism, seem to have had their own Toledoth Yeshu in the first half of the ninth century.[8] In the thirteenth century (1278), Raymund Martini, a Dominican of Spain, quoted from the Toledoth Yeshu in his *Pugio Fidei*;[9] his material was used by the Portuguese, Victor Porchet de Salvaticis, in the early part of the fourteenth century.[10] Later in the fourteenth century, two outlines of the Toledoth Yeshu theme appeared in the Hebrew *Eben Bohan*[11] by Shemtob ibn Shaprut of Spain. In 1566 Luther rendered it into German.[12] John C. Wagenseil, who had defended the Jews on occasion, wanted this booklet outlawed when he discovered it and, carefully editing the Hebrew text, he printed it—a Latin translation and a Refutation —in 1681, under the title *Tela ignea Satanae*.[13] A somewhat different text was published by Huldreich in 1705.[14]

From then on we begin to find a number of varying versions in many languages and countries. As recently as 1938, Samuel Krauss brought to light two hitherto unknown manuscripts, without title, date, divisions into chapters or much punctuation, but which he believes to have been put in writing by a copyist two centuries ago: one is in Hebrew, consisting of fourteen pages; the other is in Yiddish and runs to thirty-eight pages.[15] This is Krauss' most recent contribution in this field. His *Das Leben Jesu nach jüdischen Quellen*, published in 1902, is the most scholarly and comprehensive treatment of the subject which we have. The variant texts printed there, including three Hebrew versions, and others named, are arranged by E. Bischoff into five types: Wagenseil, De Rossi, Huldreich, Modern Slavonic, Cairo. H. J. Schonfield[16] reduces these to two basic types: the Toledoth Yeshu proper; and the Toledoth Minor which he characterizes as legends which circulated among the Jews, relating mainly to the passion and resurrection.

What exactly is the content of the Toledoth Yeshu proper? With many versions and with the widest range of variation between one version and another, there is, nevertheless, general agreement on the underlying theme and motivation. In presenting the story now, in abbreviated form, we shall follow it mainly as Wagenseil printed it. This is the most widely known version.[17]

In the year 3671 (about 90 B.C.E.),[18] in the days of King Jannaeus, a great misfortune befell Israel, when there arose a certain disreputable man of the tribe of Judah, whose name was Joseph Pandera. He lived at Bethlehem, in Judah.

Near his house dwelt a widow and her lovely and chaste daughter named Miriam. Miriam was betrothed to Yohanan,[19] of the royal house of David, a man learned in the Torah and God-fearing.

At the close of a certain Sabbath, Joseph Pandera, attractive and like a warrior in appearance, having gazed lustfully upon Miriam, knocked upon the door of her room and betrayed her by pretending that he was her betrothed husband, Yohanan. Even so, she was amazed at this improper conduct and submitted only against her will.

Thereafter, when Yohanan came to her, Miriam expressed

astonishment at behavior so foreign to his character. It was thus that they both came to know the crime of Joseph Pandera and the terrible mistake on the part of Miriam. Whereupon Yohanan went to Rabban Shimeon ben Shetah and related to him the tragic seduction. Lacking witnesses required for the punishment of Joseph Pandera, and Miriam being with child, Yohanan left for Babylonia.

Miriam gave birth to a son and named him Yehoshua, after her brother. This name later deteriorated to Yeshu. On the eighth day he was circumcised. When he was old enough the lad was taken by Miriam to the house of study to be instructed in the Jewish tradition.

One day Yeshu walked in front of the Sages with his head uncovered, showing shameful disrespect. At this, the discussion arose as to whether this behavior did not truly indicate that Yeshu was an illegitimate child and the son of a *niddah*. Moreover, the story tells that while the rabbis were discussing the Tractate *Nezikin*, he gave his own impudent interpretation of the law and in an ensuing debate he held that Moses could not be the greatest of the prophets if he had to receive counsel from Jethro. This led to further inquiry as to the antecedents of Yeshu, and it was discovered through Rabban Shimeon ben Shetah that he was the illegitimate son of Joseph Pandera. Miriam admitted it.[20] After this became known, it was necessary for Yeshu to flee to Upper Galilee.[21]

After King Jannaeus, his wife Helene (known in history as Salome Alexandra) ruled over all Israel. In the Temple was to be found the Foundation Stone [22] on which were engraven the letters of God's Ineffable Name. Whoever learned the secret of the Name and its use would be able to do whatever he wished. Therefore, the Sages took measures so that no one should gain this knowledge. Lions [23] of brass were bound to two iron pillars at the gate of the place of burnt offerings. Should anyone enter and learn the Name, when he left the lions would roar at him and immediately the valuable secret would be forgotten.

Yeshu came and learned the letters of the Name; he wrote them upon the parchment which he placed in an open cut on his thigh and then drew the flesh over the parchment. As he left, the lions roared and he forgot the secret. But when he came to his house he reopened the cut in his flesh with a knife and lifted out the writing. Then he remembered and obtained the use of the letters.

He gathered about himself three hundred and ten young men of Israel and accused those who spoke ill of his birth of being people who desired greatness and power for themselves. Yeshu proclaimed, "I am the Messiah; and concerning me Isaiah prophesied and said, 'Behold, a virgin shall conceive, and bear a son, and shall call his name Immanuel.'" [24] He quoted other messianic texts, insisting, "David my ancestor prophesied concerning me: 'The Lord said unto me, thou art my son, this day have I begotten thee.'" [25]

The insurgents with him replied that if Yeshu was the Messiah he should give them a convincing sign. They, therefore, brought to him a lame man, who had never walked. Yeshu spoke over the man the letters of the Ineffable Name—and the man was lame no more. Yet another sign did he give them. They brought a leper; he spoke the letters of the Ineffable Name, and the leper was healed. Thereupon, they worshiped him as the Messiah, Son of the Highest.

When word of these happenings came to Jerusalem, the Sanhedrin decided to bring about the capture of Yeshu. They sent messengers, Annani and Ahaziah, who, pretending to be his disciples, said that they brought him an invitation from the leaders of Jerusalem to visit them. Yeshu consented on condition that the members of the Sanhedrin receive him as a lord. He started out toward Jerusalem and, arriving at Nob, acquired an ass on which he rode into Jerusalem, as a fulfilment of the prophecy of Zechariah.

The Sages bound him and led him before Queen Helene, with the accusation: "This man is a sorcerer and entices everyone." Yeshu replied, "The prophets long ago prophesied my coming: 'And there shall come forth a rod out of the stem of Jesse,' [26] and I am he; but as for them, Scripture says, 'Blessed is the man that walketh not in the counsel of the ungodly.'" [27]

Queen Helene asked the Sages: "What he says, is it in your Torah?" They replied: "It is in our Torah, but it is not applicable to him; for it is in Scripture: 'And that prophet which shall presume to speak a word in my name, which I have not commanded him to speak or that shall speak in the name of other gods, even that prophet shall die.' [28] He has not fulfilled the signs and conditions of the Messiah." [29]

Yeshu spoke up: "Madam, I am the Messiah and I revive the dead." A dead body was brought in; he pronounced the letters of the Ineffable Name and the corpse came to life. The Queen was greatly moved and said: "This is a true sign." She reprimanded the Sages and sent them humiliated from her presence. Yeshu's dissident followers increased and there was controversy in Israel.

Yeshu went to Upper Galilee. The Sages came before the Queen, complaining that Yeshu practised sorcery and was leading everyone astray. Therefore she sent Annani and Ahaziah [30] to fetch him.

They found him in Upper Galilee, proclaiming himself the Son of God. When they tried to take him there was a struggle, but Yeshu said to the men of Upper Galilee: "Wage no battle." He would prove himself by the power which came to him from his Father in heaven. He spoke the Ineffable Name over birds of clay and they flew into the air. [31] He spoke the same letters over a millstone that had been placed upon the waters. He sat in it and it floated like a boat. When they saw this the people marveled. At the behest of Yeshu, the emissaries departed and reported these wonders to the Queen. She trembled with astonishment.

Then the Sages selected a man named Judah Iskarioto and brought him to the Sanctuary where he learned the letters of the Ineffable Name as Yeshu had done.

When Yeshu was summoned before the Queen, this time there were present also the Sages and Judah Iskarioto. [32] Yeshu said: "It is spoken of me, 'I will ascend into heaven.'" [33] He lifted his arms like the wings of an eagle and he flew between heaven and earth, to the amazement of everyone.

The elders asked Iskarioto to do likewise. He did, and flew

toward heaven. Iskarioto attempted to force Yeshu down to earth but neither one of the two could prevail against the other for both had the use of the Ineffable Name. However, Iskarioto defiled Yeshu, so that they both lost their power and fell down to the earth,[34] and in their condition of defilement the letters of the Ineffable Name escaped from them. Because of this deed of Judah, they weep on the eve of the birth of Yeshu.

Yeshu was seized. His head was covered with a garment and he was smitten with pomegranate staves; but he could do nothing, for he no longer had the Ineffable Name.

Yeshu was taken prisoner to the synagogue of Tiberias, and they bound him to a pillar. To allay his thirst they gave him vinegar to drink. On his head they set a crown of thorns.[35] There was strife and wrangling between the elders and the unrestrained followers of Yeshu, as a result of which the followers escaped with Yeshu to the region of Antioch (or Egypt); there Yeshu remained until the eve of the Passover.

Yeshu then resolved to go to the Temple to acquire again the secret of the Name.[36] That year the Passover came on a Sabbath day. On the eve of the Passover, Yeshu, accompanied by his disciples, came to Jerusalem riding upon an ass. Many bowed down before him. He entered the Temple with his three hundred and ten followers. One of them, Judah Iskarioto (Ga'isa in Aramaic),[37] apprised the Sages that Yeshu was to be found in the Temple, that the disciples had taken a vow by the Ten Commandments not to reveal his identity but that he would point him out by bowing to him. So it was done and Yeshu was seized. Asked his name, he replied to the question by several times giving the names, Mattai, Nakki, Buni, Netzer, each time with a verse quoted by him and a counter-verse by the Sages.[38]

Yeshu was put to death on the sixth hour on the eve of the Passover and of the Sabbath. When they tried to hang him on a tree it broke, for when he had possessed the power he had pronounced by the Ineffable Name that no tree should hold him. He had failed to pronounce the prohibition over the carob-stalk, for it was a plant more than a tree, and on it he was hanged until the hour for afternoon prayer, for it is written in Scripture, "His body shall not remain all night upon the tree." [39] They buried him outside the city.

On the first day of the week his bold followers came to Queen Helene with the report that he who was slain was truly the Messiah and that he was not in his grave; he had ascended to heaven as he prophesied. Diligent search was made and he was not found in the grave where he had been buried.[40] A gardener had taken him from the grave and had brought him into his garden and buried him in the sand over which the waters flowed into the garden.

Queen Helene demanded, on threat of a severe penalty, that the body of Yeshu be shown to her within a period of three days. There was great distress. When the keeper of the garden saw Rabbi Tanhuma [41] walking in the field and lamenting over the ultimatum of the Queen, the gardener related what he had done, in order that Yeshu's followers should not steal the body and then claim that he had ascended into heaven. The Sages removed the body,[42] tied it to the tail of a horse and transported it to the Queen, with the words, "This is Yeshu who is said to have ascended to heaven." Realizing that Yeshu was a false prophet who enticed people and led them astray, she mocked the followers but praised the Sages.

The disciples went out among the nations—three went to the mountains of Ararat, three to Armenia, three to Rome and three to the kingdoms by the sea. They deluded the people, but ultimately they were slain.

The erring followers amongst Israel said: "You have slain the Messiah of the Lord." The Israelites answered: "You have believed in a false prophet." There was endless strife and discord for thirty years.

The Sages desired to separate from Israel those who continued to claim Yeshu as the Messiah, and they called upon a greatly learned man, Simeon Kepha,[43] for help. Simeon went to Antioch, main city of the Nazarenes, and proclaimed to them: "I am the disciple of Yeshu. He has sent me to show you the way. I will give you a sign as Yeshu has done."

Simeon, having gained the secret of the Ineffable Name, healed a leper and a lame man by means of it and thus found acceptance as a true disciple. He told them that Yeshu was in heaven, at the right hand of his Father, in fulfilment of Psalm 110:1. He added that Yeshu desired that they separate themselves from the Jews and no longer follower their practices, as Isaiah had said, "Your new moons and your feasts my soul abhorreth." [44] They were now to observe the first day of the week instead of the seventh, the Resurrection instead of the Passover, the Ascension into Heaven instead of the Feast of Weeks, the Finding of the Cross instead of the New Year, the Feast of the Circumcision instead of the Day of Atonement, the New Year instead of Chanukah; they were to be indifferent with regard to circumcision and the dietary laws. Also, they were to follow the teaching of turning the right cheek if smitten on the left and the meek acceptance of suffering. All these new ordinances which Simeon Kepha (or Paul, as he was known to the Nazarenes) taught them were really meant to separate these Nazarenes from the people of Israel and to bring the internal strife to an end.[45]

While this is the actual conclusion of the principal part of Toledoth Yeshu, there are two supplementary chapters. One tells how Nestorius argued that the ceremonial laws of Judaism should be obeyed since Jesus had adhered to them. The other relates how Simeon Kepha, having become a Nazarene in order to save the Jews from bloodshed and exclusion from the Sanctuary, lived as an ascetic in a high tower built for him and there composed liturgical poetry like that of Eleazar ben Kalir. This poetry he sent to Jewish communities who now chant it and bless his name.

What are we to make of this fantastic story? Is it nothing but trash, sheer blasphemy? Is it the merest nonsense, too empty for serious inquiry? Or—is it a significant record for the understanding of Christianity and Judaism, and a study of the relationship of one to the other? Has it any historic value? Has it relevancy to the Bible? What shall we make of this startling document?

When we begin to probe and analyze the elements which make up the story we find a great deal that is not immediately discernible. The deeper we go the more fascinating the analysis becomes. Let us look into the essential points.

1. First, there is the account of the birth of Jesus from a human father and mother. When the Virgin Birth is not believed in there is no alternative but to accept a natural birth. If not born through the Holy Ghost, why not by Joseph, the espoused of Mary?

This is reflected in the Gospel according to John, where we read: "Is not this Jesus, the son of Joseph, whose father and mother we know? How is it then that he saith, I came down from heaven?" [46]

There is, indeed, a Syriac manuscript of the Canonical Gospels, of very early date (which two British women discovered in the Mount Sinai Monastery), in which Matthew 1:16 reads: "And Joseph, to whom was espoused Mary the virgin, begat Jesus." [47] That Jesus was born of Joseph and Mary in a normal way we know for a fact to have been the belief of the early Christians, the Ebionites.[48] The whole purpose of the genealogy of Jesus, given in the first chapter of Matthew, is obviously to indicate his Davidic descent, but the lineage is that of Joseph, the espoused of Mary, and it would be pointless were it not implied that Joseph shared in the parentage of Jesus. Ignatius, Bishop of Antioch, who was martyred between 107 and 117 C.E., is the first and only Apostolic Father to record any speculation on the miracle birth: "For our God, Jesus the Christ, was conceived in the womb of Mary, according to a dispensation of God, of the seed of David, but also of the Holy Spirit." [49]

If not by Joseph and not by the Holy Spirit, and Mary was with child, speculation leads to a point of view indicated in the New Testament itself with the verse: "Then Joseph, her husband, being a just man, and not willing to make her a publick example, was minded to put her away privily." [50] In the Apocryphal, and Uncanonical, Gospels—not as important in Christianity as the Gospels of the New Testament (Canonical) but not to be ignored either [51]—we already see definite accusations in this matter. The *Acts of Pilate* (known also as the *Gospel of Nicodemus*), of the second century, relates the charge [52] but it is refuted. The *Book of James* raises the question and at the same time protests the innocence of Joseph.[53] The Church Fathers also bear witness to this element of Toledoth Yeshu.

Justin, in the middle of the second century, records that Joseph wished to put away Mary, his betrothed, because he supposed her pregnant of another man, but he was commanded by a vision not to do so.[54] Origen relates that Celsus, in 178 C.E., had made the charge that Jesus was born out of wedlock by Panthera, a soldier, and Mary, who had been betrothed to a carpenter.[55]

Enough has now been cited to indicate the source of the material in the Toledoth Yeshu regarding the birth of Jesus. It is not mockery. It is not fabricated out of thin air. It has a history and follows a line of thought progression. Especially noteworthy is the realization that we have here a serious theological problem. Whatever unpleasantness attaches to this problem is regrettable—but unavoidable.

It is simply this. The earliest record, as we reconstruct it, tells of a natural birth of Jesus by Joseph and Mary. The Jews, and the early Jewish Christians too, believed it, for nowhere in the New Testament is there any Jewish accusation of illegitimacy. When, however, Jesus was interpreted as not only the Messiah but also the Son of God it was stated emphatically that Joseph was not the father.

"Who, then, was the father?" asked those who could not accept the Divine Sonship. Various answers were given; one of these is recorded in Toledoth Yeshu. In our discussion of the Amoraic period we saw clearly that this legend of the parentage of Jesus was not Jewish in origin; we saw also how it entered the Jewish tradition. Now we have learned why it was considered necessary to introduce it.

2. Next to consider is the item regarding Jesus and his rabbinic teachers. Here, too, we find the beginnings of the tradition in the New Testament, as told in the second chapter of Luke.[56] Details are added in the *Gospel of Thomas* which relates that Jesus was taken by the hand and led to a teacher named Zacchaeus to study;[57] also, that after he had put his elders to silence with his sagacity the scribes and Pharisees asked his mother, "Art thou the mother of this child?" and she replied that she was.[58]

Hearing this tradition, it was inevitable that someone should recall the tale in the Talmud of a sagacious lad, wise to the point of impudence, whose mother was likewise questioned regarding her child. Thus, the passage in Tractate Kallah which, as we have seen in the study of the Amoraic period, does not name Jesus and could not possibly refer to him,[59] was associated with him in the Toledoth Yeshu as a result of an analogy in circumstance.

3. Much can be told of the power of Jesus to heal and to perform other amazing deeds, as expressed in Toledoth Yeshu. We are well acquainted with the narration in the Canonical Gospels of Jesus' wondrous acts.[60] These accounts parallel remarkably those given in Toledoth Yeshu about causing the lame to walk and the dead to live. A supplementary detail, the incident in which Jesus made birds of clay to flap their wings and fly, is paralleled—interestingly enough—in the *Gospel of Thomas*.[61]

How was this power obtained? Where there was no conviction that Jesus was God, it had to be explained somehow; for, observe, Jewish tradition did not deny the astounding deeds nor did it attribute them to the work of the devil,[62] as is so often the case in religious polemics.[63]

W. M. Ramsay, for example, discloses in *The Church in the Roman Empire Before 170 A. D.* that it was the prevailing opinion in Rome that all Christians resorted to magic.[64] But the Toledoth states that the power was derived from the letters of God's Ineffable Name.

The potency of the Name is a major premise in Jewish folklore. S. Krauss maintains that the use of God's great and holy Name in this manner was originally a Gnostic practice. He therefore believes that the place given in Toledoth Yeshu to this practice is not adventitious but rather reveals to us that we must look to Gnosticism as the source of some of the strange elements in Toledoth Yeshu.[65]

The Foundation Stone of creation is a prominent feature in Jewish Midrash.[66] It is said to have been set in the Sanctuary, before the Ark. The tradition that lions guarded the Holy of Holies is preserved in the symbolism of the two lions protecting the Ark of the Torah, seen in synagogues ancient and modern.

The function of the guardian lions is similar to what the Second Targum tells of the lions of King Solomon's throne. The means of stealing the secret by concealment in a cut in the flesh is a transference to the Toledoth Yeshu of what was originally told about how Ben Stada gained the power of magic in Egypt; [67] it was applied to Jesus in the Amoraic period when Ben Stada was confusedly believed to have been Yeshu ben Pandera.[68] Thus once more we witness the Toledoth Yeshu as the combination of the Bible, the apocryphal works, teachings of the sectaries, the Talmud, folklore, the association of ideas—and a sprinkling of confusion. What was not confused was the motivation in terms of religious objectives.

4. Continuing the story in its essential development we come to the figure of Judah Iskarioto, shown in some versions as mingling among the disciples. This is none other than Judas of the New Testament.

The triumphal entry into Jerusalem, the use of Old Testament texts to prove and disprove, the amazement of the emissaries who behold the powers of Jesus—these and numerous other details relate closely to the accounts given by the Synoptic Gospels. The two separate arrests and hearings may allude to the two trials, by Herod and by Pilate.

The accusation of sorcery is given in the *Acts of Pilate*.[69] The legend of his condemnation as a deceiver who led others astray and of his being hanged on the tree on the eve of the Passover and of the Sabbath is clearly a repetition of what is in the Talmud,[70] as is also the reference to the execution of the disciples.[71]

5. A challenging item which has not previously come to our attention is the description of what takes place after the body is removed from the tree, and buried. We noticed nothing of this in the Talmud or the Midrash. As a matter of fact, it is the Gospel according to Matthew that alerts us to the possibility that the body of Jesus might have been stolen. It tells that the chief priests and Pharisees, remembering the promise of Jesus that in three days he would rise again, asked of Pilate, "Command therefore that the sepulchre be made sure until the third day, lest his disciples come

by night, and steal him away, and say unto the people, He is risen from the dead." [72] This caution is reiterated in the non-Canonical *Gospel of Peter*,[73] the *Acts of Pilate* [74] and the Patristic works of Justin and Eusebius.[75]

The garden of the Toledoth story may be adumbrated in the *Gospel of Peter* which calls the sepulchre the *garden* of Joseph; [76] also in the reference by Tertullian to a "gardener" in the same sentence which begins, "This is he whom his disciples have stolen away secretly, that it may be said that he is risen." [77] Thus, Toledoth Yeshu is almost entirely dependent on Christian sources for this incident.

Why did it find its way into a Jewish document? The answer is a simple matter of comparative theology. To historic Christianity the Resurrection was, and is, of extreme importance. Judaism continued its course on the premise that the Resurrection had not occurred. Some way, therefore, had to be found, however debatable it might be, to account for the disappearance of the body of Jesus when it was no longer in the place where it had been laid to rest.

Further reliance on the New Testament is evidenced by the correspondence of the three days stipulated for finding the body with the third day as the day of Resurrection. Moreover, the most recent publication of a version of the Toledoth [78] gives six years after the Crucifixion as the period during which there was silence among the first Christians prior to the outbreak of controversy between Peter and Paul; this corresponds to the six years when Paul began his mission among the Gentiles.[79] (This version, incidentally, states that Paul made more disciples than Jesus.)

6. The role of Simeon Kepha in bringing about a separation between the early Christians and the Jews and thus terminating hostilities is extremely interesting to observe. It reflects the historic fact demonstrated, for example, in James Parkes' *The Conflict of the Church and the Synagogue*,[80] that after the parting of the ways there was truly more internal peace than during the painful process of separation. It implies, further, that the presence of Jewish Christians, not Gentile Christians, provoked the clash with Judaism.[81] Finally, it faintly suggests an attitude that in

religion a person should definitely adhere to a clear-cut conviction, one way or the other.

The two concluding chapters refer rather to the history of Christianity than to Jesus. Not within the scope of a study of Jesus in the Jewish tradition, they need not concern us now.

7. What may be the original date of Toledoth Yeshu?

To Voltaire it appeared that this life of Jesus Christ, altogether different from that in the Gospels, was of the first century, written prior to the Gospels.[82] This guess is entirely unsupported by any evidence. Wide is the range of estimates. Klausner argues for a late date, even in its earliest form not before the tenth century.[83] J. W. Jack holds that the pamphlet of absurd legends "originated in the Middle Ages." [84] Midway between the two extremes is the conclusion reached by Samuel Krauss in his great work on this subject, namely, that the original was composed about the year 500 [85] and that the Aramaic texts, which he designates *Ur-Toledoth*, go back to the fourth century.[86] With virtual agreement, H. J. Schonfield examines the internal and external evidence and finds for the original Toledoth proper a date no later than the fifth century, probably the fourth; [87] the *Ur-Toledoth* he definitely places at about the end of the fourth century.[88]

The principal reason for this wide range of opinion in dating the document centers in the decision as to what constitutes the original Toledoth. Schonfield makes the valid point that if we regard the work as a unit in which every element must be accounted for, the date necessarily would be at the beginning of the ninth century, about half a century before first mention of it is made by Agobard.[89] Certainly, references to Eleazer ben Kalir and Simeon Stylites (if it be he who is meant in the last chapter) argue for a late date.

On the other hand, it must be countered: how much *can* be whittled away without destroying the unity and the distinctive character of the document? In many instances, if we reduce it to the utmost minimum we would find the remnant none other than the elements in the Canonical Gospels, and the date the latter part of the first century—as we observed in the analysis of the theme. In view of the fact that this is a Jewish document, with a specific purpose, we cannot consider as valid the critical editing which removes the Talmudic portions. One of these is the Amoraic story of the "impudent son," taken from Tractate Kallah, and this Tractate was not compiled earlier than about the year 500. Moreover, the possibility of having obtained this type of legend from an early Yosippon (supposedly, Josephus) is convincingly disproved by Klausner [90] and Zeitlin.[91] Hence, it is unlikely that we would find the Toledoth Yeshu—as a unified composition, a whole as it was known through the centuries, fulfilling the purpose for which it was intended—any earlier than the sixth century, at which time the Talmud was a completed and closed product. This viewpoint is not given as an exclusive one. As we have stated, depending on what is regarded as the "original" Toledoth there is room for varying opinions.

Assuming a date in the sixth century, can we narrow it further? A study of Jewish history teaches us that material which only exists by word of mouth is often put into writing at times of crisis. This is prompted by apprehension that unless this is done the inherited learning might be lost in the chaos of conquest or persecution.[92] In other words, we must look for a dramatic instance of external pressure as the factor which led to the writing of the Toledoth.

Thus, Krauss [93] selected as the determining event the Discussion which is reported to have taken place in Rome in the fourth year of Constantine the Great between the Christians, represented by Silvester, Pope of Rome, and the Jews, represented by twelve spokesmen, but especially by Zambri the magician. Certain features of the Discussion (disputation) seem to connect with the Toledoth. The wife of Constantine was named Helena, concerning whom it is recorded that she was almost converted to Judaism. Helena is the name of the Queen in Toledoth. When words failed to settle the argument it resolved itself into a contest as to which one—Silvester or Zambri—possessed the greater magic power. Zambri whispered the Name of God into the ear of a fierce bull; it was overpowering; the beast slumped and died. Zambri then challenged Silvester to restore the bull to life by invoking the Name of Jesus, doubting that he could succeed—"even if you fly." With prayer, Silvester knelt and whispered in the same ear of the bull the command in the Name of Jesus that the other Name depart and that the bull breathe again the breath of life. The bull arose and lived again. Empress Helena and her family were won to Christianity, as were also three thousand of the Jews.[94]

We recognize instantly certain similarities in this story with that of Toledoth Yeshu with respect to matching Name versus Name. In any event, Krauss refers to the persecution of the fourth century as the factor which led ultimately, if not immediately, to the composition of the Toledoth.

These elements of similarity, in all probability, did not derive from the above episode; [95] even if they did, they could have been preserved orally for a considerable time as happened with so much else in the Toledoth. Moreover, this entire event—like others of the disputations—has the earmarks of fiction. Our knowledge of it comes from George Cedrenus who lived in the Byzantine Empire in the eleventh century [96] and J. Juster, a reliable scholar on the Jews in the Roman Empire, who hold that this Discussion story originated in the East and came to the West (Rome) toward the end of the fifth century.[97]

While Krauss tells of the persecution in the fourth century, and it assuredly was a difficult one, conditions did not improve in the fifth or sixth centuries; on the contrary they deteriorated. Under Justinian the Jewish people suffered their greatest blow since the tragedy of the defeats of 70 and 135. Even after loss of their homeland they still had retained political status under Roman law. The law granted them certain rights: it may have narrowed these rights from time to time; it may have been violated again and again; but it was still the law. Emperor Justinian, however, in his legal Code deprived the Jews of their legal status, gave them no rights, made them dependent on the whim of the sovereign.[98] Synagogues were confiscated; old ones could not be repaired and new ones could not be built. In one instance Jews were forced to become converts. Justinian injected a new element of conflict with his Novella 146, issued in the year 553, which regulated synagogue worship and study, a law which Parkes characterizes as intended to undermine from within the powers of resistance of Talmudic Judaism to Christian missionary activity.[99]

This was crisis! At such a time, indeed, a Toledoth Yeshu could have been put into written form to meet the unprecedented threat. We have learned that when Justinian invaded the practice of Judaism and forbade *deuterosis*, there was the necessity to "go underground" and camouflage the sermon as liturgical poetry.[100] How likely it was to "go underground" at this time and to compose whatever else would offset the pressure and propaganda for conversion!

These things do not happen overnight. They are cumulative. Therefore, it would appear that the Toledoth Yeshu approached some definitive form toward the end of the sixth or the early part of the seventh century. With this conclusion as to its date, not too long an interval remains before someone would take note of its existence, as Agobard did in the early part of the ninth century.

8. Concerning the historical value of the Toledoth Yeshu to provide material for the life of Jesus, Klausner asserts that it is nil.[101] Other writers on this subject agree with him. Undoubtedly, we have here a conglomeration of a parody on the Gospels, with the full play of the imagination which is characteristic of this period in this type of literature in the Near East,[102] plus misinterpretation of Talmud and Midrash passages, plus excerpts from non-Canonical and Patristic writings, plus vestigial remains of sectaries, plus (as some believe) items from the Yosippon,[103] plus unwritten folk legend. But, if we remove all the "plus" accretions, is there a core—however reduced in size—of factual record of historic value?

Schonfield of England published in 1937 a challenging book [104] which undertakes the task of tracing the Toledoth Yeshu to its ultimate origin. Spurred by the words of Celsus that he could "state many other things regarding the events of the life of Jesus which are true, and not like those which are recorded by the disciples," [105] and by the words of the Gospel John, "And there are also many other things that Jesus did," Schonfield, accepting the Toledoth as a parody of an Uncanonical Gospel of a Synoptic type,[106] analyzes the entire matter and finds that the core of Toledoth Yeshu, stripped of legendary accumulation, parodies the Fifth Gospel—the Gospel according to the Hebrews—that it is similar to Mark, Matthew,[107] Luke and John, but quite different in important essentials. From this he reconstructs the Gospel according to the Hebrews. He does not claim that his proofs are complete but expresses the hope that others will continue the research.

Is Schonfield on the right track? The writer was curious to the point of inquiring. A letter to R. Travers Herford brought this interesting reply: "I know the book and have read it repeatedly. I certainly think that there is great value in his theory about the Toledoth Yeshu. And I am much surprised that so little notice seems to have been taken of it in scholarly circles. It looks as if there was a general unwillingness on the part of scholars to open their minds to a new and highly disturbing theory about Jesus. There is a great deal of bigotry and prejudice even now amongst orthodox and even liberal scholars. I can only suppose that Schonfield himself suffers under the ban against his unpopular theory." However, it must be noted that Zeitlin, not a Christian, finds no scholarly value in this theory.

There are assumptions which require further study before the conclusion can be substantiated.[108] In a review of his own studies to that date, Krauss in 1933 expressed his conclusion that the Aramaic texts of Toledoth were intended to be a Jewish reply to the Gospel of the Hebrews.[109] He was pleased subsequently to read that Schonfield was working toward a similar conclusion.[110] However, a Gospel of the Hebrews need not be *the* lost Gospel according to the Hebrews.

Schonfield assumes that this would be the only *Hebrew* Gospel, but (although it is considerably contested) C. C. Torrey argues for an Aramaic rather than Greek origin of the Canonical Gospels,[111] and Aramaic was the spoken language of the Jews of those centuries; certainly, the sources of the Greek were Aramaic; [112] further, the Gospels were available in the Syriac language in the fourth, possibly third, century in the harmonized form of the *Diatessaron*.[113] Moreover, a great deal of what is in the Canonical and non-Canonical literature must have reached the Jews by word of mouth, which they could retain because of their training in oral learning, and would explain variations in the order of events as between the Gospels and the Toledoth. His other assumption is that what is given in the Toledoth and cannot be found in the Gospels stood in Christian terms in the text of the Gospel according to the Hebrews which the composer of the Toledoth used in constructing his parody. The comment on this must be that the sources of Toledoth Yeshu are many—Christian and non-Christian, Canonical and non-Canonical, written and oral—over many centuries. At all events, we are grateful for this recent study into the nature of the document and must hope for additional light.

However, we cannot dismiss the historic value of the Toledoth. Even legends and myths reveal events, if we can interpret what they intend to tell. Whether we learn anything from Toledoth Yeshu which would give us additional information on the life of Jesus is difficult to say until we know whether this is an independent tradition traceable to the first century or is, as it at present seems to be, a reply to Christian tradition in the New Testament and elsewhere by simulating the style of the Gospels.

9. This unhistoric document discloses considerable of the history of the relations between Jews and Christians. Much of this has already been indicated.[114] No two editions of Toledoth Yeshu are identical in all points; therefore, in addition to what is common to all, each minor variation conveys a message—as to the external conditions at the time of writing (or copying), as to details in the story heard or read of Jesus and Christianity or as to the thought process, the culture and knowledge of the author and the means whereby he thought he could render a service to his oppressed co-religionists.[115]

As an illustration, Krauss found in the edition which he analyzed most recently [116] the allusion to what was probably an actual instance of a church controversy wherein a Christian was accused of protecting Jews. This particular text has Jesus begin his preaching at the age of *thirty-six*; it places particular emphasis on the role of Paul; it says that Jesus attracted a following of a million persons (reflecting the strong Christian environment in which the author lived); it evidences, on the part of the author, quite an understanding of Christian dogma. Thus, the Toledoth is of significance not only in relation to the days of its origin but in its use through the centuries.

Essentially, though, its value was subjective.[117] It did salve wounded spirits. It had theological significance. It was not blind mockery. It challenged the theology of historic Christianity. Of the Jewish communities of the thirteenth century, Grayzel writes: "nor is it unlikely that the Jews referred to the Toledot Jeshu as to an authentic tradition." [118] Reading it, they found that it was more difficult to yield thereafter to the pressures to accept Christianity.[119] They understood more clearly the logic of Judaism. This interpretation of the subjective value of the Toledoth Yeshu is supported by S. Krauss: "It ought also to be added that many of the legends have a theological background. For polemical purposes it was necessary." [120]

How widely these booklets were read and how many persons they influenced is open to speculation. In twentieth-century America their existence is unknown to all but the limited number of students in this field. Even in the Middle Ages, the historian Graetz maintains that very few Jews had copies of "these absurdities." [121] Klausner believes that they had a wider circle of influence.[122] We do know that none of the eminent Jewish scholars of the centuries refer to Toledoth Yeshu. So far as we can tell, they paid no attention to it. Judaism in the Middle Ages was rich in content and sufficiently absorbing to hold the complete interest of the Jewish people.[123] Their attention was diverted when attempts were made to lead them to the baptismal font: then they necessarily had to give thought to the doctrines associated with Jesus.

## SECTION B

## DISPUTATIONS AND POLEMICS OF THE
## MIDDLE AGES

Summing up the record of the Middle Ages, which he dates
from 315 to 1791, Jacob R. Marcus writes: "The medieval world
was a world of polemics and religious disputations. There is hardly
a century since the rise of Christianity in which Christian works
were not written against Judaism and replied to by Jews. Disputations occurred frequently, too frequently for the Jews, who
entered with no alacrity into such discussions in which the opponents were also the judges." [1]

To tell even a part of all that is summed up in that paragraph
would take volumes. Solomon Grayzel did, in fact, write a volume
on the Church and the Jews of just one century—the thirteenth
century. There is in the English language no comprehensive presentation of the Jewish polemics and disputations of the Middle
Ages.[2] References to the material are to be found in the Jewish
encyclopedias, books of Jewish history and literature, and in scattered studies.

Of the Christian viewpoint we have *Adversus Judaeos* (1935)
by A. L. Williams. Still, when there are two sides in a debate it is
instructive to know what the other side has to say. Williams himself makes this point [3] in notifying us that there are two versions
of the public disputation held in 1263 between Pablo Christiani
and Moses Nahmanides. While the two accounts agree in substance, the one recorded from the standpoint of the Dominicans
gives the victory to Pablo, while the Hebrew version claims for
Nahmanides the winning decision. Naturally! However, Williams
concedes that an impartial study of the two versions "leaves little
doubt that the latter is truer to the facts."

### 1.

In these disputations not much theological progress is observed.
Once the lines of polemic battle were drawn in the earlier dis-

167

putations they became the line-up for the theological arguments of the succeeding generations: scarcely ever was anything new added. There was a simplicity to this entire matter. The medieval Church, wherever it enjoyed temporal power to enforce its wishes and was so disposed, desired that Jews recognize their sinfulness in not having accepted Jesus as the Christ, that forthwith they become baptized as Christians *or else* their sacred books would be burned, their religious study and practice encumbered, their possessions confiscated, their lives tormented with all manner of prejudicial infringement to the point of exile and even death.

The alternative—baptism or expulsion—was set early, in the time of the Visigothic kings of the Spanish territory. In 589, King Reccared I accepted Roman Catholicism for himself and made it the religion of the state. Immediately, anti-Jewish laws were enacted and pressure was brought to bear.

We have, for the record, the very first document of allegiance to the new faith submitted by Jews forced to accept Christianity. It was sent in 654 by the Jews of Toledo to King Recceswinth. Among other declarations it stated: "We believe that Christ is the son of the living God." [4] Although the Arabs invaded in 711 and overthrew the Visigothic Kingdom, this pattern, worked out in the seventh century, was followed by Spain in the centuries of church control, culminating with the dread Inquisition.

In view of the vast amount of anti-Jewish polemic literature during the first millennium of the Christian era, it truly is amazing how little there is on the Jewish side in the way of attack *or* defense. In the previous chapters we investigated the Jewish record to the sixth century when the Talmud was completed (and we included the continuing Midrash compilations which run many centuries beyond). We now look into the subsequent centuries and find a very minimum until we reach the thirteenth century when there is an outbreak of public debates, in which Jewish leaders are compelled to participate and therefore to give heed to a subject which to them was not of primary interest.

It may be that the documentation of these intervening centuries was more complete but that the documents have been lost or destroyed. Here and there we can reconstruct some of the material. An incident of the ninth century catches our attention.[5] In 839 the aristocratically born Frenchman, Bodo, Deacon of the Palace of King Louis, on a visit to Rome, became a proselyte to Judaism, changed his name to Eleazar, and married a Jewish woman. Paulo Alvaro of Cordova, a Christian of Jewish descent, wrote four letters meant to win Bodo back. To these Bodo replied. We have only fragments of Bodo's replies, as found in Alvaro's quotations. The controversy, apparently, revolved about the correct interpretation of Old Testament verses as to whether Jesus was the promised Messiah, as to the doctrine of the Trinity and as to who was the true Israel. We gather that it was his understanding of the message of the Bible prophets that convinced Bodo to become a Jew. Amulo, Archbishop of Lyons, referred bitterly to Bodo in his treatise written some eight years later.

## 2.

One of the earliest documents extant, of Jewish polemics in relation to Christianity, which comes to us directly from the Jewish source, dates from the first half of the tenth century.[6] Only recently have we known of its existence, comprising ten leaves of a Genizah fragment.[7]

At first it was thought to be a polemic against Karaism and other sectaries, or a missing part of a work by David al-Mukammas, but in 1938 (after he studied the two latest leaves which had turned up) Jacob Mann identified it more accurately as a polemic against Islam, Christianity, the Samaritans, and Jewish separatists.[8] It is written in Hebrew, in archaic style. The name of the author is unknown; he probably lived in Babylonia or Persia.

It is the opinion of this early polemicist that the Nazarenes really wanted Judaism but were led into Christianity by a distorted claim that this was the "new Israel" and the "new covenant" of prophecy. They go astray, he says, following a strange God who would give birth to a son by a Jewish woman, one who died as mortals die; that this error of incarnation is perpetuated by the use of ikons and paintings showing all phases of his earthly life. He brings together three verses [9] by which, he asserts, Christians claim the Trinity—teaching Jesus as the Father, Son and Holy Spirit. In defense of Judaism the author stresses that the Law is not abrogated, that the Exile is not meant as punishment for Israel's sins, that the prophetic promises are yet to be fulfilled.

There is nothing remarkable here, except the odd interpretation that Jesus *is the entire Trinity*. The main value of this document, besides its early date, is its criticism of Jewish heterodoxies as well as of Christianity and Islam.

Beginning with the eighth century there were religious stirrings in Jewish life in the East, stimulated greatly by the evolving Islamic culture. Messianic pretenders came to the fore. The Talmud and even the Bible were challenged. There was a breaking away into separatist sects. The spokesmen of rabbinic Judaism, the traditional Judaism, rose in its defense and in the course of meeting the internal challenge, used the opportunity to defend it also against the external challenge of the other religions. It was really necessity rather than opportunity. Considering that some of the Karaites interpreted Jesus and Mohammed as prophets, the Rabbinites had to reply to this point. Polemic literature, therefore, began to appear.

Contemporary with, or possibly earlier than, the unnamed author mentioned above, is a man concerning whom we have more definite information, but not as much as we would like to have. Of his date we can be no more specific than to state that he is referred to as no longer among the living in the year 937. Of Babylonian origin, his name is David ibn Merwan al-Mukammas—sometimes called David ben Merwan al-Rakki.[10] It appears that in Nisibis he was converted to Christianity by Nane, a philosopher and physician, from whom he thoroughly learned the Christian doctrine. Then he returned to Judaism and vigorously defended it. M. Harkavy, who discovered in the Leningrad Imperial Library (in 1898) fifteen chapters of his main work, *The Book of Twenty Chapters*,[11] suggests that the name Al-Mukammas (related to the Arabic word for "grasshopper") means "the leaper," in that he made a double leap—once from Judaism to Christianity, then from Christianity back to Judaism.

Of the development of Christianity, David al-Mukammas tells, as reported by Kirkisani in his historical account of the Jewish sects, that regulations not found in the Gospels nor in the Torah but established by the early Christian leaders were attributed by them to Paul and Peter, as revelations from Jesus, and that when further regulations were required they were formulated by the 318 bishops in council at Nicea—and these are believed in as laws of God. Various authorities make similar regulations, and Christians choose which to follow. These things are possible because proof from the Gospels is not required when accepting opinions. Thus, he traces to Constantine the origin of the cross, the building of churches and the killing of Arius for the latter's stand regarding the Messiah. Such are the men who determine the forms of worship.

Al-Mukammas then turns his attention to New Testament criticism and finds discrepancies in the lineage of Jesus. He perceives disagreement between the genealogy listed by Matthew and that listed by Luke. Also, the descent in both cases is traced through Joseph, whereas the Gospels state that Joseph did not beget Jesus. Further, certain names in the lists of ancestors are not to be found in the Old Testament nor in Jewish tradition.

In *The Book of Twenty Chapters*, written in Arabic, Chapters 9 and 10 deal with the divine attributes. In defense of God's unity, Al-Mukammas teaches that when we say "God lives" we do not mean that life is a separate attribute but that it is identical with, and eternal like, God; Christians err in making a distinction whereby Wisdom is the Son, and Eternal Life is the Holy Spirit, for this implies composition rather than absolute unity. God's attributes are inseparable from His being. God cannot have form; failure to understand this, he charges, is another error of Christianity. The old claim of the abrogation of the Law, he refutes in a treatise on the subject, included in his commentary on Genesis.

In addition to the importance of his own views, Al-Mukammas

was the means whereby the Karaite, Kirkisani, and the leading
Rabbinite protagonist, Saadia, derived their knowledge of Christian dogma and philosophy.[12]

### 3.

Of these two, let us trace first the references to Jesus in the
Karaite tradition. Karaism, strictly defined, is a sect which ultimately broke away from Judaism and has survived into the
twentieth century. It is estimated that in our generation the
number of Karaites in the United States amounts to no more
than one hundred families.[13] Nevertheless, it is a sect which has
a history of twelve hundred years and at one time threatened the
entire structure and nature of what George F. Moore terms
"normative Judaism" and certainly aroused rabbinic (normative)
Judaism to re-evaluate and re-express itself.

The main concept in Karaism is the rejection of the Oral Law
as developed in the Talmudic literature. It is a return to Scripture
and a life based on its plain meaning, although in the course of
time the Karaites developed their own traditions and at times
adopted rabbinic interpretations as well.

Islam, in its rise and expansion in the seventh century, is recognized as a strong influence in Karaism. At the end of that century, Abu Isa al-Isfahani of Persia, the forerunner of Karaism,
acknowledged the prophetic mission of Jesus and Mohammed to
their respective peoples (the Gospels as guidance in Christianity,
the Koran in Mohammedanism, even as Jews have their own
literature) and added himself to the list as the final messenger
of the Messiah sent to save Israel.[14]

Anan ben David, of the latter half of the eighth century, looms
prominent among the antecedents of the sect. But the name
*Karaites* is not found until the middle of the ninth century in the
writings of Benjamin ben Moses al-Nahawandi. It is of interest
to mention, in passing, Benjamin's teaching that a specially created
angel performed the deeds of creation, not God Himself—a theory
which bears some relationship to the Logos idea.

Jacob Kirkisani (Abu Yusuf Yakub al-Kirkisani, in Arabic),

of the first half of the tenth century, interests us in particular. It is in his *Book of Lights*,[15] an important work written in Arabic in 937, that we learn of his dependence on David al-Mukammas for his knowledge of the origins of Christian teaching. In it we learn, in fact, the history of Jewish sects from the time of King Jereboam, and among these, in historical order,[16] we are told of Yeshua, known as Jesus son of Mary, who the Rabbinites say is "the Son of Pandera"; that he lived at the time of Yehoshua ben Perahyah, who is said to have been his uncle; that this happened at the time of Caesar, King of Rome, in the days of the Second Temple, when he was crucified.[17] We observe here the old chronological error which places Jesus a hundred years earlier than indicated in the Gospels. The author commits other errors too. For instance, he relates that the Torah which the Jews have is not the one given through Moses, but a new Torah given by Ezra.[18]

Kirkisani presents an exposition of Christianity in Chapter VIIIa, stating at the outset that Jews differ considerably among themselves with regard to Jesus. Some assert his claim to be a prophet; others deny it. Rabbinic tradition records this in Sanhedrin 107b of the Babylonian Talmud.[19] Rabbinites admit the miracles of Jesus but attribute them to magic and to the use of the secret Name.[20] Benjamin al-Nahawandi, he reports, counts Jesus among the five Jews who presumed to call themselves prophets, to whom the Daniel verse (11:14) applies. (A later Karaite writer, Yefeth ben Ali, refers this verse to the pupils of Jesus).[21] Some of the Karaites hold Jesus to have been a righteous man who taught in the manner of Zadok [22] and Anan; the harm the Rabbinites sought to do to Anan, Kirkisani says of his Rabbinite foes, they succeeded in doing in their opposition to Jesus.

The Christianity which became historic, he goes on to relate, was introduced and established by Paul who claimed to be a prophet and who ascribed divinity to Jesus. "He [23] did not make any (new) laws at all, and he did not declare anything to be obligatory. He asserted that religion consists merely of humility. Therefore, they assert that their fasts and prayers are not obligatory, but are only a matter of free will. He did not prohibit any kind of food at all; on the contrary, he permitted all animals, from the gnat to the elephant."

It is rather the Christianity of his day which Kirkisani criticizes as heresy. "They say that the Creator is one substance in three hypostases; that He is one in three and three in one, for, according to them, He is living and knowing; but life and knowledge are two qualities of the substance, therefore the substance is one hypostasis and the two qualities are two hypostases, together three hypostases." They assert, he explains, that Jesus is the prophetically promised Messiah; that as the Son, he is one of the three hypostases; that Jesus is divine and human, the personification of the Creator who is the substance.

They maintain, he adds, that the prophetic promises, such as the rebuilding of the Temple, already have come to pass; that Torah laws were given to Israel in wrath; that the doctrine of the three hypostases was not revealed by God until the time of Jesus because humanity could not comprehend it earlier; that the Word is as old as God. Moreover, they base their claims on ambiguous passages in the Old Testament. It is here that he quotes with approval the critique of the Church and the Gospels which he learned from David al-Mukammas.

In Chapter VIIIb Kirkisani sets out to refute that Jesus was a prophet and performed miracles. He offers the thought that Mohammed, in order to facilitate acceptance of himself, and seeing the strong belief of Christians, accepted Jesus as a prophet (but not a God) and born of no mortal father. Moslem theologians accept the Christian tradition of Jesus' miracles (which prove him to be a divinely empowered prophet), for there is the testimony of eye-witnesses, but they do not accept the Christian doctrine of Jesus' divinity because it is but the product of analogy, reasoning and speculation.

To this Kirkisani replies that the witnesses to Jesus' miracles are the four Evangels and Paul who also were prophets and performed miracles. If their testimony is to be trusted regarding the miracles of Jesus why not also regarding the divinity of Jesus, for it was Paul who announced the doctrine of the Trinity and said that Jesus was the Son of God? In fact, more people saw the miracles of Paul than those of Jesus, thus giving added weight to the prophetic truth of the traditions Paul handed down.

However, if the Moslems hold that the Trinity idea is not true, it being contrary to reason, then he (Paul) who proclaimed it, is not a prophet or a worker of miracles, nor are the traditions concerning him based on reliable witnesses, nor can one believe that many people witnessed miracles performed by him. The argument is the more cogent regarding Jesus whose witnesses were fewer, and it cannot be proven that he was a prophet. If Abu Isa's attributing prophecy to Jesus and others is unfounded, then his claim that he himself is a prophet is proved false, too.

The chapter concludes with a polemic against belief in Mohammed as a prophet and with a defense of Moses' status. The ultimate purpose of the critique is disclosed in the closing sentences, to prove that Abu Isa is false in his claim to prophecy. And, he adds, the pretense of Yudghan, another pre-Karaite pseudo-Messiah, is too shallow to bother disproving.

As we shall soon learn when we shift our attention to Saadia Gaon—Kirkisani's contemporary and mighty defendant of the traditional Rabbinite position in the internal controversy within Judaism—the Karaite ideological rebellion was fought out, and victory was gained by the side of traditional Judaism (the Rabbinites) not without having exerted a wholesome, stimulating effect upon rabbinic thought and culture.

Before leaving our study of Jesus in Karaite literature we should attend to two more items briefly, without taking the time to go into the polemics found in the Bible commentaries of Yefeth ben Ali or in the writings of lesser lights.

The outstanding Karaite of the twelfth century was Judah ben Elijah Hadasi of Constantinople. He began in 1148 the writing of *Eshkol Hakofer*, which means "A Cluster of Camphor," an interesting phrase taken from Song of Songs (1:13) and used in the sense of our term "Encyclopedia." It is written in quasi-rhyme. Moreover, each sentence of the 379 lengthy sections begins with a succeeding letter of the Hebrew alphabet, from the first to the last letter, at times in reverse order and at times arranged in acrostic to spell out the author's name or that of his father.

The main divisions are treatises on each of the Ten Commandments. Under the Second Commandment, which prohibits other gods, the author refutes Sadducees, Samaritans, Christians and especially Rabbinites. The polemic against Christianity (alphabets 98 partly, 99 and 100) was deleted by censors but restored by W. Bacher from a Vienna manuscript.[24]

For information on Christianity this encyclopedic work depends on Mukammas, Kirkisani and the Yosippon.[25] There is not much that is original. It opposes the Christian use of certain Old Testament verses as allusions to Jesus, places Jesus in the time of Queen Helene (as in the Toledoth Yeshu), refutes the Incarnation, the Divine Sonship of Jesus, the Trinity, the Virgin Birth, the Gospel genealogy of Jesus, the Abrogation of the Law—and, for good measure, attacks the Rabbinites for conceding that Jesus performed miracles by use of the Name of God, as well as for leaning toward Dualism by reason of undue emphasis on Divine Justice and Divine Mercy.

In contrast to the above, a Karaite of the sixteenth century—Isaac ben Abraham Troki—wrote a remarkable polemic but, inasmuch as it was acceptable to rabbinic Judaism, it will be considered in relation to that century in the main course of our investigation.

The final observation with regard to Karaism and indicative of its vanishing status in Jewish history is an episode of the nineteenth century.[26] Simhah Bobovich, a Karaite of influence in the Crimea, assigned Abraham Firkovitch, the Karaite leader, to prepare proof that Karaism antedated rabbinic Judaism and had no hand either in the crucifixion of Jesus or in the Talmud.

Firkovitch gathered much valuable material on Karaism. He then tried to show that Karaites lived in the Crimea as early as the seventh century B.C.E. and therefore could not possibly have participated in the events in the life and death of Jesus. To do this he doctored certain of the dates. The result was the granting by Russia to the Karaites of civil rights of equality denied to Jews. Thus, the connection with Judaism was severed.

But, Karaism now has virtually died. The latest count as of 1932, estimated only 12,000 Karaites in the world.[27] In these years after the havoc of World War II one wonders to what further extent their scant number has dwindled.

### 4.

We must now return to the main stream of Jewish tradition where we left it temporarily in the first half of the tenth century.

Saadia ben Joseph, who was born in Fayyum, Egypt, in 882, and died in Sura, Babylonia, in 942, accomplished more than any other Jewish leader in meeting the Karaite schism head-on and gaining a complete victory for rabbinic Judaism. Saadia Gaon (*Gaon* being the title of eminence of the president of the Babylonian schools of learning in the post-Talmudic period), presided over the school of Sura and wielded considerable authority and influence by reason of his strong personality, his profound knowledge of the Bible, Talmud and philosophy, and his insight into the issues and needs of his generation.

A systematic thinker, he realized the necessity of working out a dogmatic presentation of Judaism. This would require a formulation of the essential doctrines, such as the Unity of God, the Messiah, the Law. Inasmuch as the status of the person of Jesus had been introduced into the Karaite-Rabbinite controversy, there was that added reason for him to express a position as to Jesus.

In his opus magnum, *The Book of Beliefs and Opinions*,[28] he makes specific mention of Christian doctrine in four regards. In Chapter V of his Treatise on God [29] he writes: "Christians erred when they assumed the existence of distinction in God's personality which led them to make of Him a Trinity and to deviate from the orthodox belief." [30] He then offers the refutation based on reason, but he also invokes the aid of the One God.

To reply to the uneducated who believe in a crass materialistic Trinity would be a simple task. In Chapter VIII of this Treatise he states clearly that epithets applied to God which have the appearance of anthropomorphism are to be taken only as figurative descriptions but not in any material sense such as would apply to human beings. Elsewhere [31] he goes so far as to say that, in

Scripture or in our speech, if any expression is used concerning God or His handiwork it is undoubtedly meant to be taken in a figurative sense if it contradicts the demands of sound reason.

His reply is particularly to the elite who declare "that only a thing that is living and omniscient is capable of creating" and thus by rational speculation "recognize God's vitality and omniscience as two things distinct from His essence, with the result that these become for them a Trinity." In his rebuttal, Saadia holds that they have but this alternative: to believe that God is or is not a physical being. "If they believe that He is a physical being, then they are on a par with the common herd of their people who are accordingly subject to whatever refutation has been presented of the view of those who anthropomorphize God. If, on the other hand, they do not believe God to be a physical being, their allegation of the existence within His essence of distinction, with the result that one attribute is not identical with the other, is equivalent to an allegation on their part that He is really a physical being. They merely used another term to express the same thought. For anything that harbors distinction within itself is unquestionably a physical being.

"We have, then, established the fact that these three matters constitute one attribute. It is only impossible for a human being to combine them in speech as the mind does by means of its cognition. One might cite as an analogy to the above the case of him who says that he does not worship the fire but the thing that burns and gives light and rises upward, which is in reality nothing else than fire."

Saadia's own words have been quoted here, rather than paraphrased, so that we may know precisely what he seeks to convey. To explain further, he adds that because a human being is seen alive at one time and dead at another, we believe that his life is distinct from his essence. "Therefrom we infer that there is something in him by virtue of which he lives and which, if it is removed from him, causes him to die." Likewise, man is ignorant when knowledge is removed. Therefore, we do not assume that man is essentially endowed with life and knowledge. "Since, however, it is really out of the question that there be found a time in which the Creator of the universe is not living nor endowed with knowledge, as is true in the case of man, it follows of necessity without any doubt, that He is intrinsically alive and possessed of knowledge."

Moreover, trinitarian theologians select God's essence, vitality and omniscience, as an artificial means of supporting a doctrine of Trinity which has been told them. But—what of God's omnipotence, or the fact that He sees and hears? If it be argued that these latter are included in God's living and knowing, it can be answered that omniscience makes unnecessary the mention of His living, since only He who is alive can know anything.

As for Scripture verses—such as II Samuel 23:2, Psalm 24:4, Job 33:4, Psalm 33:6—offered as proof of the Trinity, Saadia charges those who thus use these verses with unfamiliarity with the Hebrew language. What the Bible intends to convey is the thought that God created all things by means of His word, His command, His will or His wish; that He created them with intent, as borne out by Job 23:13; also, that He created all with one breath, not piecemeal, as shown by Isaiah 48:13, Psalm 33:6, Psalm 18:16. In fact, besides *spirit* and *word*, Scripture mentions God's *hand, eye, anger, mercy*; why should not these also be regarded as properties of God?

Incidentally, at this juncture Saadia denies the co-existence with God of an eternal word (Logos) in the creation. He explains that wisdom (Proverbs 8:22) was not an instrument wherewith He created. The meaning is that God created all things wisely.

The second specific reference to Christian doctrine is in Chapter VII of the same Treatise. It tells of four sects who believe in the Trinity: the first holds that the body as well as the spirit of Jesus derived from the Creator; the second, that the body was created, the spirit having emanated from the Creator; the third, that the body and spirit were created, but an additional spirit derived from the Creator; the fourth and most recent sect holds that Jesus was a prophet, and interprets the sonship as an expression of esteem.

Saadia refutes the fourth sect of Christians with his arguments on the Messiah and on the Abrogation of the Law (described later). The first sect he refutes, in addition to these two points, by the argument against the theory which asserts that the Creator of bodies has created them out of His own substance. He gives four proofs in favor of creation in time, four proofs in favor of *creatio ex nihilo*, and these five objections—"that an eternal being, that is subject to neither form nor quality nor dimension nor limit nor place nor time, can be so changed that a part of it becomes a body possessing form and dimension and qualities and place and time and other attributes belonging to corporeal beings"; "that the All-Wise, Who is immune against all pain and unaffected by action and not subject to accidents, should choose to turn a portion of Himself into a body so that He would become exposed" to such evils; that a righteous God would "hurl a portion of Himself into such misfortunes," deserved or undeserved; that a portion of God would accept the command of the remaining parts so as to receive impression, shape, form and pain; "that it is inconceivable that One endowed with intelligence, Who is capable of averting pain from portions of Himself, would not avert it." [32] The third sect he refutes with the additional obstacle that it is impossible for a created physical being to become God through the association with it of a divine element; that the argument that something of this nature did happen—that the presence of God on Mount Sinai, in the Burning Bush, or in the Tent of Meeting, would make these objects deities also—is a case of going from bad to worse. The second sect is refuted by all of the preceding objections combined.

The two remaining sections where we know without doubt that Christian teaching is meant are those which Saadia offers in rejoinder to the stand of the fourth sect.

All of Treatise VIII is given over to discussion of the promised Redemption and the Messiah yet to come. Specifically it mentions in Chapter IX the Christian claim that the fulfilment of God's promises began 135 years before the destruction of the Second Temple. Saadia, in reply, interprets Daniel 9:26, "an anointed one shall be cut off," as a reference is not to one particular person (Jesus) but to the cessation of the priesthood with the annihilation of the Sanctuary; he further contends that the chronological calculation based on the Daniel prophecy does not work out to the time of Jesus.[33] These arguments he appends to the lengthy one which takes up most of the Treatise, giving proofs from Bible texts, from history and from personal observation, as evidence that the Redemption and the Messiah will definitely come in the future.

To refute all four sects of Christians, Saadia makes clear his position on the Law, too. He devotes Chapters VII to X of Treatise III to a rational and textual defense against the premise that the Mosaic Law had been abrogated and the Jewish people doomed. In the development of this theme Saadia takes an important stand with regard to Moses and miracles. He places Moses on the highest pinnacle of human achievement, as the supreme medium for divine revelation. Then he takes note of the protest that, if belief in the mission of Moses is based on his miracles, why can that not be the basis of belief in someone else's mission?

Our belief in the mission of Moses is not based solely on his miracles and marvels, is the Jewish reply. "The reason for our believing in him, and in every other prophet, is rather the fact that he first called upon us to do what is proper. Then, when we had heard his appeal and we saw that it was proper, we demanded from him miracles in support of it and, when he performed them, we believed in him. If, however, we had felt that the appeal he made at the beginning was not proper, we would not have demanded any miracles from him, for miracles are of no account in supporting the unacceptable." As an example, if a claimant of prophecy commands, in the name of the Lord, adultery or theft or threatens to bring a flood upon the earth or teaches that heaven and earth were created thoughtlessly while the Lord was asleep—his message is not sanctioned by either reason or tradition, and therefore he would not be asked to submit a miracle as a sign of his mission. We would not listen to anyone, no matter what marvels he performs, who wants us to give up such rational convictions as that truth is good and lying is objectionable.

This completes our inquiry into the work of Saadia, mostly polemic, sometimes apologetic—for the mood so easily shifts from one to the other. The presentation has been somewhat lengthy, but purposely so. Other than the briefer exposition by Al-Mukammas, and apparently dependent upon it in some of its ideas, this *Book of Beliefs and Opinions* is the first thorough and systematic answer of rabbinic Judaism to Christian doctrine based on Jesus. It employs philosophy, Scripture, logic, history, personal observation. Many of the viewpoints are to be found in later Jewish literature and, having examined them here in some detail, it will not be necessary to do so again.

Not least in significance is the fact that Saadia gained his objectives. He saved Judaism from the messianic pretenders of his day, the heretics, the critics of religion, of the Bible and of the Talmud; he saved Judaism from odd influences of a seething Islamic searching and from the Karaite threat to traditional Judaism. As for Christianity, he did not resort to legends but to reason and revelation. His primary interest was not to win converts from Christianity but to teach Jews an appreciation of their own values and insights.

### 5.

As our investigation moves into the eleventh century we come to learn that besides the methods, already observed, of replying to the Gospels and of analyzing philosophically the doctrines of Christianity, there is yet another way in which Judaism was upheld. It is the way of exegesis.

From the very beginning of the Christian tradition, attention was directed to an interpretation of words, verses and chapters in the Old Testament which would validate the Christian teachings concerning Jesus. It is found in the New Testament. It is prominent in the writings of the Church Fathers and is known as the *Testimonia*. This procedure is part of the Jewish heritage in Christianity; interpretation of the word of God as a guide for truth is an ancient and honored practice in Judaism, at least as old as the times of Ezra the Scribe of whom it is written that he and his associates "read in the book, in the Law of God, distinctly: and they gave the sense, and caused them to understand the reading." [34] It is natural, therefore, to expect that the Jewish teachers would record *their* interpretation of the disputed passages. This they did in the Talmudic and Midrashic literature, in an unorganized manner, as opportunities presented themselves.

The philosophers, such as Saadia, likewise employed Scripture to support the force of logic. The writing of commentaries became a specialized field in the Gaonic period. Saadia, for example, is as distinguished for his translation of the Bible into Arabic [35] and for his Bible commentaries as for his philosophy. As we get into the eleventh and twelfth centuries, though, we reach the high point in the exegesis of the Bible—and of the Talmud too.

Solomon ben Isaac, better known as Rashi, of France (1040–1105), wrote commentaries which even to this day are indispensable for an intelligent study of the Bible and Talmud. His work is so vast that we could not begin to itemize the many instances in which, without mention of Jesus or Christianity, he molded the Jewish tradition of emphasis on the unity of God, the future expectation of messianic redemption, the unfulfilled historic role of Israel. This is his most valuable contribution.

Less important are his several comments on the specific mention of Jesus in the Talmud. He follows the plain meaning without much theory on his part.

Concerning the passage which tells of Ben Stada bringing magic from Egypt by a cut in his flesh,[36] Rashi comments that this device was used by Jesus because Egyptian magicians forbade the export of secrets of magic. Here we see that Rashi accepted the confused identity of Ben Stada and Jesus, and his explanation of the Egyptian prohibition may be either an assumption or a tradition still extant in his day. The phrase "burns his food in public," as applied to Yeshu the Nazarene,[37] Rashi interprets literally, as alluding possibly to some ritual of worship. In the reference to Balaam, "Woe unto him who makes himself to live by the name of God," [38] Rashi says it means Balaam; he does not attribute it to Jesus, although we are puzzled as to how and when Balaam made himself God, except as explained in our earlier discussion of the passage. In the story of R. Eliezer's arrest for *Minuth*,[39] Rashi makes the odd assertion that the *Minim* arrested Eliezer; it must have been incredible to Rashi that the great rabbi would be suspected of *Minuth.*

Already in his day it was required that the term *Minuth* be explained. In one place when he sees the word *Minim* he comments that it refers to "disciples of Yeshu"; [40] "turned toward *Minuth*" he interprets, "those drawn to the error of Yeshu and his disciples are called *Minim*"; [41] "those who engage in sorcery" evokes the comment, "who entice and lead astray through sorcery, like the Nazarene." [42] Yet in B. Hullen 13b he applies the term to idolators, in B. Abodah Zarah 26b he defines it as referring to idolatrous priests, Jews or Gentiles. We see how far back the problem existed of properly identifying the term.

The Tosafists of the twelfth and thirteenth centuries, who followed in the footsteps of Rashi, were likewise limited by the literary and historical knowledge of their times and they too could be mistaken, as we have seen with regard to the interpretation of *Ben Netzer.* [43]

Whatever scant information relevant to Jesus is to be found in Rashi, the Tosafists, Abraham ibn Ezra (1092–1167) or the other great exegetes is incidental and unorganized. However, when we reach Joseph Kimhi (1105–1170) we find the first deliberate, actual unit of polemic-apologetics, with emphasis on exegesis. His *Book of the Covenant* [44] sets forth a sample debate, written by Kimhi at the request of his students for a compilation of prophetic verses wherewith to reply in a disputation. The Christian spokesman is called the *Min*; the Jewish, the *Maamin* (believer).

At the outset there is a discussion of the Trinity. The *Min*, admitting that he cannot prove the Son (in the Trinity) through the intellect, attempts to do so through Scripture, insisting that Isaiah 9:5 could not possibly refer to a human being. The *Maamin* replies that his opponent, like Jerome who translated the Bible faultily, wrongly vocalizes the Hebrew consonants, rendering the word in the future instead of in the past tense. The correct translation, accordingly, should be: "His name *is* called (not "shall be called") Prince of Peace."

This verse is not a prediction of Jesus, as one reads it in the translation of Christian tradition: "Wonderful, Counsellor, The

Mighty God, The Everlasting Father, The Prince of Peace." More accurately, Kimhi teaches, it refers to King Hezekiah, already born, to whom God gave appellations applying to his times: *Pele*, "the Lord performed wonders through him"; *Joez*, "he was counseled to walk in the godly way"; *El-Gibbor*, "God strengthened him against his foes"; *Abi-ad*, "He added fifteen years to his life"; *Sar-shalom*, "the Almighty made Hezekiah a prince of peace." This is the method of exegesis.

Joseph Kimhi then argues against the credibility of incarnate deity, using Genesis 1:3 for support. He opposes also the concept that Jesus took on human flesh in order to redeem the righteous from hell, brought on by the original sin. The *Min* protests that one who wants to believe has no need to explore the words of Jesus, even when reason may incline against them; he concedes good conduct on the part of the Jewish community, but of what avail are good deeds if there is no faith? In reply the *Maamin* insists on the correctness of his own faith: reason will not allow him to belittle God as capable of becoming incarnate; indeed, were this concept true, God would not punish him for refusing such belief, since his refusal is prompted by a sincere wish not to diminish His glory.

The talk then turns to the subject of miracles. Like Saadia, the *Maamin* holds that miracles do not prove divinity; the prophets also performed them, but claimed no godship. He asks, "If when, as you say, God took on flesh, did Jesus then possess the soul of God? If so, why did he cry out that God had forsaken him? If it was a human soul that he possessed and you assert that after his death the divinity dwelt in him, then it is in no wise different from what is true of any other human being."

In defense of God's oneness, Kimhi insists that a ship can have but one captain; if one God contains all power, why have more than one? There are many species in creation but one Creator.

The discussion then centers on the Messiahship of Jesus: if Jesus is meant to be the prophet, referred to in Deuteronomy 18:15–19, to whom the people will not hearken, it must be remembered that the same Old Testament designates Moses as the greatest prophet. To the argument that certain passages must be taken allegorically, not literally, the retort is given: "Only that which cannot be accepted literally has to be taught allegorically; if one bids a servant ride the horse upon the water the meaning must be allegoric; and some instruction, such as circumcision, is to be understood both literally and allegorically."

The interpretation is debated of quite a number of Bible verses: Genesis 49:10; Jeremiah 32:14 coupled with Daniel 10:12, 24–26 (Kimhi follows Saadia's calculation for the date of the Messiah); Isaiah 45:1; Psalm 110:1; Psalm 72:1; Genesis 18:1–3; Psalm 87:4; and the much disputed Chapters 7 and 8 of Isaiah. After covering still other points where interpretations are given always on the basis of reason combined with Scripture, the author concludes: "If you are asked questions other than these I caution you to review and reëxamine these explanations and from them learn how to answer others."

David Kimhi (1160–1235) of Narbonne, France, follows in the footsteps of his father Joseph. In his polemic, *Disputation*,[45] he reiterates many of his father's views, supplementing them here and there. He carries on a debate with a young Christian scholar. In the opening he challenges the idea of the Virgin Birth from several points of view.

The greater part of the brief composition, though, is directed against the possibility of Jesus having fulfilled the specifications prophesied concerning the Messiah: the twelve tribes of Israel have not been reassembled (Isaiah 11:12); the Temple and the City of David have not been rebuilt (Ezekiel end; Zechariah 8:9; Isaiah 2:3); Jesus has not inaugurated universal peace (Isaiah 9:6), nor does he rule over the kingdoms of the earth (Psalm 72); nor have the nations beaten their swords into ploughshares (Isaiah 2:4). Pressed by the Christian protagonist to concede that Jesus did indeed revive himself so that his disciples should believe in him, David Kimhi protests that, if the purpose was to win faith in him, Jesus should have appeared in resurrected form in the presence of all the people, especially of the court that sentenced him, not merely to several women and disciples.

To the assertion that God gave the Natural Law to govern man until the time of Moses, that then the Written Law (O.T.) was

revealed, to be in effect until the time of Jesus when the Evangelical Law (N.T.) takes over, the answer is given: "Does God, or
does He not, know the future? If He knows, He should have
given the Evangelical Law, which is supposed to be the best, to
Moses; and it would have been obeyed even in those days. Why
did Moses command that one may not add to the Law nor take
away from it? Why does the Psalmist say that the Law of the
Lord is perfect? If it needs changing it is imperfect. Jesus himself
said that he did not come to destroy the Law. Finally, would it
be merciful of God to wait 3500 years until the coming of Jesus
to save humanity from original sin?"

In addition to this document we have David Kimhi's *Answers
to Christians* [46] which is a posthumous collection of the polemic
passages scattered in his Commentary of the Bible, especially in
the part which covers the Psalms. By this time, however, there
is sufficient indication of how exegesis was employed in the
polemic-apologetic literature of the Jewish tradition.

### 6.

More of the nature of apologetics than polemics is the defense
of Judaism by the philosopher-poet, Judah Halevi of Spain, who
by the year 1140 completed *Kitab al Khazari: The Book of Proof
and Argument in Aid of the Despised Religion.* [47] This remarkable
defense of Halevi's faith is written in dialogue style and is built
upon the framework of a romantic story, said to have taken place
in the middle of the eighth century. This account relates how the
Khazar monarch, Bulan II, was converted to Judaism (which he
previously had despised) as the final step in a search for true religion, a search in which the rival claims of philosophy, Christianity, Mohammedanism and Judaism are debated.

In support of his belief the Christian scholar [48] admits the
Jewish Torah as revealed, but adds that God later became incarnate through the Virgin: seemingly a man, apparently a prophet,
he was truly God—Messiah and Son of God. God is One, though
terms of the Trinity are used. Those who thus accept Jesus are the
true Israel. To this presentation the Khazar king responds that the

conclusion is not logical and, not having grown up in the Christian faith, he therefore cannot accept it.[49]

The defense of Judaism argues for a pure concept of God's unity.[50] Except for the Tetragrammaton (YHWH) which stands for the actuality of God, the various names given to the deity are merely relative attributes and predicates. Human beings may speak of Him as merciful or just; in doing so they but express the working of God's eternal laws upon their own lives: in essence the Lord is an impartial Judge Who does not change from one attribute to another. Positive attributes would be anthropomorphic. We can apply to Him only negative or relative attributes. This is Unity.

In telling of rabbinic tradition,[51] Halevi mentions Yeshu the Nazarene as the disciple of Yehoshua ben Perahyah. This is one more instance of the Talmudic problem we have already discussed.

Halevi discards philosophical speculation as a means of finding religious truth, for heretics and unbelievers can turn it to their own use. True belief derives from direct revelation, or prophetic insight, given to Israel as the people of God.[52] The two greatest miracles are, indeed, God's revealing Himself to mankind through the prophets, and the preservation of Israel.[53] The humiliated condition of the Jewish people, so painful after the Crusade of 1096, Halevi interprets in terms of the Suffering Servant [54] doing God's work. As illustration, he cites the reverence of Christians for those who in the early days followed Jesus and suffered all manner of humiliation; divine power is truly with the humble.[55]

As in the promise expressed by Isaiah, the day is coming when the rejected will be honored. This ardent expectation of a messianic future for Israel and Palestine is couched by Halevi in poetic creations which are regarded as unsurpassed since Bible days.[56] While a special pleader for his own people, still this poet-philosopher maintains that Christianity and Mohammedanism may appear to reject Judaism but actually they do prepare the way for the expected Messiah. When he is ultimately acknowledged, all peoples will be as one tree—and the root, Israel, will then be honored.[57]

## 7.

In the generation after Judah Halevi, Judaism was blessed with its greatest philosopher since Bible days—Moses Maimonides—often referred to as Rambam, from the initials of his name. He was born in Cordova, Spain in 1135 and died in Fostat, Egypt (Old Cairo) in 1204.

In his lifetime Maimonides achieved eminence in several areas of research. Famous as a practicing physician, he wrote valuable medical treatises. Ten have survived to this day.[58] In the field of Jewish learning, he penned an Arabic commentary to the Mishnah; compiled *Sefer Hamitzvoth*, an Arabic codification and interpretation of the 613 laws of the Torah; composed in Hebrew the more important *Mishneh Torah*, known also as *Yad Hahazakah*, or simply as the "Code," an unparalleled gathering and systematic arrangement of the Jewish Law which had accumulated during fifteen centuries and influenced the codifications of succeeding generations; and, greatest of all, created the *Moreh Nebuchim* ("Guide to the Perplexed"), written in Arabic, with the purpose of harmonizing Aristotelianism with the views of Judaism, a masterpiece which succeeded in guiding Christian [59] and Mohammedan as well as Jewish thought up to and including modern times. Little wonder that tradition has coined the encomium: "From Moses (of the Bible) to Moses (Maimonides) there is none like unto Moses."

In this vast literature there is amazingly little of a polemic nature, at least as relates to Jesus. This is the more notable in view of the fact that for years, beginning at the age of thirteen, Maimonides, together with others of his family, was forced to migrate from one country to another by reason of the fanatical Almohades who decreed the acceptance of Islam, or exile.

To his persecuted brethren he sent epistles of comfort and hope. In *Iggereth Hashemad* he came to the aid of those upon whom Mohammedanism was imposed by force but who remained Jewish at heart. In *Iggereth Teman* he replied forcibly to Mohammedan charges and offered encouragement to the Jews of Yemen (Southern Arabia) to wait for the true Messiah. In its present form this epistle contains no reference to Christianity but there is evidence that in an uncensored version it stated that suffering came to the Jewish people because of the historic effort to replace Judaism with religions similar to it. One of these (Christianity, in contrast to the Mohammedan persecutors) did not cause ultimate harm to Judaism, for it expanded by winning Gentiles as adherents, even though Jesus meant his message for his fellow Jews.[60] In Maimonides' opinion Jesus was a Jew, for his mother Mary was a Jewess.[61]

Further specific mention by Maimonides is the item in the *Mishneh Torah* which regards the Nazarenes of Palestine as idolators.[62] This view is based on the limited opportunity he had to observe the use of images in Palestine and was modified in later Jewish literature.[63]

Of greater importance, however, is the passage found only in uncensored manuscripts and editions of the *Mishneh Torah*: [64] "Even of him (Jesus) who imagined that he was the Messiah, but was put to death by the Court, Daniel had previously prophesied; as it is said, 'Also the children of the violent among thy people shall lift themselves up to establish the vision; but they shall stumble.' [65] Has there ever been a greater stumbling than this? For all the prophets declared that the Messiah will be the deliverer of Israel and their saviour, gathering their dispersed ones and confirming their commandments. But he caused Israel to perish by the sword, their remnant to be dispersed and humbled. He induced them to change the Torah and led the greater part of the world to err and serve another besides God.

"No human being, however, is capable of fathoming the designs of the Creator, for their ways are not His ways, neither are His thoughts their thoughts. All these events (relating to Jesus) and even those relating to him who succeeded the one referred to (Mohammed), were nothing else than a means for preparing the way for the King Messiah. It will reform the whole world to worship the Lord with one accord; as it is said, 'For then will I turn to the peoples a pure language that they may all call upon the name of the Lord to serve Him with one consent.'[66] How will this be? The entire world has been filled with the doctrine of the Messiah, the Torah and the Commandments. The doctrines have been propagated to the distant isles and among many peoples, uncircumcised of heart and flesh. They discuss these subjects which contradict the Torah. Some declare these Commandments were true, but are abrogated at the present time and have lost their force; while others assert there are occult significations in them and they are not plain of meaning—the King has already come and revealed their hidden significance. But when the (true) King Messiah will in fact arise and succeed, be exalted and lifted up, they will immediately all recant and acknowledge the falsity of their assertion."

In this spirit Maimonides, when asked by correspondence whether one may teach Christians the Commandments and the doctrine of retribution, replied in the affirmative. Christians, he held, do acknowledge the Torah as revealed to Moses, although they do sometimes give to it wrong interpretations. If properly instructed, many of them may recant.[67] In a like vein he advised a proselyte that, even though not of Jewish parentage, he might indeed recite the prayer, God of *our fathers*. If Jews trace their descent from Abraham, Isaac and Jacob, he might well trace his from the Creator of the Universe.[68] Alluding to the rabbinic teaching that the pious of the Gentiles have a portion in the world-to-come,[69] and that the Gentile who concerns himself with the Torah of Moses is equal to the high priest,[70] Maimonides asked of non-Jews nothing but a sincere intention to attain to a pure faith in God and to purity in conduct.[71]

## 8.

The several instances cited above are practically all the statements of Maimonides concerning Jesus. However, as was explained in the chapters dealing with the Talmudic material, we must take cognizance of indirect references as well. There may not be actual mention of Jesus but from what is said we may infer an indirect allusion to Jesus. In such cases, what is recorded can be of much greater significance than some of the confused and legendary items wherein the person of Jesus is specified. This is a fact which is generally overlooked in studies of this theme.

Support for this thesis is not too difficult to find. For the sake of economy in time and space we shall introduce here but one quotation as confirmation. In an authentic work on the history of Jewish literature, the introduction to the chapter on philosophy and theology states: "It is only when the nation or the group emerges from its seclusion and comes in contact with other nations and the respective cultures meet, that the religious ideas of one group begin to be tested, analyzed and explained in the light of the ideas of the other group. First, as a result of the testing and analysis, doubts as to the exact meaning of the religious principles arise, and secondly, there arises on the part of the adherents of the attacked religion a desire for defending it, for reinterpreting its principles in the light of the stronger or prevailing culture, and very often to prove its identity with the most elevated principles of that culture, and thus a philosophy arises." [72]

On this basis we can survey Jewish philosophy and theology during the period of the Christian Era, particularly in countries where there was contact between Jews and Christians, and by noticing what is emphasized in the Jewish viewpoint we can discover indirect allusions to Jesus and to the religion centered in him. This must be done, though, with the utmost caution, lest one jump to hasty conclusions.

Points of emphasis in many, if not most, instances will prove to be no more than reiteration of earlier traditions intrinsic in Judaism, or they will prove to be the natural product in the evolution of thought and emotion. Still, there remains what appears to have a definite bearing on our subject: for example, as K. Kohler observes, the spiritualization of the God idea by the philosophers of the Spanish-Arabic period served, among other purposes, to "emphasize opposition to every human representation of God, especially the God-Man of the Christian Church." [73]

When we looked into the works of David al-Mukammas, Saadia and Judah Halevi, we saw that the mention of Jesus was an integral part of the entire philosophic approach. This was especially true of Saadia who referred the reader to various portions of his book for his refutation of Christian traditions about Jesus.

Now that we have reached Maimonides, the greatest of the philosophers, it is appropriate to survey the writings of some of the philosophers who do not necessarily name Jesus but who may have implied him. We shall limit ourselves again to the possible allusions to Jesus—without attempting to enter into the wider field of Christian doctrine and practice.

Solomon ibn Gabirol (c.1021–c.1058) was the first Jewish philosopher in the western part of the Old World. He was the first, too, of all of the philosophers in Spain, whether Christian, Jewish or Moslem.

In these pages which relate to the relationship between Judaism and Christianity it is pertinent to report that, by some strange accident of history, Ibn Gabirol was regarded as a Christian, or possibly a Mohammedan, philosopher until about one hundred years ago (1845) when the error was discovered and made known.[74] His philosophic work, *Fountain of Life*, written originally in Arabic, was translated into the Latin *Fons Vitae* in the middle of the twelfth century at the request of Archbishop Raymond of Toledo. The name, Ibn Gabirol, was corrupted through translation into Avencebrol, then Avicembron, finally Avicebron—and Avicebron became an important source of study for the Christian scholastics of the thirteenth century!

Basing his ideas on neo-Platonism, Ibn Gabirol carries his reasoning to the point where he introduces a Divine Will wherewith the Creator comes into closer contact with what He has created. This concept is reminiscent of the Logos, which in Christianity is Jesus, the second person in the Trinity: hence, the acceptance of Ibn Gabirol into Christian theology. The paradox is the more striking in view of the fact that Ibn Gabirol's poetry found a place in Jewish liturgy, poetry such as *Song of Unity*, and *The Royal Crown* which praises God Who is One in every possible meaning of oneness.[75]

God's unity is emphasized as the basis of all else, in conduct as in belief, by Bahya ibn Pakuda in his *Duties of the Heart* (*Hoboth Halebaboth*),[76] written in the early part of the twelfth century. He adopts the arguments of Saadia on the subject and supplements them too: in his view the burden of proof is on the shoulders of him who seeks to prove more than a unity.

In the matter of attributes, though, he distinguishes between the permanent or *essential* ones—Existing, One, Eternal—which are really one and inseparable and are meant only for the purpose of denying that which is opposite, and the *active* attributes which are merely human expressions as to how God affects human life. Why does Bahya examine and reëxamine the thought of God's oneness in every possible light? Is there not the likelihood that he is meeting a challenge, the challenge of Christian Trinity put forth directly, or indirectly through the medium of Mohammedan polemics?

As we follow the main trends in Jewish philosophy,[77] without stopping to go into the lesser variations, we come to Abraham ibn Daud of Toledo, Spain (1110–c.1180), whose *Exalted Faith*[78] is the first attempt to harmonize Aristotle's philosophy with Judaism. On an Aristotelian foundation he proves God, Whose essence is unity and Who cannot be associated with any other being. He is incorporeal. There are neither essential nor accidental attributes; attributes are merely negative and relative. Anthropomorphisms in the Bible are to be understood metaphorically. He who sees multiplicity in God's nature is like a person whose eyes are not coördinated and who sees double.

Ibn Daud's argument against the abrogation of the Jewish Law seems definitely to be a defense against Christianity.[79] It is interesting to note that of the medieval Jewish philosophers he was the first to itemize the dogmas of Judaism. Of the six he enumerates, three are: God is One; God has no positive attributes; Moses is supreme and the Torah is eternal.

What Ibn Daud introduced, Maimonides developed to the fullest. We have already dealt with Maimonides' specific references to Jesus. Let us now explore the indirect allusions.

Maimonides states that, beginning with childhood, people must be informed that God is One, that none besides Him is to be worshipped, that He is incorporeal, that there is no similarity in any way whatsoever between God and His creatures. [80] God possesses no attributes, composition or plurality: He is absolutely One. [81] When we seek to describe Him, it can only be by use of negative attributes.[82]

Arguing against intermediation between God and man, Maimonides comments that even idolators do not believe that God is in the images of stone or wood. Idols are worshipped because they represent the agent between God and man.[83]

There are eleven degrees of prophecy whereby God's will is ascertained, but Moses is above any of them. Israel's belief in Moses and the Torah is not founded on miracles, for they create doubt that perhaps they were done by magic. Israel believed in Moses because at the time of the revelation they saw it with their own eyes and heard with their own ears. Therefore, if a prophet were to arise, perform signs and wonders, and refute the prophecy of Moses, he is not to be given credence.[84] The Torah of Moses is not to be abrogated.[85]

With conviction Maimonides believes in the future coming of the Messiah, a great prophet, but not greater than Moses. He holds that the Balaam passage of Scripture prophesies two Messiahs: one, David who redeemed Israel from the troublers of his day; also, a later Messiah who will bring redemption in the future. The latter need not perform wonders, such as reviving the dead. Of Davidic descent, he will meditate on the Torah and induce Israel to walk according to the Oral and Written Law, fight the battles of the Lord, rebuild the Temple. If he does not succeed, or is slain, he is not the Messiah. The days of the Messiah will be the time when the kingdom will revert to Israel who will return to the Holy Land.[86]

Maimonides sums up his views of Judaism in a list of thirteen dogmas.[87] In this Creed are affirmations of God's unity, God's incorporeality, His exclusive claim to be worshipped, Moses' supremacy as a prophet, the immutability of the revealed Torah, the Messiah who is yet to come: these six of the thirteen appear to have a definite relationship to the Jewish record concerning Jesus, without actually naming Jesus.

The Creed expressed so well the fundamental beliefs of the people that it quickly became the theme of Jewish verse in all

countries where Jews dwelt. The best known poetic setting is the
*Yigdal* which entered the liturgy of the Synagogue, for the first
time, apparently, in 1578.[88] It is the opinion of K. Kohler that
"the Maimonidean articles of faith were adopted into the liturgy
because of their emphasis on the absolute unity and indivisibility
of God, by which they constituted a vigorous protest against the
Christian dogma." [89]

Now that we have examined in some detail the possibility of
indirect references to Jesus in the works of the greatest Jewish
philosopher of the Middle Ages it will not be necessary to repeat
the process with regard to those who follow, except where some
new element or approach should be noticed. It so happens that
after the time of Maimonides we get into the thick of the public
disputations which break out in the thirteenth century. In many of
these the Jewish philosophers were forced to take an active part.

## 9.

In the medieval period the first actual reply on record to a
specific document against Judaism was written in about 1170 by
Jacob ben Reuben of Huesco, Spain. The Dialogue of Joseph
Kimhi between the *Min* and the *Maamin*, as we have seen, was but
an exercise in disputation—an example of how a Jewish protagonist
might answer charges. The fact that it was composed for the purpose of instruction intimates that public debates must have been
taking place. Now, with Jacob ben Reuben we get down to actual
cases, for in writing *Wars of the Lord* [90] he gave vigorous reply to
Peter Alphonsi (1062–1110), also of Huesco, although it is not yet
a face-to-face meeting of contestants.

Alphonsi had been Moses Sephardi, a Jewish physician to King
Alphonso I of Aragon. At the age of forty-four he was baptised,
accepted the name Peter and added Alphonsi in honor of his monarch. Then he wrote a *Dialogue* to show the superiority of Peter
Alphonsi over Moses Sephardi: himself now *versus* himself then.[91]
He defended Christianity as against Judaism, Mohammedanism and
speculative philosophy. In addition to the interpretation of Bible
verses and the criticism of Jewish practices, Alphonsi attacked the

Talmud and Midrash—one of the earliest instances of what later became frequent—by taking literally the Haggadah which is really meant as fanciful allegory and inspirational imagery.[92] He opposed also the purported references to Jesus in the Talmud.

These were the accusations which Jacob ben Reuben answered. Then he launched his own offensive, directing attention to contradictions in the Gospels and Acts of the New Testament.

There were others later on who took Alphonsi to task. We need not here spend any further time on them. The three elements worth noticing are: first, the date of this earliest actual give-and-take; secondly, the injection of attack on the Talmud into the dispute; third, the hostile initiative taken by an apostate Jew.

Now we arrive at the thirteenth century, a century which brought untold misery to the Jews in Spain and France by reason of supposed Talmudic reflections upon Jesus. The real reason, of course, was the Jewish resistance to enforced apostasy. The erstwhile Jew, Nicholas Donin of La Rochelle, France, complained in 1239 to Pope Gregory IX that Jews are not easily converted, for the reason that the Talmud contains blasphemies against Jesus and Christianity. Thereupon, in 1240, the Pope ordered the authorities in France, Spain, Portugal and England to seize all Jewish books and examine them.

The only one to obey the order vigilantly was King Louis IX of France. That year a public disputation was commanded between Donin and Yehiel ben Joseph, distinguished rabbi of Paris (one of the Tosafists), accompanied by three other rabbis.[93]

We who read of this typical disputation share emotionally in the tragic drama as we visualize the scene: the King and Queen, the dignitaries of the powerful State Church supported by the supreme authority of the Pope, the aroused public opinion, the bitterness of the apostate Jew who sought at whatever cost to make an impression of zeal in his newly acquired faith, the respectful pleading of the Jewish scholars to abandon this useless public contest which they knew could end in only one way—disaster for them and for their co-religionists. For judges were not impartial, the subject touching upon the person whom Christians worshipped as God was so fraught with danger and, deprived of legal rights or safeguards, the Jewish community would suffer even were their representatives victorious in debate. With assurances of personal safety to the participants, given by the Queen, the disputation began.

To the charge that the Talmud contained much nonsense Rabbi Yehiel explained that the Haggadah of Jewish tradition consists of parables to stir the imagination but that one is not bound to accept it in the way that one must accept the legal guidance (Halachah) of the Talmud. One of the valuable purposes of the Talmud is to give a proper explanation of difficult Bible verses, such as the stories of Lot's wife turning into a pillar of salt, the power of speech given to Baalam's ass, the episode of Jonah's gourd; whoever does not study the Oral Law cannot understand the Written Law (Scripture). However, although he himself had found hidden interpretations in what seem to be strange passages of Haggadah, one who does not wish to regard them seriously need not do so.

To the amusement of the audience, Nicholas Donin heaped ridicule upon the Talmud. Then, to arouse the priests to violent, anti-Jewish action, he cited what he termed rabbinic blasphemies against Jesus.

In each instance he was proven wrong by the Jewish representative. Concerning the quotation of B. Gitin 57a [94] R. Yehiel answered that it referred to Jesus, but not to *the* Jesus of Nazareth who certainly did not deny the Torah. Concerning B. Sandhedrin 43a [95] he replied that there is no verification of the reported facts, for it happened so long ago; further, why blame Jews today for what their ancestors might have done centuries ago?

Concerning B. Sanhedrin 67a he responded that the allusion is not to Mary, mother of Jesus, for she was of Jewish flesh and bone; the Mary whom the Talmud calls Magdala lived hundreds of years after the time of Jesus of Nazareth; moreover, Ben Stada was not Jesus, the former having been stoned in Lud, not crucified in Jerusalem. Concerning B. Sotah 47a and Sanhedrin 107b R. Yehiel argued that the incident of Yehoshua ben Perahya happened in the days of King Jannaeus, two hundred years before the Christian Era and that the Jesus named there could not be the Christ.

The priests then questioned the validity of the explanation that different persons named Jesus could be meant. The rabbi supported his position by reminding his questioners that not everyone named Louis was alike, that some were kings of France and some were not; that in fact, two people in a city could have the same name and even die on the same day but they were not one and the same person. An unexpected turn was given to the discussion when the Queen reprimanded the priests for insisting and trying to prove that these unpleasant things *were* said of Jesus; in doing so, she said, they were disgracing their own religion.

Other charges were made and refuted, but they do not relate to our subject. The disputation closed with the Church dignitaries inquiring whether they, according to the Torah, could be saved and Yehiel responding that the Torah teaches that they need but perform the seven Noachian laws to be assured salvation. Jews, he added, pray for the welfare of the nation where they reside happily and securely, even as taught in the Mishnah Aboth.

As comment upon this disputation we observe that Yehiel of Paris was correct in larger measure than has hitherto been appreciated.[96] Study of our theme up to recent years sought to find in rabbinic literature every possible allusion to the Jesus of Christianity wherever the name Jesus, or a presumed substitute therefor, was noticed. Now, however, as clearly demonstrated in Chapters II and III of this volume, we have good grounds for agreeing with Yehiel that every mention of Jesus is not necessarily Jesus of Nazareth, and that certainly Ben Stada and Balaam are not originally intended to refer to the person upon whom the faith of Christ is built.

A rabbinic colleague in the Paris disputation, Judah of Melun, who was denied contact with Yehiel during the hearing, gave expression to his own views and answered similarly: the Talmudic references to Yeshu are not applicable to the founder of Christianity.

Paying no attention to the logic brought out in the debate, the church tribunal in 1242 and again in 1244 burned in Paris many carloads of the Talmud and other books of rabbinic Judaism. There was a temporary let-up, but in 1247 Odo, Bishop of Tusculum, reported to Pope Innocent IV that the rabbinic writings contained "so many unspeakable insults that it arouses shame in those who read it, and horror in those who hear it," [97]—and again the Talmud was burned.

## 10.

A counterpart of this disgraceful event took place in Barcelona, Spain. Again an apostate, Pablo (or Paulus) Christiani, instigated the trouble. This time, however, Pablo sought to prove that the Talmud *taught* the divinity and Messiahship of Jesus.

King Jayme I of Aragon in 1263 arranged in his palace a polite debate between Pablo and Moses ben Nahman (Nahmanides),[98] with a royal guarantee of free speech. It was agreed that the conversation would be conducted in gentlemanly fashion, making this disputation an exceptional one. It was agreed that no attempt would be made to convert from one belief to another. It was agreed to discuss whether the Messiah had come or was to come, whether the Messiah is a man or God incarnate, whether Jews are holding to a correct faith. Actually, only the first two questions were covered.

To Pablo's claim that the Talmud teaches Jesus as Messiah and God, Nahmanides replied that the Talmud was compiled five hundred years after the time of Jesus. If the rabbis of the Talmud believed in Jesus, as Pablo asserted, why did they continue to observe Judaism, why did they not accept Christianity as Pablo had done, Pablo who understands their words better than they themselves do?

Confronted with Genesis 49:10, Nahmanides discussed this verse, "The sceptre shall not depart from Judah, nor the ruler's staff from between his feet, until Shiloh come." [99] He persuaded Pablo that because the Jews of his day had no Davidic King this was not proof that the Messiah (Shiloh) had come; the verse could refer to a temporary cessation of Davidic rule, to an interruption in the times before Jesus. Pablo objected that the interruption of the Babylonian exile amounted to but seventy years and could be termed temporary but not the exile in the Christian Era of one thousand years, that such duration must be regarded as cessation indeed; but Nahmanides negated Pablo's argument by reminding him that the verse speaks of Judah not having a ruler, but does not speak of the entire people of Israel.

He refuted also Isaiah 52:13-15; Isaiah 53; Psalm 72:8 and Daniel 9:25-27 as Bible evidence of the Messiah having come.

Pablo then quoted Haggadic tales [100] as evidence of Talmud teaching that the Messiah had come at the time of the destruction of the Temple. Thereupon, Nahmanides corrected this by saying that the stories tell of the Messiah having been born, but it is not the same as having *come*: Moses was born long before he came to lead the Exodus from Egypt; David did not become king the moment he was born; the Messiah will not *come* until Elijah shall anoint him. In any event, the Haggadah is sermonic illustration by individual teachers. It does not possess the authority of the Bible nor of the legal portion of the Talmud. He preferred to believe with the Sages who taught that the Messiah would be born close to the time when the exile of Israel should end, that he would die in glory and his son would reign, the feature of the Messianic Era being that Israel then would no longer be subjugated by alien powers.

Moses ben Nahman then made the significant statement that the Messiah is not of primary concern in Judaism. "You, O King," he said, "are more important to us than the Messiah.[101] If, despite obstacles and humiliation, I observe my faith, by your consent, my reward is great. But when the Messiah, flesh and blood King of Israel, shall come and set his law upon the world I will have no choice but to observe the Jewish law, and my reward will not be as great."

He proceeded to explain to his monarch that the real problem between Judaism and Christianity is in the God concept. The King could accept the doctrine of incarnation of the deity because he had been taught it from childhood, but it was irrational to one not so indoctrinated, Nahmanides took occasion also to refute the doctrines of Original Sin, Salvation from Hell through Jesus, Vicarious Atonement.

Nahmanides then presented his calculation, based on Chapter 9 of Daniel, as to when the Messiah would come. It was his hope that only ninety-five years remained before the Messiah would appear. Parenthetically we might mention in this connection that, when Abraham ben Samuel Abulafia came to Rome in 1280 and presented himself to the Pope as the Jewish Messiah, he may have done so prompted by information which came to him of this disputation, particularly the statement of Nahmanides that the Messiah would come only after having appeared by divine command before the Pope with a request for Jewish liberation.[102]

The second question, whether the Messiah is God incarnate or entirely human, occupied the lesser part of the disputation. Alluding to Isaiah 11 and Genesis 49:10, Nahmanides defended his position that the Messiah would be a human being. As for the latter Bible reference, he interpreted the word *Shiloh* as related to *Shilya*,[103] which means "placenta," and used this as proof that the Messiah would be of normal human birth and of entirely human nature. Pablo offered Psalm 110:1 as proof of Jesus' divinity; but his opponent explained, with supporting evidence, that "The Lord saith unto my lord" means no more than "God said to David."

On the final day of full argument Nahmanides submitted to the King the thought that if Jesus in his lifetime endeavored in every way to prove that he was divine and could not convince the Jews of his day, how could disputants of the thirteenth century, remote from the times of Jesus, who certainly did not know him as well as did his contemporaries, believe that they could succeed?

Nahmanides was questioned on the Trinity. He, in return, asked what Pablo meant by the Trinity. Is it that the Godhead is formed of three bodies, as of people? Are there three intangible bodies, like souls or angels? Is it an object composed of three things, as bodies are composed of four elements? Pablo replied in the negative to these definitions, but gave his own: Wisdom, Will, Power.

In rejoinder, Nahmanides agreed that God is wise and not foolish, that He wills without suffering sensation, that He is powerful and not weak—but to speak of the Trinity is entirely erroneous. In the Creator, wisdom is not an accident, but He and His wisdom are one; He and His will are one; He and His power are one: Wisdom, Will and Power are one. Even if they were accidental attributes, God still would be not three but one, with three accidental attributes.

The King, repeating what he had been taught, suggested an analogy: wine has flavor, color and bouquet—three things which are yet one. Nahmanides pointed out the error: the red color, the flavor and the bouquet in the wine are three separate things: one may be found without the other, for there are red, white and other colors in wine, and so with the flavor and bouquet. Moreover, the red color or the flavor or the bouquet is not a species like the wine which fills the vessel, but the wine is the body which has three accidents—there is no unity. We could really say, if we were forced to accept the erroneous view, that the Godhead is fourfold: God, His Wisdom, His Will, His Power. Furthermore, God lives; this too is an attribute; therefore He is fivefold: God Himself, Wisdom, Will, Power, Life. Nevertheless, Pablo insisted that he believed in a complete unity which has in it a Trinity—which is so profound that even the angels and heavenly hosts cannot comprehend it. In final rejoinder Nahmanides replied: "Is it not clear that a person does not believe what he does not comprehend, that, if so, the angels do not believe in the Trinity?"

Thus the disputation ended. As supplement, for a fuller understanding of the viewpoint of Moses ben Nahman, it should be added that in his philosophical writing he maintained that everything is the handiwork of God; hence, everything that touches our lives is miraculous. Miracles, in other words, are in the regular scheme of nature and history. It is in the light of this thought that we must review everything Nahmanides said concerning the Messiah. Also, in his basic assertion that God is constantly and immediately in us and everywhere about us Nahmanides disproves, as Solomon Schechter aptly points out,[104] the charge against Judaism "that the rigid monotheism of the Jews makes God so transcendental that He is banished from the world. As we see, it is just this assertion of this absolute Unity which not only suffers no substitute for God, but also removes every separation between Him and the world."

Having failed in the disputation, Pablo reversed his tactics and persuaded Pope Clement IV to order (in 1264) confiscation of the

Talmud in order to examine it for *hostile passages concerning Jesus*, and, if found, its consignment to the flames. The King of Aragon did *not* burn the rabbinical literature, for he felt that some sections of it supported Christianity. But he did give the Dominicans authority to obliterate from the Talmud anything which was regarded as offensive. Thus, in 1264, was introduced Christian censorship of rabbinic literature.

As an interesting sidelight, it may be mentioned here that on an occasion prior to the year 1270 a dispute took place in the monastery of Cluny, France, between a visiting knight and a Jew, regarding the Virgin Birth. So convincing were the arguments of the Jewish spokesman that the knight was reprimanded for the incident, with the admonition that as a result some Christians might have been made into disbelievers.[105]

It became obvious that the need had arisen for Christians themselves to study the language of rabbinic literature. Now for the first time in Western Europe since the days of the Church Father Jerome, there came upon the scene a Christian protagonist, not a convert from Judaism, who was equipped with a knowledge of the sources as a weapon for attack (a policy encouraged by Raymund de Penaforte).

Raymund Martini, a Dominican monk in Spain during the second half of the thirteenth century,[106] wrote *Capistrum Judaeorum* [107] and especially *Pugio Fidei*,[108] to show that, by his reading of the sources, rabbinical literature as well as the Bible acknowledged Jesus as both Messiah and Son of God. He built his thesis upon the interpretation of Old Testament texts which had been quoted and refuted many a time before his day, and upon passages in the Haggadah which he adduced as evidence that the authorities of the Talmud and Midrash *taught* the Incarnation and Divinity of the Messiah (Jesus), Original Sin, the Resurrection and Ascension of the Christ. Some of his rabbinic quotations are not to be found anywhere and there is doubt as to their authenticity.[109]

Reply to these strange assertions was made in pamphlet form by Solomon ben Abraham ibn Adret (1235–1310), disciple of Nahmanides and outstanding Talmudist of his day, surnamed

"The Rabbi of Spain." With moderation he reiterated the fancy-free nature of Haggadah and, more important, corrected fallacious interpretations of the quoted passages, giving their plain sense. In addition, his work includes a defense against Mohammedan polemic and against belief that the Mosaic Law was abrogated.

A final word as to *Pugio Fidei* is to mention its extensive use by later Christian writers, by Geronimo de Santa Fé and Peter Galatinus, with no acknowledgment that this was the source; and by Victor Porchet de Salvaticis, with acknowledgment. This repetitiousness made for monotony in the charges and counter-charges as they dragged on through several centuries. There were repeated examinations of the Talmud, Christian censorship carried out by converted Jews, and, to avoid complications, censorship by the Jews themselves—which resulted in obliterating from the Talmud much which referred neither to Jesus nor to Christianity.

## 11.

In the thirteenth, fourteenth and fifteenth centuries the list of disputations and disputants becomes a rather lengthy one.

Moses of Salerno, of the first half of the thirteenth century, appears to be the first Jew in Italy to reply in kind to the Christian polemic which had been flourishing there for some time. He was followed by others there, notably Solomon ben Yekuthiel and Abraham Farissol.

In France there was the Official family (indicating that they probably held some official posts) which engaged in scholarly disputations with Dominicans, Franciscans, bishops and royal father confessors, even with Pope Gregory IX and Pope Gregory X. The family included Nathan ben Meshullam, of the twelfth century, who regarded the undue length of the Jewish exile as punishment for the deification of a man (Jesus); his son, Joseph ben Nathan; his son's son, Nathan ben Joseph Official; and his great-grandchild, Joseph ben Nathan Official, designated the Zealous One, who compiled in the second half of the thirteenth century the discussions of his family and of other French rabbis in a work called *Yosef Hamekanne*, a title which became known in a later edition as *Teshuboth Haminim*.

In Provence, or southern France, Mordecai ben Yosifiah wrote *Mahazik Ha-emunah* and Meir ben Simon composed *Milhemeth Mitzvah*. Isaac ben Nathan refuted *The Letter of Rabbi Samuel*, an Arabic letter supposedly written about 1072 by a rabbi of Morocco, telling of his acceptance of Christianity.[110] The authenticity of this letter is much in doubt.

In Spain considerable controversy was stirred up by Abner of Burgos, physician and Talmudist, who, in approximately 1330, was baptized at the age of sixty. As a Christian, he became known by the name Alphonso of Valladolid. Writing in Spanish and Hebrew, he sought in *The Offering of Zeal* to prove Christianity by the Talmud and Midrash, and in *The Wars of God* he refuted Jacob ben Reuben's reply to Peter Alphonsi. In return he was now answered by quite a few on the Jewish side, the more prominent being: his former friend, Isaac ben Joseph ibn Pulgar, who wrote (between 1335 and 1345) *The Support of the Religion*,[111] harmonizing Judaism and philosophy, itemizing the thirteen superior qualities of Moses, insisting that Jesus was not the Messiah foretold by the prophets but that the Messiah was yet to come;[112] Shemtob ben Isaac ibn Shaprut, of the fourteenth century, who had held a disputation with Cardinal Don Pedro de Luna (later Pope Benedict XIII) and controversies with apostates from Judaism, and had compiled (1385) *The Touchstone*,[113] in dialogue form, covering fourteen volumes of refutation of many polemic points and also a fifteenth volume answering Abner of Burgos in particular; and Moses Cohen of Tordesillas, a contemporary, who wrote *The Support of the Faith*.[114]

In the continuing story of the give-and-take between the representatives of the one religion and those of the other a lighter note is introduced in an incident that is truly stranger than fiction. Isaac (ben Moses Halevi) Profiat Duran[115] (c. 1350–c. 1415) had been forced to accept Christianity against his will; so too his friend, David Bonet Bongiorno. To escape the duress prevalent in Spain and live unhampered Jewish lives they both agreed to meet at a point of embarkation and make the voyage to Palestine. Upon reaching the appointed place Duran found a letter from Bonet stating that Paul of Burgos (who had been Solomon Halevi and after conversion to Christianity had risen steadily to the position of Archbishop of Burgos) [116] had convinced him of the truth of Christianity; he was going to remain a Christian and he advised Duran to do likewise.

Duran wrote Bonet a letter of reply which has become known in history as *Al Tehi Kaabothecha,* which are the opening words of the epistle and of each paragraph and mean "Be Not Like Your Fathers." With satire so veiled that one must look a second time for the true intent, Profiat Duran advised his former friend not to be like his fathers who did not believe in a God Who could be born in human form, who did not believe in Original Sin, the Eucharist, the Abrogation of the Torah. The ambiguity of this letter was such that some of the church apologists quoted it as a defense of their own religious views and, not understanding the Hebrew title, referred to it as *Alteca Boteca.*

The serious and important work of Profiat Duran was written in 1397 at the request of his disciple, Hasdai Crescas. Called *Kelimath Hagoyim,* it consists of twelve chapters. Nine of these offer a systematic and historical critique of the basic principles of the Christian religion: against verses which might indicate such doctrines it arrays New Testament quotations to refute belief in Jesus as God, in the Trinity, Incarnation, Redemption, Abrogation of the Law. It submits, too, the contention that such matters as Abrogation, Transubstantiation, Baptism, the Papacy are without New Testament authority. The three remaining chapters subject the writings of some of the Church Fathers to criticism for misquoting and misapplying a number of Old Testament passages. *Kelimath Hagoyim* is a principal product in Jewish polemics.[117]

Profiat Duran's influence and arguments are definitely seen in the polemic written toward the end of the fourteenth century by Hasdai Crescas who is better known in the field of Jewish philosophy. His contribution to the defense of Judaism through philosophy will be considered shortly when we take up study of the place of Joseph Albo in our theme. In Crescas' polemic there is little that goes beyond Duran, except his particular philosophic approach to the questions of Jesus as Son of God, the Incarnation of God, the Trinity.

Of especial interest is his assertion that the Second Advent of Jesus was actually awaited in the lifetime of his followers and that only after their disappointment did they project it into the future. According to Christian doctrine, he explained, after the Antichrist had come and caused confusion there would be the Second Coming.

A new element in the course of medieval polemics is the fact that Hasdai Crescas wrote in the Spanish language, not in Hebrew or Latin, so that his Spanish-speaking, non-Jewish neighbors might be made aware of his viewpoint. That he succeeded is proven by the many replies his polemic evoked. With the original title *Tradato*, it was translated in 1451 into Hebrew as *Bittul Ikkere Hanotzerim*.[118]

In 1394 a specific charge was introduced in Germany by a Jewish convert, who changed his name from Pesah to Peter, to the effect that the *Alenu* prayer composed by the Talmudic Amora, Rab, in the first half of the third century, was insulting to Jesus. It reads: "For they bow down and pray to naught and vanity, unto a god that cannot save." But these phrases are from Isaiah 45:20 and antedate Jesus. Moreover, at the time the prayer was composed in Babylonia, Christianity was virtually unknown there.[119] How far-fetched accusations can be!

Among prominent Jews arrested to give an accounting was Yom-Tob Lipmann of Mühlhausen who, when subsequently released (the others were put to death), wrote during the early years of the fifteenth century a brilliant answer to critics of Judaism.

The book carries a famous title, *Sefer Hanitzahon* ("Book of Victory"). This designation was used by several French and German writers in their arrangement of Bible verses whose alleged proof of Christian doctrine they refuted. The oldest, *Nitzahon Yashan Noshan*, seems to have been composed in the middle of the thirteenth century; another, *Nitzahon Yashan*, the old but not the oldest Book of Victory, comes from the latter part of that century.

The work by Lipmann is by far the most comprehensive. Armed with his knowledge of Bible exegesis, rabbinics, philosophy and mysticism as well as of Latin, the New Testament and current Christian literature, the author expounds Judaism for the benefit of the learned who do not blend their knowledge with Judaism, the heretics and Karaites, the observant Jews who do not understand the deeper interpretations, and the Christians—and these four categories he symbolizes by the four sons in the ritual story of the Passover Seder.

The arrangement is interesting. Beginning with the first word in Genesis and continuing through the order of the chapters of the Old Testament, each controversial verse receives comment. The material is divided into 354 sub-sections to symbolize that a Jew should give thought to his religion each day of the (lunar) year. For added value as a reference source-book there also is an index-like grouping of subject matter.

To avoid duplication we shall describe this type of polemic more fully when we come to study the compilation by Isaac of Troki.[120] One fact is obvious. This *Sefer Hanitzahon* made an intense impression. Beginning with the countercharge in 1459 by Stephanus Bodeker, the Bishop of Brandenburg, a veritable anti-Lipmann literature resulted, with Theodore Hackspan, Christian Schotan and John C. Wagenseil as contributors.

The situation is reversed in the next incident to come to our attention. This time an advocate of Christianity opened the gates to a flood of Jewish response. In 1413 the converted Jewish physician of Benedict XIII, one Joshua ibn Vives-al-Lorki,[121] who had assumed the name Geronimo de Santa Fé and had assisted Vincente Ferrer, the Dominican friar, in the preaching crusade which invaded synagogues throughout Castile for converts, persuaded the quasi-Pope to call a disputation in Tortosa to prove, out of the very Talmud, that Jesus was the promised Messiah. The Jewish view was upheld by twenty-two scholars; the meetings covered a period of a year and nine months (1413–14). As in an earlier century, when this procedure failed, Geronimo then accused the Talmud of blasphemy and published his complaints in two treatises.[122] The net result was a papal bull in 1415 forbidding study of the Talmud and especially the reading of *Mar Mar Yeshu* (a probable reference to the Toledoth Yeshu), with severe penalties provided.

Many were the rebuttals to Geronimo. There were the replies made by Don Vidal Beneviste in the disputation itself. Isaac ben Nathan of Provence wrote a refutation. Solomon ben Simon Duran (Rashbash) of Algiers—whose father, Simon ben Zemah Duran (Rashbaz) had written (1423) the important chapter *Kesheth Umagen* ("Bow and Shield") of the *Mogen Aboth* commentary as a polemic against Islam and Christianity—battled Geronimo in 1437 with his *Melhemeth Mitzvah* ("The Battle of Duty").[123] In many regards, from the standpoint of Jewish theology, the most significant reply was that of Joseph Albo (c. 1380– c. 1444) of Aragon.

Having taken a courageous part in the dismal Tortosa disputation, Albo felt deeply the need not only to refute specific charges against Judaism but to enlarge his undertaking and restate the principles of his religion in order to clarify what is primary and what is secondary. Drawing upon the thinking of those who preceded him—Maimonides, Gersonides, Crescas, Simon Duran—he modified their views here and there and produced in 1428 the notable *Sefer Ha-Ikkarim* ("Book of Principles").

## 12.

When we pick up the thread of the philosophic-theological trend in medieval Judaism where we left it after Maimonides, we learn of Levi ben Gerson (1288–1344), known also as Gersonides, who in his *Milhamoth Adonai* ("Wars of the Lord") went boldly even beyond Maimonides in seeking to harmonize Aristotelianism with Judaism. He maintained that where the meaning of the revealed word in the Bible is not clear it should be interpreted strictly in conformity with reason but at the same time he acknowledged that revelation, as in the Old Testament, is not subject to error like human reasoning. He believed that there was ultimately complete agreement between the Torah and the logical approach to truth. Among his viewpoints we find a minimising of miracles; also, that God's attributes do not imply multiplicity in divinity. These assertions may be indirect allusions to Christian belief.[124]

Hasdai Crescas changed the direction of the philosophic inclination in Judaism away from Aristotle and ultra-rationalism to a more emotional traditionalism. Better known than his polemic which we noticed earlier was his philosophic work, *Or Adonai* ("The Light of God"). It is regarded as having had an extensive influence upon many thinkers, including Spinoza.

Beginning with the nature of God, he examines every approach and in each case emphasizes that God must be One in the most absolute sense of oneness. But his ultimate reliance is on Scripture: "Hear, O Israel, the Lord our God, the Lord is One." [125]

Crescas then reëxamines critically the Thirteen Articles of Faith stipulated by Maimonides and develops a set of principles with more differentiation. Before aught else is the "great root" of all religions: belief in the existence of God. Out of this, first, are the "fundamental principles of the Torah": God's omniscience, providence, omnipotence, purpose, prophecy and free will for man. Second, are the "true beliefs" essential to avoid heresy, but not indispensable for Torah to exist: creation *ex nihilo*, immortality, reward and punishment, resurrection, eternity of the Torah, supremacy of Moses' prophecy, validity of the priestly *Urim* and *Tumim*, belief in the coming of the Messiah; to these are added practical dogmas as to the efficacy of prayer, the priestly benediction, repentence, Atonement Day, the four other Holy Days. Third, are "opinions" deriving from tradition, such as: the world is eternal, many worlds are possible, God's essence cannot be known, and others. There is a definite indication of apologetic-polemics in this formulation.[126]

The next major formulation of the principles of Judaism was by Joseph Albo, the last of the important Jewish philosophers of the Middle Ages. Because of his experience in disputation he realized the need to uphold Judaism as the true religion, and not merely to prove basic things regarding God such as all religions could and did accept.[127]

Albo, in arranging the dogmas, resorted to the analogy of a

tree. First are the three "roots" (*Ikkarim*): the existence, revelation and retribution of God. Each has "auxiliary roots" (*Shorashim*) or derivative principles: from the existence of God are derived unity (without composition or multiplicity), incorporeality, timelessness, perfection; from the revelation of God are derived prophecy, authenticity of the messenger; from the retribution of God are derived God's knowledge, providence. Altogether there are eleven dogmas. To deny the eight "auxiliary roots" is to deny the three main "roots." The true religion agrees with these principles—if, in addition, the one who offers these principles in God's name speaks directly from God, as Israel witnessed that God did address Moses directly. The ability to perform (genuine) miracles shows merely that the person so gifted is considered worthy by having had this power endowed, but does not prove that he is sent by God to promulgate a new Law.

Lesser than these eleven dogmas are six "branches," denial of which makes a Jew a sinner but not a heretic. They are: creation *ex nihilo*, Moses is superior to all other prophets, the Torah is immutable, human perfection is attainable by proper observance of a single one of the commandments, resurrection, Messiah. Thus, belief in the future coming of the Messiah is not fundamental. The Torah can exist without it.

Joseph Albo's classification of the dogmas has become a popular influence in Jewish life since the fifteenth century. The indirect allusions to Jesus are clearly discernible.

In addition, there is one entire chapter (Book III, Chapter 25) of direct reference. It is in the form of a discussion with a Christian scholar who claims four defects in the Torah of Moses: unlike the teaching of Jesus, it contains extraneous matter; "it expresses the divine mysteries alluding to the Trinity in a very obscure manner"; it speaks only of material, not spiritual, happiness; it is defective in forms of worship and standards of conduct. "All these statements are untrue," Albo answers—and he proceeds with his argument.

As preamble, a number cannot be odd *and* even at the same time, a body cannot be in two places at the same time: these things the mind cannot conceive; therefore, they cannot be. If we seek to believe in impossible things, why was reason given to man?

First, everything in the Torah of Moses, if properly understood, helps to explain the laws; did not Jesus command his followers to obey the Law of Moses? Second, the Torah stresses divine unity and incorporeality; we can know God solely by His ways. Third, to believe in God being three and also one is as impossible as two contradictories being possible at the same time. Fourth, there is promise of spiritual as well as material reward; sacrifices are a concession to habit but are meant to purify life; practice of usury relates only to idolators. Countering with a critique of transubstantiation, differing genealogies of Jesus, errors in Acts 7:14-16, 13:21, interpretation of Genesis 49:10, Isaiah 7:14, Jeremiah 31:15 as messianic evidence, Albo denies that the Old Testament is superseded, but proclaims (from Psalm 19:18): "The Law of the Lord is perfect."

A pertinent question of interest to the modern reader is the one introduced in Chapter 24 of Book I in *Sefer Ha-Ikkarim*. May, or should, one investigate his own religion to see whether it is true? May he adopt another religion if it appears to be truer? Here is Albo's answer. Investigation shows doubt; where there is doubt there can be no firm belief; reward for belief will be found only when it is firm and doubt-free. On the second part of the question, whether one should investigate another religion and accept it when it seems to be truer, his reply is that one may learn of a third religion and on investigation be won to *it*; this could continue until one has examined *every* religion, but he can never be satisfied, for there may be a still truer religion which is unknown to him: hence doubt will remain and he will not be saved by his belief.

A problem arises. There is trinitarian and there is monotheistic religion. If only one of these leads to happiness and a person may not budge from his own religion, he is punished by being forced to remain in a false religion. The solution lies in the fact that all religions agree that one of them (Judaism) is divine; their criticism is merely that it was superseded by their own. Therefore, non-Jews should investigate their religion to ascertain whether they are justified in opposing what they admit in the first instance to be divine, Jews should investigate whether their own divine law is eternal, and wherein change might occur. For it to be *divine* law, investigation must show, first, that beyond removing human wrongs it is not in opposition to the eleven aforementioned "root" and "auxiliary root" principles and that it arouses a desire for human perfection, and, secondly, that the messenger of God "proved his authenticity, as one sent by God to transmit a law"—namely, not simply that he could perform miracles but that there must be direct proof as in the case of Moses, when all Israel witnessed that God spoke to him at Sinai (Deuteronomy 5:27; Exodus 19:9), as explained in Chapter 18 of Book I.[128]

Can there be, then, only *one* divine religion? Chapter 25 of Book I answers that from the standpoint of God, the Giver, there can be only one. The receiver, mankind, includes many variations in character, disposition and habitat, and therefore there will be varying customs and conventions; but the basic principles are the same, depending as they do upon the Giver. Happiness is attained by Israel through the supreme Law of Moses. Other nations gain happiness through the Noachian Law (also divine), as the rabbis teach: "The pious ones of the nations of the world have a share in the world-to-come." [129]

Albo's *Book of Principles* has been described with this amount of detail in order that we may gain more intimate knowledge of the thinking of those days than we can from a mere cataloguing of names and disputations.

For the continuity of the record we shall now list representative names of the remaining centuries, pausing for detail only when a particular item calls for attention.

In the fifteenth century, in addition to those already named, there were the following. Hayim ibn Musa of Bejar in 1456 opposed Nicholas de Lyra with *Maggen Veromah* [130] ("Shield and Spear") which advocates the literal meaning of the Old Testament, clear of philosophical meandering or the variations of the Septuagint and Vulgate, and which refuses to accept Christian proofs from the New Testament, Josephus, the Targum, Haggadah, or obscure passages. Joseph ibn Shemtob of Castile, in addition to translating Crescas' polemic and writing a commentary on Profiat Duran's satiric epistle, engaged in disputations before the King, wrote polemically and died a martyr.

Don Isaac Abravanel (1437–1508), whose *Yeshuoth Meshiho* ("The Salvation of His Anointed") is a collection of polemic-apologetic references in his Bible commentary, particularly on the Book of Daniel, offers two items of interest. He comments on Genesis 50:20 and tells that Joseph absolved his brothers from any blame for what they had done to him, since it was God's way of fulfilling His will, for good. In this comment we see an interpretation of the Trial and Crucifixion. He expatiates on the Messiah-to-come, but holds that he will be *impersonal*: this reveals a trend in later Jewish thought in which the Messiah, in contrast to the concept of Jesus as the Christ, is made colorless, approaching anonymity.[131]

The biography of Don Isaac Abravanel brings to light many tragic details of the Spanish Inquisition, begun with the Auto-da-Fé in 1481 and culminating with the Expulsion in 1492. This too, alas, is part of the record of Jesus in the Jewish tradition.

As we move into the sixteenth century we learn of John Pfeffer-korn, a baptized Jew of Germany, who revived (in 1509) the charge against the Talmud treatment of Jesus, harking back to the slanderous inventions of his prototype, Donin. It appeared as if another public burning of the Talmud was to be witnessed. The Emperor appointed a commission of inquiry which included John Reuchlin, Christian scholar of Hebrew. Reuchlin, who was as eager as any other to encourage baptism of Jews, nevertheless found nothing objectionable in the Talmud. The Christian leaders divided for and against Reuchlin's finding. A controversy ensued, disclosing internal weaknesses in the structure of Christianity, and this became an important factor in the creation of the Protestant Reformation.[132] This, too, was a result of the purported references to Jesus in the Talmud.

One item of good news to report is the fact that Pope Leo X consented to the printing of the Babylonian Talmud in Venice in the year 1520 by a Christian, Daniel Bomberg. This was the first printing of the complete Talmud.[133] The Palestinian Talmud came soon after.

Yet, a generation later, in Italy, there was another confiscation and burning of the Talmud, by order of Pope Julius III in 1553, because of its supposed slander of Jesus. This was not the first attack against the Talmud in Italy. As a matter of fact, in 1270 the apostate, Manuforte of South Italy, denounced the Talmud as blaspheming Jesus and Mary, so that Jewish homes were searched by order of the King, and volumes probably were burned. In 1322 there was a Talmud conflagration in Rome by papal decree; in 1426 there was confiscation of Jewish books in Savoy and Milan, through incitement by an apostate, Vicenzo. But the tragedy of 1553 was more disastrous than these because it was more widespread and more lasting in dire consequences. The evil effects of the decree were felt in all lands controlled by the papacy. Jewish petitions for leniency resulted the following year in an order which allowed retention of the Talmud on condition of severe censorship of anything which might possibly refer to Jesus or Christianity. Yet, in 1559 in one town alone, in Cremona, ten thousand Jewish books were burned. Without let-up, confiscation and conflagration went on and on, well into the eighteenth century.[134]

## 13.

Six names are selected to represent the sixteenth century.

Solomon ibn Verga, born in Seville in 1460, was exiled to Portugal in 1492. Forced to pronounce allegiance to Christianity in 1497, he renounced it nine years later and escaped to Turkey where he died in 1554. In *Shebet Yehudah* ("Tribe of Judah") he compiled a valuable record of the disputations and persecutions of those bitter centuries.

Abraham Farissol of Italy already has been mentioned. Don David Nasi of Candia wrote *Hodaath Baal Din* ("Testimony of the Plaintiff") which turns to the New Testament for verification of Judaism, a reverse twist on the usual practice. His brother, Don Joseph Nasi, an official of state, wrote a treatise in Portuguese which is *Ben Porath Yosef* ("Joseph Is a Fruitful Bough") in the Hebrew translation. Abraham ibn Megas, physician to the Sultan of Turkey, wrote *Kabod Elohim* ("The Glory of God"), which shows reliance on Profiat Duran and is both a polemic on Christianity and an apologia for Judaism. Isaac ben Abraham of Troki (near Vilna), the sixth in our list, wrote *Hizzuk Emunah* ("Strengthening of Faith"); praised by Voltaire as a masterpiece, this polemic calls for description.

The author, strangely enough, was a Karaite, yet his book became a favorite among Jews generally. The volume was completed by his disciple the year after Isaac Troki's death (1594).[135] It has been often translated, notably into Latin by Wagenseil (1681), who then offered a vigorous Christian reply and began a stream of refutation reaching into the twentieth century.[136]

The booklet [137] was intended for fellow Jews only, to strengthen them in their faith; thus considered, it is more of the nature of apologetic than polemic literature. Its value lies in its clarity, its appeal to reason as well as to Scripture, and in the author's knowledge not only of the New Testament and other Christian literature but also of the work of the anti-trinitarian liberals (Simon Budni, one of them) in the Christian circles of Poland of that time. *Hizzuk Emunah*, in turn, was utilized by the liberals and anti-clericals of the eighteenth century.

A question by a Christian scholar opens the subject: "Why do you Jews refuse to believe that Jesus Christ was the Messiah, evidence concerning him having been given by the true prophets in whose words you believe?"

Immediately in the first chapter of the hundred and fifty which make up the book the answer is summarized, with a profusion of Bible references. The Gospel quotations from the Prophets do not relate to Jesus, nor was he the Messiah, as proven by: (1) his pedigree, for he was not of Davidic descent; (2) his acts, in that (by his own words) he brought the sword instead of peace, set children and parents apart (as in Matthew 10:34), and did not rule over peoples; (3) the period in which he lived, since they were not the predicted "latter days"; (4) the prophetic promises not having been fulfilled, in that one universal kingdom and one religion were to prevail, idols and false prophets and profanity were to disappear, sin was to be no more in the world, the war with Gog and Magog was to precede the era of world peace, peace was to reign in the animal kingdom, Israel was to be restored and freed from troubles and anxieties, the Shechinah in the form of prophecy and wisdom and knowledge was to return to Israel. No one as yet has fulfilled these predictions.

Considerable amplification follows this opening statement, as one moves into the heart of the book. In the few introductory chapters there is refutation of the claim that God favored those who accepted Jesus but rejected Israel; faith maintains that "the Lord thy God will turn thy captivity, and have compassion upon thee, and will return and gather thee from all the peoples whither the Lord thy God hath scattered thee" (Deuteronomy 30:3). Then, starting at Genesis, Chapter I, verse 1, and continuing through the books of the Old Testament, each disputed word, phrase or passage is explained. In this manner, most of the basic teachings of Judaism and Christianity are appraised.

Chapter XLIII then rejects the Apocrypha as a source of evidence, since it is neither prophetic nor revealed. The remaining seven chapters of the First Portion of *Hizzuk Emunah* supply answers to Christian divergencies from the Old Testament.

The Second Portion, beginning with the assertion that Jesus never intended a new Law, reviews the New Testament from Matthew to Revelation, occupying one hundred chapters for interpretation. This mass of evidence follows the well-trodden paths of discussion. Its greatest asset, indeed, is its simple, straightforward movement toward its objective.

### 14.

The seventeenth century may be summarized, similarly, by the selection of six salient names.

Zalmon Zevi Openhausen wrote (1615) *Der Jüdische Theriak* ("The Jewish Medicine") in reply to Frederick von Ittingen, formerly a Jew known as Samuel Brenz, who attacked the Talmud and Jewish practice. Answering the supposed Talmudic references to Jesus, Openhausen demonstrated that some other Jesus of earlier date was meant. The work was reissued in a Yiddish version.

Jacob of Venice wrote *Disputation*,[138] a clear and convincing reply to a former disciple, Saul, who became Peter Paul, a Christian polemicist. Jacob found it necessary, in the main, to explain that Haggadic passages in rabbinic literature are to be understood as allegory and illustration.

An unidentified Jewish spokesman participated in a disputation in Ferrara, Italy (1617), against Don Alfonso Caracciolo on the question of the abrogation of the Law. To support the Jewish position he relied on the work of Joseph Albo.[139]

Manasseh ben Israel, of Marrano parentage, a rabbi in Amsterdam, wrote *Hope of Israel* (1650) to describe the conditions required among Israel before the Messiah would come and the Jews could return to Palestine. This volume was of important help in gaining Cromwell's permission for the Jewish people to resettle in England. In *Vindication of the Jews* he presented a defense of his people.

Judah Leon de Modena, a rabbi in Venice who was frequently brought into religious arguments, wrote *Maggen Vehereb* ("Shield and Sword") in 1644. It deals with Original Sin, Trinity, Incarnation of God, Immaculate Conception, Virgin Birth, non-existence of Midrashim quoted by Peter Galatinus.

Of particular interest is the section—Chapters Nine and Ten of Part III—which presents a sympathetic view of Jesus, in contrast to the critique of Christian doctrine. This seventeenth-century Jewish writer portrays Jesus as an eclectic teacher who selected the best there was in the three groupings of Judaism of his day, although following the Pharisees in greater part. Yet, while adhering to the Written Law, he departed from the Pharisees on specific practices. The noteworthy instance was that of the ritual of washing the hands. This led to opposition by the Pharisees, who sought to prevent the disruptive formation of yet another sect. Jesus, however, won to him the *Amme Ha-aretz*, the people of the land.

Jesus, Modena continues, did not ascribe divinity to himself.

He used the phrase "son of God" to mean that he came as a messenger of God to teach humility, repentance and the victory over the inclination to wrong-doing. It was only by those who came afterward that he was accorded the role of the Messiah.

Modena is to be regarded as a forerunner of the modern method of analyzing the elements of the New Testament and relating them to the facts as given by Josephus. He anticipates also the spirit of the modern Jewish interpretation of Jesus.[140]

Toward the close of the sixteenth century (1695), Isaac Lupis wrote *Kur Metzaref Ha-emunoth* ("Purifying Crucible of Belief") concerning his disputation at Marseilles with Fra Francisco and the baptized Jew, Don Pedro,[141] with the Prince as judge.

Fra Francisco holds that the central issue is whether the Messiah *had* come; if not, he admits, the Mosaic Law is still valid. He asks why Jews regard the Talmud so highly when, as the apostate had informed him, it is crude nonsense.

Isaac Lupis replies that certain of the quotations from the Talmudic literature are misquotations while others do not even exist, but the important thing is to understand the Talmud. Haggadic passages in the Talmud and Midrash are individual opinions and employ metaphor, allegory, hidden expressions, hyperbole, analogy and fanciful dreams—for the purpose of homiletic illustration. Not everyone appreciates this method of finding hidden meaning in Scripture; acceptance of it is purely optional.

After a pointless discussion of well-worn Haggadic tales concerning the coming of the Messiah and oft-repeated Old Testament predictions, the controversy shifts from theme to theme, touching on Original Sin, Redemption from Hell, Abrogation of the Law, Baptism, etc. The disputation ends with disgust expressed by the Prince at the poor showing of Don Pedro. "If I were not a confirmed Christian," he said, "I would consider that the truth was with the Jews."

## 15.

At the opening of the eighteenth century, Johann Eisenmenger of Germany published *Entdecktes Judentum*,[142] a supposed exposure of the hostile attitude of the Talmud toward Jesus and Christianity. The historic memorandum that for a bribe of 30,000 thalers the author offered to destroy the edition gives a fair example of his integrity. Incalculable harm was done during the eighteenth and nineteenth centuries by this study which is as inaccurate as it is malicious—and it is a pity to see it read by theological students of our generation as though it were authentic.[143]

As recently as 1757, Jewish representatives again were called to task in public disputation to answer to charges against the Talmud. This time it was caused by the Frankists, followers of Jacob (Leibovicz) Frank—a Jewish pseudo-Messiah—who complained to Bishop Dembovski, of Poland. As a result of the forced disputation, thousands of copies of the Talmud were confiscated and burned.

What irony there is in history! In the very same year, 1757, Jacob Emden, rabbi in Germany, wrote: "The Founder of Christianity conferred a double blessing upon the world: On the one hand he strengthened the Torah of Moses, and emphasized its eternal obligatoriness. On the other hand he conferred favor upon the heathens in removing idolatry from them, imposing upon them the seven Noachian precepts. Added to this, he imposed upon them stricter moral obligations than are contained in the Torah of Moses. There are many Christians of high qualities and excellent morals. Would that Christians would all live in conformity with their precepts! They are not enjoined, like the Israelites, to observe the laws of Moses, nor do they sin if they associate other beings with God in worshipping a triune God. They will receive a reward from God for having propagated a belief in Him among nations that never heard His name: for he looks into the heart." [144]

### 16.

The medieval period for the Jewish people ends in 1776 (or 1791). It ends with the declaration of human rights, with the respect accorded in a democracy for each man's religion.

New forces made themselves felt within Christianity and within

Judaism. The Bible came to be understood in a new light, rendering antiquated much of the discussion of proof by Scripture. Baruch Spinoza (1632–1677) bequeathed to the eighteenth century a political-religious-philosophical outlook which helped bring about the end of medievalism. Study of the new period must begin with him and with the question as to whether he can be regarded as representative of Jewish or Christian thought—or both. With him begins an estimate of Jesus which belongs to our times.

Indicative of the new day was an incident in the life of Moses Mendelssohn. This eighteenth-century Jewish philosopher had expressed in private conversation his view of Jesus as a great ethical teacher. On the basis of this reported conversation the Swiss pastor Lavater challenged Mendelssohn to accept Christianity. The latter replied that the proprieties of intimate discussion had been violated and, further, that Judaism recognizes the right of each to follow his own religious tradition and yet to see worth in "the other person's religion." Lavater later expressed regret for what he had done. In the action of these two men we perceive the working of the modern spirit.

In uneven fashion, with some communities of the world still backward and others breaking new ground, sure signs appeared in the eighteenth century that the day of forced conversions, disputations and polemics was to be no more.

# JESUS IN RELATION TO THE TOTALITY
# OF JEWISH LIFE

Perspective is an important requirement in a picture. It gives dimension, proportion and interrelation to the subjects of the composition and bestows upon them an aspect of reality.

The portrayal of Jesus in the Jewish tradition likewise requires perspective. Otherwise, it would be unfinished. In addition to assembling the individual items, pertinent to our theme, in Jewish life and literature of the past seventeen or eighteen centuries, and in addition to examining and understanding them, point by point, it is necessary, finally, to see the entire collection of items in relation to the totality of Jewish life. Only then will the picture be complete and true.

It is reasonable for one to ask questions such as these: All that I have read in the foregoing pages of this chapter, when summed up, is it a prominent part of the Jewish tradition? What is its proportion in the entire scene? Did the Jews think often of Jesus?

The answer to these questions is to be found by placing the complete record regarding Jesus, as set forth in this study, into the framework of Jewish history and literature. We can then see both as a single whole.

It will be discovered that in terms of amount as well as degree of intensity of interest there was considerable variation, according to specific circumstances, in each century and in each environment where the Jews lived.

A rather accurate perspective may be gained by a perusal of the well-balanced and highly regarded volume, *Jewish Life in the Middle Ages,* by Israel Abrahams. These are the chapter headings: Life in the Synagogue, Communal Organization, Social Morality, Home Life, Courtship and Marriage Customs, Trades and Occupations, The Theatre, Fashions of Apparel, Charity, Care for the Sick and Captive, The Scope of Education, Pastimes and Amusements, Personal Relations and Relations with Non-Jews. These captions indicate the full background for what we have considered about Jesus.

The fact is that for long periods large sections of the Jewish people lived in countries where the Mohammedan, Persian, or other religions flourished and where Christianity was scarcely known. This important factor must not be disregarded in a comprehensive evaluation of our subject.

Wherever they lived in a Christian environment, they conducted themselves in accordance with their inherited faith, some being more pious than others, some leaning to the rationalistic, some to the mystical, some to the other expressions of Judaism—but to all of them Judaism was *their* portion. At the same time, they respected the sincere convictions of their neighbors. In the post-Talmudic centuries they did no active proselytizing (although the conversion of certain Arab tribes and the Khazars are notable exceptions). Hence, in the normal course of events there was no call to argue among non-Jews the merits of Judaism or to challenge Christians on their theology regarding Jesus.

When, however, disabilities were imposed upon those who desired to be loyal to their Judaism and attack was let loose upon them, they responded in terms of self-defense and of some counter-attack. Polemic was answered with polemic. When political power commanded public disputation, and the Jewish leaders had no choice but to take part, they faced the test in a forthright manner. They upheld their own inherited faith, vigorously defending their right to serve God as their ancestors had done. When pressed to accede to viewpoints regarding Jesus which did not accord with Jewish tradition they naturally marshaled every exegetical and philosophical argument in support of their position. Disputations, though, were far from a desirable phase of Jewish life.

"I do not think that there is in the whole domain in literature," Solomon Schechter wrote, "less profitable reading than that of the controversies between Jews and Christians. These public disputations occasionally forced the Jews themselves to review their position towards their own literature, and led them to draw clearer distinctions between what they regarded as religion and what was folklore. But beyond this, the polemics between Jews and Christians were barren of good results. If you have read one you have read enough for all time. The same casuistry and the same disregard of history turns up again and again." [1]

Thus the legends of the Toledoth Yeshu, interesting as they may be in the several respects shown in our analysis, came to be recognized as folklore. The discussion of the Toledoth took up a considerable part of this chapter because there were challenging elements which called for elucidation. But in the perspective of Jewish history it did not loom large. The best proof of its unessential nature is the fact that the leaders of Jewish thought and life did not make use of or allude to it.

Even in the authentic rabbinic literature, one Jewish spokesman after another stressed the need to differentiate between the fanciful and the actual, between folklore and the facts, identified respectively as Haggadah and Halachah.

In the perspective of history, if we look for some constructive result of the deplorable disputations, we find that they sharpened in Judaism the definition of the concept of God, the Messiah, the Torah, the people of Israel.

This brings us to the second half of the inquiry as to the relationship of Jesus to the totality of Jewish life. Seeing that in the Jewish tradition Jesus was not held to be the Savior or Messiah or Son of God, what was there in Judaism to inspire and uplift Jewish life, corresponding to the values Christians found in the person of Jesus?

The motivation for asking this question is neither apologetic nor polemic. It arises quite naturally when one has come to the concluding stage of the exposition of the Jewish interpretation of Jesus.

The religion which was actually lived by the Jewish people consisted of standards of belief and behavior set forth in the codifications of rabbinic law, culminating in the *Shulhan Aruch* of the sixteenth century; study of the inherited lore by adults as well as children in the *Beth Hamidrash* of each synagogue; worship in the synagogue, as *Beth Hatefillah*, comprising prayer, reading of the Torah and Haftarah, and the sermon; use of the synagogue as *Beth Hakenesseth*, a communal center for philanthropy, social activity and every phase of community welfare; and family religion in the home. All this radiated from an ardent faith in One God.

Volumes could be, and have been, written on each of these aspects of Jewish life in the post-Talmudic period. For those who seek more detailed information of the essentials of the Jewish tradition a selected bibliography is supplied in the chapter on Literature Analysis.[2]

For the purpose here, however, of answering the question germane to our theme, it should suffice to summarize briefly the salient facts.

Taking literally the words of the Holy Bible,[3] "Thou shalt keep His statutes and His commandments which I command thee this day, that it may be well with thee and thy children after thee," a behest often reiterated and reëmphasized as the motif of the Old Testament, Jewish tradition gladly accepted the revealed Will of Heaven [4]—the Written (Old Testament) and the Oral Law (Talmud and the full rabbinic teaching derived from it)— as the most direct and intimate relationship possible for man with God. No intermediary was considered necessary.

The traditional Jew determined unconditionally to obey the precepts,[5] moral and ritual, personal and social, as the means of gaining mastery over self, of practicing righteousness and lovingkindness, of finding well-being and abundant living here and reward in the hereafter, and thus of coming nearer and nearer unto Him in whose likeness man has been created. This was to be the means of finding all that could be meant by "salvation."

To this end, the Talmud and the commentaries, the codifications of creed and practice,[6] the Questions on procedure under unprecedented conditions and the Answers given by rabbinic teachers,[7] the customs [8] and newly instituted ordinances [9] were developed— covering each and every item for a person's days on earth, reaching into matters of worship, conduct, study, aspiration, etiquette, clothing, diet, hygiene, business, profession, charity, justice, social relations, domestic relations, and the relations between Jew and non-Jew. It included everything. Nothing was overlooked, from the cradle to the grave and beyond, to translate into reality the words of Psalm 16:8, "I have set the Lord always before me," which are announced as the theme in the opening paragraph of the *Shulḥan Aruch*.

Judaism was coextensive with life. It was abundantly satisfying.

Moreover, in addition to stressing the unity and spiritual nature of God and His intimate and direct relationship to all His children, the theology and worship promised that redemption was yet to come to Israel and to all humanity. The Torah was not abrogated, its promises not yet fulfilled, and Israel still had a unique destiny.

Throughout the Middle Ages, the synagogue, the school, the home, and the daily conversation, no less than the formal sermon, reiterated unshaken belief in these truths.[10] They made of life a spiritual adventure, the doing of God's work. Who could ask for more than this?

The Jew found abiding value in this living tradition, even as the Christian did in the person of Jesus.

Now that we have touched upon the relation of Jesus to the totality of Jewish life, the portrayal of the Jewish tradition concerning him thus gains an added dimension and becomes the more understandable.

# CHAPTER V

# CONCLUSION

# V

THE record concerning Jesus in Jewish tradition now has been described and analyzed. To what conclusions does it lead us?

At the very beginning, when we set out upon an investigation of the record, we gave thought to the importance of the inquiry and determined what our objectives would be. There was no assurance that the sources would yield all that we should like to know. Documents, traditions, history and literature tell us just so much—and nothing more. The best we can do is to examine most carefully what is available and to interpret it most reasonably, without forcing what is not there.

What, then, have we found?

We were surprised to learn that there was not in English literature a continuous account of the attitude of the mother religion, Judaism, toward Jesus—the Christ of Christianity. We now have it. The story of eighteen centuries of Jewish tradition has been related in these pages, setting forth the explicit references to Jesus together with what may be regarded as indirect allusions.

The nineteenth and twentieth centuries belong to the contemporary scene, and the modern Jewish viewpoint has been reflected by the recent authors who have been quoted in the various sections of this volume.

The earliest portion of the record is that contained in the Talmud and Midrash. A primary objective, therefore, has been the reconstruction of the expurgated material and an interpretation of what has been much misunderstood. All rabbinic passages which possibly might allude to Jesus are assembled here.

These were scrupulously translated, for when dealing with original sources where there is controversy much depends upon accuracy of translation. The task, then, was to segregate the earlier part of the rabbinic record, the Tannaitic—belonging to the first two centuries of the Christian Era—from that which is later, or

Amoraic. Finally, there was the requirement to interpret the passages with unwarped judgment. Thus we arrived at a more accurate understanding of the Talmud and Midrash.

It was important for many reasons to differentiate between what is a genuine reference to Jesus and what has been erroneously believed to refer to him. We discovered that, particularly in the earlier centuries, there is far more that does not truly allude to Jesus than that does. Yet, even the lesser amount that remains is significant.

We compared the Talmudic evidence with the accounts of the Gospels and the Church Fathers and we realized that in the Tannaitic period none of the bitterness is shown by Jews toward Jesus which is recorded in the Christian literature.

Best remembered were: the power to heal in his name; a Pharisaic-like exposition of Scripture attributed to him; the fact that he left disciples; and an unhistoric tradition of the circumstances of his trial and death.

Since he was regarded as a Jew, there was still within Judaism, at the beginning of the third century, association with the followers of Jesus. One passage in the Talmud seems actually to name the Gospels and quote a specific teaching, but there are opposing opinions about this.

Nothing is recorded of Jesus' preaching and rules of conduct because, presumably, these in the main were in accord with the accepted teachings of the time.

Nothing is mentioned explicitly of Jesus as the Son of God or the Messiah, nor of his miraculous birth or resurrection. In these respects it is possible to see indirect references in the charge of leading Israel astray and in the passages which tell that God can have no Son.

In fact, the indirect references—if they truly are allusions to Jesus—are more significant than those which specifically mention his name.

Especially is it true of the later rabbinic record that the teachings of the unity and incorporeality of God, the belief that the Messiah was yet to come, the emphasis on Moses and the Mosaic Law, and the decline in the status of miracles, are more important in revealing the Jewish attitude than are those passages where Jesus is actually mentioned.

The specific references of the Amoraic period which name Jesus are mainly homiletical and theological. Scriptural texts are adduced to interpret the nature of Jesus and his disciples. There is further reference to healing in his name. His doctrine is regarded as a departure from Judaism.

The passing of several centuries led to the confusion of Jesus with Ben Stada and of Mary with Mary Magdalene. We sought to understand how those errors came to be.

The Babylonian Amoraim, moreover, were removed by distance and environment as well as in point of time from the possibility of first-hand knowledge. Their sayings on Jesus, therefore, are characterized by an atmosphere of unreality. It is to be remembered that the teachers of the Talmud tended "the vineyard of the Lord" for the followers of Judaism. This was their primary interest. All else was incidental.

Another objective in this study was the seeking of information which could help in determining the question of the historicity of Jesus. We found that the difficulty of fixing exact dates of Talmudic material presented a problem. Yet, with a fair degree of probability we were able to date at least one Tannaitic passage at about 95 c.e., which is as early as any non-Canonical source, and earlier than considerable portions of the New Testament. On the basis of possibility we were able to date another passage at 73 c.e., which is the approximate date of the earliest Canonical Gospel.

We sought an answer as to why Judaism did not assent to the Messiahship of Jesus. We found that it was because Jewish tradition did not regard the required messianic conditions as fufilled with his coming. Judaism, therefore, adhered to the hope that in days ahead God would bring redemption. But there was no unanimous opinion as to when the Messiah would come and what his exact role would be.

Inevitably, legends came to cluster about the name of Jesus. They were not originally Jewish, for these same legends attached to other personages of ancient times. They were, in fact, used by Christian writers to refer to the Antichrist.[1] Mingled with rabbinic passages which originally had little or no relevancy to Jesus, but were applied to him, they became the Toledoth Yeshu.

There is, we noticed, the theory that from the Toledoth Yeshu one can reconstruct the lost Gospel according to the Hebrews, an independent source of the life of Jesus. It is a challenging theory but not wholly proved. What is fairly evident is that the contents of the Toledoth Yeshu are so arranged as to constitute a reply to the Gospels and Acts of the New Testament.

The significance of this legendary *Life of Jesus* is its subjective value, which in our day we understand by the psychological term *displacement*, which is defined as a "protective mechanism, used primarily to release emotional tension built up by repressed memories or immediately irritating circumstances." [2] We find that these legends assumed no important role, but that the Jews of the Middle Ages channeled the greater part of their energies to a joyous fulfillment of the requirements of Judaism.

Considering the aggressions against Judaism during the period which history describes as the *dark* Middle Ages, it is significant to read the characterization of the Toledoth Yeshu by one who gave it thorough study: "The Jewish legends relating to Jesus appear less inimical in character when compared with the parallel passages which are found in pagan authors and Christian sources, more especially as such legends are fixed and frequently occurring themes of folklore; and imagination must have been especially excited by the historical importance which the figure of Jesus came to have for the Jews." [3]

From a study of this portion of the historic record we learn that expressions of opinion must be understood always in the light of the then existing conditions—the general cultural level, the presence or absence of prejudicial regulations, the degree of political enlightenment. This fact leads us to the conclusion that a particular viewpoint regarding Jesus must be related to the century and environment in which we find it. Always care must be exercised not to quote a statement or passage as applicable for all time. When a position in the Jewish tradition persists it gains in importance. But viewpoints which pertain to medievalism should not be carried over indiscriminately and regarded as valid in modern times.

This is true correspondingly with regard to the Church and spokesmen of Christianity, in relation to Judaism.

The spectacle of compulsory disputations and polemics on the Talmudic references to Jesus—supposed or real—and the resultant burning and censorship of the Talmud belong to that type of abuse of religion which the world recognizes in the word Inquisition. The pity is that the accusations were so groundless, the suffering so unjustifiable. Especially now that we have examined the record of the Talmud, this becomes clearer than ever!

One of the incidental results of the destruction of rabbinic literature may have been the annihilation of what might have contained precious historic documentation, never restored, of the beginnings of Christianity. This is a hypothesis, to be sure, but it is interesting to know that Samuel Krauss, who had spent forty years in the study of this theme, held to a suspicion that more than one literary product which would now be invaluable was thus destroyed.[4]

The polemic and apologetic literature of the Middle Ages assumed a recognizable pattern. Verses of the Old Testament were quoted by Christian representatives to validate belief in Jesus as the Messiah and Son of God, in the Trinity, Incarnation of Deity, Original Sin, Redemption through Jesus, and other such doctrines of the Church. They argued God's rejection of the Jews for not having accepted Jesus, the Abrogation of the Mosaic Law and the errors of Judaism. Jewish representatives likewise quoted the Old Testament, but to prove the very opposite and, at times, they launched into historical and literary criticism of the New Testament.

The attack upon the Talmud was on two fronts. One was the charge of insolence in the passages dealing with Jesus. The analysis in the third and fourth chapters of this book reveal how unfounded indeed was the complaint on this score. That Jewish polemicists of the Middle Ages recognized the unreliability of many of these passages as references to Jesus is truly amazing, considering that they did not possess the historic and literary tools we use in modern scholarship.

The other phase of attack took rabbinic literature to task because of certain extravagant Haggadic passages. The answer was simple and to the point, yet had to be repeated over and over. It was that one does not take seriously what was meant to be no more than a stimulating play of the imagination, a daring illustration, a fable, a legend or even "humorous by-play to enliven heavy discussion," to use the phrase of Solomon Schechter, who adds that a controversialist who takes such matter seriously fits the category described by Johnson's famous statement to Boswell: "Let us get serious, for there comes a fool." [5]

Amazing, indeed, was the turnabout executed by some of the polemicists who criticized the Haggadah for statements supposedly critical of Jesus, after having relied on it until they were refuted, for proof that the Talmud taught Jesus as the Christ.

It is generally understood that the aim of the disputations was to win converts to Christianity. A probable factor not generally recognized was the desire to recondition the thinking of many who had been Jews and had become Christians under duress, so that their assimilation into the new environment might be facilitated.[6] Similarly, the polemics of the New Testament and of the Church Fathers appear in a new light when seen not as an obvious attack upon those who do not accept the supernatural character of Jesus but as an effort to strengthen neo-Christians in their new allegiance as well as to weaken the Judaic ties of the Jewish Christians who managed to persevere for four centuries and more. This is but one illustration of how our study, as a by-product, clarifies elements in the history of Christianity. This, too, was one of our objectives.

In the course of our inquiry we necessarily learned much about Judaism. We traced the evolution of the rabbinic tradition. We were made aware of the internal challenge of Karaism, reflecting the new Mohammedan thinking, and the introduction into the dispute of a renewed evaluation of Jesus.

We caught a glimpse of the thinking of medieval Jewish philosophy and the formulation of dogma in Judaism. The theologian-philosophers in particular bring to us a realization that in reaching conclusions regarding Jesus which differ from those in Christianity they did so through a sincere interpretation of Scripture and through the logic of their thinking based on specific premises. To us it means that differing viewpoints need not imply unfriendliness. They arise from early training, from inheritance of a tradition, from honest conviction.

We gained some knowledge of Bible and Talmud exegesis and the codification of Jewish law. Above all, we became acquainted with the fact that in the Jewish tradition the Jew found a spiritual way of life which exalted him and consecrated his days on earth.

In our opening chapter we resolved that, as an added purpose of this investigation, we would, if possible, ascertain something of the relationship between Christianity and Judaism—two religions whose history and nature are so uniquely enmeshed each with the other. This information might be of current value to the modern Jew and the modern Christian who live together as neighbors and share the responsibility and the privilege of building a God-centered world.

What have we found?

In our study of the relations between populations of two religions we must not overlook the practical aspect of social intercourse between these peoples. In large measure they must have shared economically, culturally, spiritually. They were, after all, neighbors, as long as they were permitted by the higher power to remain neighbors. If there was illness, misfortune or unhappiness in a home, the neighbor—whether Christian or Jewish—must have responded in a neighborly manner. In extending the needed help, the neighbor was prompted by the spirit of religion, a spirit in which fine points of differentiation between Tritheism, Trinity, and Monotheism receded into the background, at least while coping with a human problem of the moment.

To understand the relationship throughout these many generations of God's children, Christians and Jews, an analogy will help. We open the morning newspaper and read of several automobile accidents in our part of the country but not of the hun-

dreds of thousands of cars which afford pleasure to their occu-
pants without unpleasant mishap. We read of divorces, especially
among persons whose names are newsworthy, but not of the
happiness and love in the millions of homes which constitute the
stability of our country. We read of crimes but relatively little
of the day-to-day decency exchanged between man and his fellow. We read of the dislocations in industry at a particular time
but not of the sixty million persons who will be at their assigned posts building a strong economy. Whatever is extraordinary, shocking, tragic or painful is written into the record. Also
whatever is heroic and dramatically virtuous finds a place therein.
Neither of these two extremes characterizes the life of the average
person. Yet the bulk of humanity is made up of average people—
with average virtues and average vices. The bulk of humanity
may not create spectacular news but *the bulk of humanity is the
life of the world.*

This reasoning suggests to us the importance of reading between the lines as well as what is printed in the lines of the past.

James Parkes recognized this truth. Writing of the *Conflict of
the Church and the Synagogue* and relating the hostilities of the
theologians and legislators, he appended to each phase of the
story of the first eight centuries of the Christian Era a reminder
that the average Jew and Christian did enjoy mutual friendship.

Of the critical fourth century he writes that "though so far
this chapter has dealt almost exclusively with official and unofficial
manifestations of hostility, it would be a mistake to assume that
during this period all Christians and Jews hated each other. The
canons of the councils and the violence of such as Chrysostom
both have their origin in the friendly relations between local
Jewish and Christian communities. Trouble, when it comes, comes
clearly from the ecclesiastical or imperial authorities, and not
from the populace. . . . But the problems facing the leaders were
different from those facing the 'man in the street,' Jew or Christian, and in daily life the two monotheists must still have much
in common in the face of a not-yet-dead pagan world. At this

period it is doubtful if the stories of the Sepher Toldoth Jeshu were more believed than the fantasies of the Christian pulpit." [7]

Even of the Byzantine empire, where social relations had deteriorated, Parkes can state "that, where there was no direct reason for the contrary, relations between Jews and Christians were not unfriendly. Local Christians did not necessarily approve of the doings of the monks, and the councils in the east as well as in the west had to cope with close social relationships between Jews and Christians. All references to Jews are not hostile. Anecdotes are retailed by various chroniclers showing their [8] compassion for Christian suffering, their admiration for Christian piety, and their desire to assist Christians in distress." [9]

Hence, even in manifestations of malevolence there may be discerned at times an undercurrent of friendly disposition. Another example is the disgraceful law in certain of the European lands which segregated the Jews into their own neighborhoods.[10] As stated explicitly in the Cortes of Toledo (1480), one of the reasons for it was the determination of Christian authorities to terminate the constant association of Jews and Christians.[11] Unhindered, therefore, it was the natural thing *to associate* with each other.[12]

During even the darkest stretches of the Middle Ages there are signposts along the highway of the centuries which point to brotherly Jewish attitudes to Christianity [13]—in the spirit of the rabbinic teaching that "the righteous among the Gentiles have a share in the world-to-come." [14] All peoples may find salvation in their own discipline.

We observed the thinking of Saadia Gaon, of the tenth century, to the effect that Christianity differs from Judaism in that it personifies the attributes of God.[15] We have seen that the twelfth century's greatest poet, Judah Halevi,[16] and the greatest philosopher, Moses Maimonides,[17] depicted Christianity as helping to prepare the way for the Messiah—a viewpoint often repeated.[18] We took cognizance of the consecrated spirit of Jacob Emden of the eighteenth century.

In the eleventh century, Solomon ibn Gabirol expressed in his

majestic poem, *The Royal Crown* (read by Jews on the important
Eve of Atonement, after Services), an attitude which recommends
itself to the most enlightened liberal of our own twentieth
century:

Thou art the God of Gods, and the Lord of Lords,
Ruler of beings celestial and terrestrial,
For all creatures are Thy witnesses
And by the glory of this Thy name, every creature is bound to Thy
service.
Thou art God, and all things formed are Thy servants and
worshippers.
Yet is not Thy glory diminished by reason of those that worship
aught beside Thee,
For the yearning of them all is to draw nigh Thee.[19]

The *Sefer Hassidim* written in the twelfth century by Judah
ben Samuel of Regensburg, Germany, became in medieval Jewish
life an accepted guide of ethics and morals. In it we read: "That
which the Torah ordains for Israel, is meant to promote love and
peace among all human beings." [20]

Also in the twelfth century, Maimonides taught, besides what
has previously been quoted, that a Jew should perform all acts of
charity for non-Jews even as for Jews, to visit the sick, to bury
the dead, to support the needy, for Scripture teaches: "The Lord
is good to all; His tender mercies are over all His Creation"; also,
"Her ways are ways of pleasantness, and all her paths are
peace." [21]

In the fifteenth century, the "preacher's preacher," Isaac Arama,
who influenced Jewish preaching for five hundred years, spoke
forth as follows: "We can discern a special providence in the fact
that it is among Christian and Mohammedan nations that we are
scattered. For, in whatever distorted a form, our Torah has
become the property of these nations; at least, they subscribe to
the essential principles of our faith. We are thus privileged to live
in an environment in which, though we suffer much sorrow and
pain, the perpetuation of Judaism is assured." [22]

The sixteenth-century codification of Jewish law in the *Shulhan*

*Aruch* states the duty of a Jew to give to non-Jewish charity; [23] to deal honestly, the same law applying to Jew and non-Jew alike; [24] to treat even a slave, when non-Jewish, with courtesy, not to degrade him by word or act, not to bully or scornfully entreat him, but to address him gently and listen to him courteously; [25] when seeing a Christian sage, to speak the blessing: "Blessed art Thou, O Lord, King of the Universe, who hast imparted Thy wisdom unto man." [26]

Summed up in these several citations are not haphazard remarks of incidental nature. They are the expressions of the foremost authorities in Talmud, exegesis, philosophy, moral piety, preaching, liturgy, and the standard code of Jewish practice. Their messages blend as one, telling of the common denominator which unites Christian and Jew.

These declarations and views are set forth here as evidence of an important element of the Jewish tradition. The fact that there is this component—added to the fact that a good part of the Jewish tradition disagreed with the theology relative to Jesus but generally maintained silence on his ethical teaching—supports the inference that the Jewish tradition held in esteem the superb parables of Jesus and his venture by word and example to lead men to God and the good life.

This degree of agreement does not imply relinquishment. It does not suggest that the time has come for the Jew to give up his Judaism or the Christian his Christianity. Both great traditions, besides this extent of agreement, possess distinctive viewpoints which are uniquely their own and of enduring value.

The part of the heritage that is held in common does signify that the two may join forces in important endeavors and work together to bring humanity closer to the Kingdom of Heaven on earth.

An impressive result of clarifying the record concerning Jesus is the clearing of the heavy haze of medieval error. This is necessary for the spirit of the modern age. In a day when we believe in freedom of religion we accept the principle that each religion has its inherent right to express itself unhampered, to bring the most abundant life to its devotees. In this spirit there is neither the polemic nor the apologetic approach. It is agreed, rather, that each religion speak its truth with vigor.

This concept, for example, is expressed in the idea of a volume such as *The Religions of Democracy*.[27] In the pages within the two covers a Protestant, a Catholic and a Jew describe what each faith has to offer toward the building of a democracy which stands to benefit from the best there is in all three.

Similarly, in *Judaism and Christianity Compare Notes*[28] a Jewish teacher tells of Judaism and a Christian teacher tells of Christianity, each with conviction, but without crowding, insulting, or apologizing to the other. Both viewpoints are contained in a single volume as a symbol of that which binds together all who seek for spiritual values in life and the road leading to God.

Perhaps it can be understood now why it was necessary for a Jew to write of the Jewish record concerning Jesus. The nature of the theme demands it. The general acceptance of such authorship on this theme may serve as another signpost of the more enlightened spirit in the civilization of modernity.

Literature Analysis

TO FACILITATE an orderly listing of the literature relevant to
our theme we may divide it into two general categories as pertaining to:

I. *The Talmudic Period,* which includes both the Tannaitic * (dealt
with in Chapter II) and the Amoraic * (dealt with in Chapter III) and

II. *The Post-Talmudic Period,* which includes the Gaonic [1] and the
later medieval (dealt with in Chapter IV), extending beyond the
fifteenth century, the termination of the Middle Ages in general history, to 1776—the year of the birth of democracy, which to the Jew
has meant the beginning of the Era of Emancipation, the true entry
into the Modern World.[2]

The Talmudic Period constitutes a suitable unit because, while there
may be differences of opinion as to which passage is Tannaitic and
which is Amoraic, the fact is that they are both contained within the
Talmud.* The Tosefta * comes well within this scope; it is, in fact,
mainly contemporaneous with the Mishnah.* There is a question with
regard to the Midrashim: * some are early, and fall in place in the
Talmudic Period; others are late, and belong to the Post-Talmudic
Period; for the purpose of bibliography and study, however, we include the Midrashim as part of the Talmudic Period.

When history is dynamic there are no sharp dividing lines. The
momentum of forces in an earlier era is felt in a later one. Likewise,
results seen in a later era have their beginnings in an earlier one. So, in
the Post-Talmudic Period, we find legends built upon casual and
incidental items in the rabbinic literature, these legends taking form
before the actual completion of the Talmud. Again, controversies in
the Middle Ages over Talmudic references to Jesus have their roots in
the Talmud. The literature of the Middle Ages grew out of the roots
in the Talmud as well as out of those in the Bible. But since this phase
of our inquiry differs in essential regards from the previous one, as
seen in Chapter IV, it calls for a separate bibliography.

## I. THE TALMUDIC PERIOD

Within this general section we introduce sub-groupings: A. *Original
Sources;* B. *Literature Specifically on This Theme;* C. *General References.* The first two of these will be discussed as well as itemized.

* These terms are explained in Chapter II.

## A. ORIGINAL SOURCES

1. The Holy Bible
   The Jewish Publication Society translation of the Old Testament [3] (O.T.) into English and the King James translation of the New Testament (N.T.) are used.
2. The Apocrypha and Pseudepigrapha of the Old Testament, ed. by R. H. Charles, 2 Vols., 1913. New English edition is in preparation by Dropsie College, Philadelphia; Book I published by Harper, 1950.
3. Mishnah—here referred to as M.
4. Palestinian Talmud (Yerushalmi)—here referred to as P.
5. Babylonian Talmud (Babli)—here referred to as B (Baraitha portions of the Talmud are designated Ba).
6. Tosefta—here referred to as T.
   An enumeration of the extant manuscripts and older editions, valuable for reinsertion into the text of censored material, is given by Strack, *Introduction to Talmud and Midrash*, pp. 79–86.[4]
   These are referred to in the Original Text as follows:

R = de Rossi ms. of Mishnah, from 13th cent., in Parma.

A = Berlin ms. of Mishnah, from 13th cent.

C = Cambridge Univ. Library ms. of Mishnah, ed. by W. H. Lowe.

L = Leiden ms. of Palestinian Talmud, used for printing Venice Talmud.

Mu = Munich ms. of Babylonian Talmud, 1343.

O = Oxford ms. of Babylonian Talmud (oldest that is dated), about 1123 C.E.

F = Florence ms. of the Babylonian Talmud, second oldest extant, completed about 1176 C.E.

Pa = Venetian edition of printed Palestinian Talmud, 1523.

N = First ed. of printed Mishnah, Naples, 1492 f.

V = Venetian (first) printing of Babylonian Talmud, 1520–22.

E = Tosefta code, formerly in Erfurt, now in Berlin.

Vi = Vienna code of Tosefta.

Z = Zuckermandel, M. S., comparison of early Tosefta texts (compiled 1880–82, Passewalk).

*Sefer Dikduke Soferim* [5] *(Variae lectiones in Mishnam et in Talmud Babylonicum)*, Raphael Rabbinovicz, Munich, 1868–1886, 16 Vols.

(17th published by Ehrentreu, Przemysl, 1897). This invaluable collection of the variant readings in the oldest editions uses the 1721 Frankfort-on-Main edition of the Babylonian Talmud as the foundation and makes use of the Oxford and Munich manuscripts; however, it does not cover all of the Talmud [6] nor all of the early manuscript material.[7] Rabbinic passages or words (and those in the standard commentaries) believed to allude to Jesus or Christianity and therefore deleted or mutilated by the censors, are collected in printed booklets:

> *Kuntres Lemal'oth Hesronoth Hashas,*[8] or the shorter title with only the last two words; Königsberg, 1860; Cracow, 1895; often in manuscript or printed without date or place of publication.
>
> *Kebutzath Hahashmatoth,*[9] no date or place of publication; some reprinted in Cracow, 1893.
>
> *Sefer Hashabath Abedah,*[10] (possibly) Lemberg, 1858.
>
> *Kuntres 'Omer Hashikchah,*[11] no place given, 1861.
>
> Separate pages printed in Amsterdam, 1708, by Simeon Shammash and his brother, Isaac; meant to be pasted in the proper place in the Frankfort-on-Main Talmud edition.[12]

*Der Babylonische Talmud Herausgegeben nach der editio princeps,* Lazarus Goldschmidt; Vols. I, II, III, VII, Berlin; Vols. IV, VI, VIII, Leipzig; IX, Haag; 1897–1935.

> Restores censored matter, based on Venice ed. (1520–23); mainly follows *Dikduke.*
>
> Translates into German; also gives brief comments.

*Ozar Habaraitot,* Michael Higger, New York, 1938–42.

> Assembling and classification of the Baraithoth.

*Seven Minor Tractates,* ed. by Michael Higger, New York, 1938.

7. The Midrashic Literature, in the various collections.

The principal Midrash collections are: [13]

Tannaitic Midrashim

> *Mechilta,* ed. by J. Z. Lauterbach, Jewish Pub. Soc., 1933–34, also Eng. trans.; M. Friedmann ed., Vienna, 1870, used here.
>
> *Sifra,* ed. by M. L. Malbim; Reprint, Vilna, 1924.
>
> *Sifre,* ed. by Horovitz, Leipzig, 1917; completed by L. Finkelstein, 1935. M. Friedmann ed., Vienna, 1864, used here.

Pesikta De Rab Kahana, S. Buber ed., Lyck, 1868.

Midrash Rabboth to the Pentateuch and Five Scrolls

> The Vilna edition (1843–45) is used.
>
> English translation by H. Freedman and Maurice Simon, London, 1938.

Tanhuma (Yelammedenu), S. Buber ed., Vilna, 1885. Psalms, 1891.
Pirke De Rabbi Eliezer, ed. by G. Friedlander, London, 1916; also Eng. trans.
Tanna Debe Eliyahu, ed. by M. Friedmann, Vienna, 1902.
Pesikta Rabbathi, ed. by M. Friedmann, Vienna, 1880.
Midrashic Thesaurus
  Yalkut Shimeoni, Vienna ed., 1898.
  Midrash Hagadol, ed. by Schechter, Cambridge, 1902; Hoffman, Berlin, 1913; E. N. Rabbinowitz, New York, 1932.
Minor Midrashim assembled in
  *Beth Hamidrash*, Adolf Jellinek, new ed., Jerusalem, 1938.
  *Otzar Midrashim*, 2 Vols., J. D. Eisenstein, N. Y., 1915.
Haggadic selections translated by Louis Ginzberg in *The Legends of the Jews*, 7 Vols., Jewish Pub. Soc., 1909–38.
Original Talmudic and Midrashic references gathered and appended to the works of this theme by Laible, Herford, Strack, Zeitlin.
  COMMENTS ON THE TEXTS are given by:
    Richard von der Alm, *Die Urteile heidnischer und jüdischer Schriftsteller der vier ersten christlichen Jahrhunderte über Jesus und die ersten Christen*, Leipzig, 1865.
    Christian Schottgen, *Horae hebraicae et talmudicae*, Dresden, 1742, Vol. II, pp. 839–871.
    Daniel Chwolson, *Das Letzte Passamahl Christi und der Tag seines Todes*, Leipzig, 1908, pp. 85–125.
    Samuel Krauss, *Das Leben Jesu nach jüdischen Quellen*, Berlin, 1902, pp. 181–194.
    And in the works on this theme, named below.[14]

## B. LITERATURE SPECIFICALLY ON THIS THEME

THE EARLIER LITERATURE is given by Hermann Strack in the Introduction to Laible's, *Jesus Christus im Thalmud*, Leipzig, 1900, and in Strack's own *Jesus, die Häretiker und die Christen*, Leipzig, 1910.
  Only the following need be mentioned again here:
R. M. Meelführer, *Jesus in Talmude* (Latin), Altdorf, 1699.
J. A. Eisenmenger, *Entdecktes Judenthum*, Frankfort, 1700.
A. C. Werner, *Jesus in Talmude* (Latin), Stade, 1731.
Nitsch article in *Theologische Studien und Kritiken*, 1840, pp. 115–120.
  I. M. Jost, *Geschichte des Judenthums und seiner Secten*, Leipzig, 1858, Vol. I, p. 405.

F. Hitzig in *Zeitschrift für wissenschaftliche Theologie*, 1865, pp. 344–347.

A. Geiger, *Jüd. Zeitschrift für Wissenschaft und Leben*, 1868, Vol. 6, pp. 31, 305.

F. Perles, in *Monatschrift für Geschichte und Wissenschaft des Judenthums*, 1872, p. 267.

Theodor Keim, *Die Geschichte Jesu von Nazara*, 1867–73; English translation, London, 1873–77. One of the earliest of recent Christian scholars to pay attention to Jewish sources, in reconstructing the life of Jesus.

G. Rösch in *Theologische Studien und Kritiken*, 1873, pp. 77–115 and 1878, pp. 516–521.

Bernhard Pick, *The Talmud—What It Is And What It Knows About Jesus*, New York, 1877, pp. 113–123; also, *Jesus in the Talmud*, New York, 1913.

J. Levy, *Neuhebräisches und Chaldaisches Wörterbuch*, Leipzig, 1876–88; articles on various names of Jesus.

Joseph Stein, "Bileam und Jesus" in *Jüdisches Literaturblatt*, 1881, nos. 31, 32.

Alfred Edersheim, *Life and Times of Jesus the Messiah*, London, 1883.

R. Sinker, *Essays and Studies*, Cambridge, 1900, pp. 58–79.

Theodore Zahn, *Forschungen zur Geschichte des Neutestamentl. Kanons und der altkirchliche Literatur*, Leipzig, 1900, Vol. 6, pp. 266–269.

## THE PRINCIPAL COMPLETE WORKS ON THE THEME

1. Heinrich Laible, *Jesus Christus im Thalmud*, Leipzig; 1st edition, 1891; 2nd edition, 1900 (96 pages of text; 19 pages of appendix).

The value of this work is enhanced by an Introduction of H. Strack, consisting of Bibliography, and an Appendix by G. Dalman, *Die Talmudischen Texte (über Jesu)*, giving the Hebrew and Aramaic texts culled from uncensored sources. An English translation of the German was made by G. Dalman and A. W. Streane, Cambridge, 1893.

As to the place of this study, Herford, with characteristic humility, acknowledges that in the portion of his own book relating to Jesus he made constant use of Laible's work, claiming for himself not much more than a rearrangement of the material and a modification of some of the conclusions,[15] an opinion with which W. Bacher in his review of Herford's book agrees.[16]

However, Laible does err in some of the translation and in many points of interpretation, especially in identifying passages as references to Jesus, without sufficient grounds. Further, he gives none of the indirect allusions. Most serious, however, is the unabashed hostility in Laible's treatment of Judaism, hostility inherited from the bitter Middle Ages and detrimental in what should be a scholarly pursuit of objective truth.

2. R. Travers Herford, *Christianity in Talmud and Midrash*, Williams and Norgate, London, 1903 (397 pages of text, 36 pages of appendix).

This eminent British scholar and friend of Judaism, who has dedicated a long lifetime to studying the Jewish background of Jesus, has written on our theme the work best known in the United States and England. The critical reviewer, W. Bacher, terms it a storehouse in which are contained all the relevant original texts, judged with scientific width of view and with noteworthy impartiality.[17]

This well-printed, substantial volume gives the original text, the translation, the interpretation and discussion and, as full measure, an excellent index.

While inquiry into the Talmud allusions to the *Minim* (sectaries) is only indirectly of concern to our inquiry, it should be noted that Herford did pioneer work in gathering the references to the *Minim*, as Laible's book had done with the passages relating to Jesus.

The deficiencies are mainly such as are inevitable in any pioneer effort in the field of scholarship. A student of this subject must begin with Herford's volume but should not terminate his study with it.

As Strack did not fail to point out,[18] Herford presents the original Talmud texts generally as arranged by R. Rabbinovicz, without further checking into the older manuscripts for additional and, at times, more correct variant uncensored readings; this may seem trivial but is actually of great importance. Also, careful checking will show errors—not many or serious—in the spelling of words in the original texts.[19] Again, it will be found that not all passages relating, or which might be considered as relating, to Jesus are included,[20] and that several references are placed among those of the *Minim*,[21] when their importance as passages concerning Jesus should have dictated their location in this category.

Moreover, there are inaccuracies in translation,[22] to which Bacher, in his searching review, calls attention. They have created erroneous impressions.[23] Yet, we must concur with Bacher that these are overshadowed by the great conscientiousness which distinguishes Herford's work.[24]

The most serious shortcoming is in designating as rabbinic references to Jesus those passages which cannot be so regarded.[25] The fault is not entirely Herford's. He but follows the lead of Laible (and in noteworthy instances corrects Laible's biased viewpoint) and of those commentators who preceded Laible.

3. Hermann L. Strack, *Jesus, die Häretiker und die Christen nach den ältesten jüdischen Angaben*, Leipzig, 1910 (128 pages, incl. original texts).

Commendable is Strack's purpose,[26] expressed in the Preface, to offset anti-Jewish attitudes fostered by purported Talmudic interpretations of Jesus. To this objective is coupled Strack's scholarship and desire for accuracy. Few Christians have approached Strack's profound knowledge of rabbinic literature. He compared the oldest manuscripts extant, as well as the earliest printed editions, and prepared a careful arrangement of the original texts, separating the Tannaitic from the Amoraic passages. But he, too, has placed in the *Minim* section several references of importance which should have been included in the portion relating to Jesus.[27]

Strack adds a chapter on early Jewish attitudes to Jesus as reflected in the Greek and Latin writings of the early leaders of the Church. Thus, he transmits the expressions, from the Greek, of Justin Martyr (c. 155–160), Pionius (d. 250), Origen (wrote c. 225), Eusebius of Caesaria (d. 339), Epiphanius (d. 403), Andreas, Archbishop of Crete (d. *circa* 720), John of Damascus (d. *circa* 754), Epiphanius the Monk (d. 813); and from the Latin, Tertullian (d. *circa* 220), Agobard, Archbishop of Lyon (d. 840), Amolo, his successor (d. 852).

It is questionable whether this chapter adds particularly to the value of his work. A more complete record in the original languages of this type of reference is to be found in Migne's *Patrologia Latina, Patrologia Graeca* and Graffin's *Patrologia Orientalis*. A selection of the more significant utterances is translated into English by A. Lukyn Williams in *Adversus Judaeos*.[28] The serious objection to the inclusion by Strack of this chapter is that which already has been discussed—the unreliability of polemic writing as source material regarding the religion that is being attacked.[29]

In the translation and interpretation of the rabbinic material Strack makes important corrections. It is regrettable that his work is in mere pamphlet form, the section dealing with Jesus consisting of only forty-

seven pages, with twenty pages of text, and not nearly as readable as
Herford's. It is not translated from the German into English and
therefore is precluded from reaching those who do not read German
and from doing for the average reader in English-speaking countries
the good the author may have contemplated. There is a minimum of
commentary, confined mainly to footnotes, limiting continuity and
development of the material, so that on important points one cannot
tell whether the author does or does not credit certain passages as
truly referring to Jesus.[30] Some of the passages identified with Jesus
cannot be so regarded,[31] while others have been omitted.[32]

4. Joseph Klausner, *Jesus of Nazareth*, published and copyright by
Macmillan, 1925 (pp. 17 to 47 of the total 434 pages).

Originally published in Jerusalem in 1922, as *Yeshu Hanotzri*, this is
the first scientific study, by a Jew, in modern Hebrew, of the life,
times and teaching of Jesus.

Although this is not an instance of an entire volume dealing with
our thesis yet Klausner expresses in these thirty pages the gist of the
Tannaitic record so succinctly and so ably that it merits a place among
the fuller treatments.

Still, the brevity limits the usefulness of the presentation. There are
no original texts given. The bibliography is scanty.[33] The translation
of some passages is given, not of others. The author does not follow
the orderly chronology of the material. He makes no sharp and clear
division in the arrangement of the material between that which is historically acceptable and that which is not. There is no room for complete discussion of references not accepted. The Amoraim are all too
quickly brushed aside.[34] However, these are shortcomings attributable
mainly to the fact that a discussion of our theme in *Jesus of Nazareth*
is but a small part of a larger task, and the author himself speaks of it
as "this brief study on Jesus in *Talmud* and *Midrash*." [35] Finally, there
are conclusions which are open to challenge, as we have seen in Chapter II.

## BRIEF BUT VALUABLE STUDIES

W. Bacher, "Travers Herford's 'Christianity in Talmud and Midrash' " in the *Jewish Quarterly Review*, old series, Vol. XVII (1905),
pp. 171–183. Important corrections as to translation and interpretation.

R. Travers Herford, in J. Hastings' *Dictionary of Christ and the
Gospels*, Edinburgh, 1908, Vol. 2, pp. 876–882. Good summary of
viewpoint of his book.

Samuel Krauss, article "Jesus—Jewish Legends of" in *Jewish Encyclopedia*, New York, 1907, Vol. VII, pp. 170–173.

Samuel Krauss, "Jesus in History and Legend" in *The New Era* (periodical), New York, Vol. 6 (1904–05), pp. 19–27, 153–162. Excellent comments on Talmudic record.

*Otzar Yisroel* (Hebrew Encyclopedia), New York City, 1911, article by the editor, J. D. Eisenstein, on "Jesus in Talmud and Midrash," Vol. V, pp. 229–231.

Jacob Z. Lauterbach, *Jesus and His Disciples in Talmud and Midrash*, at present available in manuscript, being edited by Lou H. Silberman for publication.

A. Meyer, "Jesus im Talmud," in Hennecke's *Handbuch zu den neutestamentlichen Apokryphen*, Tübingen, 1904, pp. 47–71.

Solomon Zeitlin, article, "Studies in the Beginnings of Christianity," in *Jewish Quarterly Review*, new series, Vol. XXXIV (1923), pp. 133 ff. Important critique of the treatment in Klausner's *Jesus of Nazareth*, at the same time giving Zeitlin's questioning of the historic value of the Talmudic record of Jesus.

Solomon Zeitlin, "Jesus in Early Tannaitic Literature," in the *Chajes Memorial Volume (Abhandlungen zur Erinnerung an Hirsch Perez Chajes)*, Vienna, 1933, pp. 295–308. Insufficiently known critique of Herford's and Klausner's conclusions; limited to a consideration of the earlier Talmudic record, gives text, translation and keen, scholarly analysis.

Solomon Zeitlin, article on "The Halaka in the Gospels and Its Relation to the Jewish Law at the Time of Jesus," in *Hebrew Union College Annual*, Vol. I (1924), pp. 357–373. Presents Talmudic evidence; challenges its worth in ascertaining the historicity of Jesus.

George F. Moore, article in *Harvard Theological Review*, Vol. 16 (1923), pp. 96 ff. Mild critique of Klausner's *Jesus of Nazareth*.

Jehoshuah Guttman, article on Jesus in rabbinic literature, in *Encyclopedia Judaica* (German language), Berlin, 1932, pp. 78–79.

Simon Cohen and collaborators, article "Jesus of Nazareth" in *Universal Jewish Encyclopedia*, Vol. 6, pp. 83–87; also, article on "Christianity" by Ernest Jacob, Vol. 3, p. 181.

R. Travers Herford, article on "Jesus in Rabbinical Literature," in *Universal Jewish Encyclopedia*, New York, 1942, Vol. 6, pp. 87–88. Herford accepts critique of his earlier work and retracts certain of the conclusions of his book.

R. Travers Herford in J. Hastings' *Encyclopedia of Religion and Ethics*, Scribner's, 1928 ed., Vol. VII, pp. 551–552.

## C. SELECTED GENERAL BIBLIOGRAPHY

(IN ADDITION TO LITERATURE NAMED ABOVE)

Pertinent articles on the various subjects and personalities are to be found in alphabetical arrangement in:

*The Jewish Encyclopedia*, 12 Vols., Funk and Wagnalls, 1901–06.

*Otzar Yisroel*, Hebrew Encyclopedia, 10 Vols., New York, 1907–13.

*Encyclopedia Judaica*, in German, 10 Vols., Berlin, 1928–34.

*The Universal Jewish Encyclopedia*, 10 Vols., New York, 1939–43.

*Ha-Encyclopaedia Ha-Ivrit*, Hebrew Encyclopedia, 16 Vols. planned; 1 completed, Israel, 1949.

FOR GREATER UNDERSTANDING OF THE TALMUD AND MIDRASH, AND THE DEVELOPMENT OF RABBINIC JUDAISM

*The Babylonian Talmud*, translated into English, with valuable foot-notes, 34 Vols., Soncino Press, England, 1935–48.

Herbert Danby, *The Mishnah*, entire Mishnah translated into English, Oxford, 1933.

Louis Ginzberg, *A Commentary on the Palestinian Talmud*, New York, 1941.

C. G. Montefiore and H. Loewe, *A Rabbinic Anthology*, Macmillan, London, 1938.

Solomon Schechter, *Some Aspects of Rabbinic Theology*, Macmillan, 1909.

A. Cohen, *Everyman's Talmud*, London, 1932; Dutton, 1949.

J. Z. Lauterbach, *The Pharisees and Their Teachings*, Bloch, 1930; also in *Hebrew Union College Annual*, Vol. VI, 1930.

Hermann L. Strack, *Introduction to the Talmud and Midrash*, 1st edition in German, 1887; Eng. trans. of 5th edition, Jewish Pub. Soc., 1931.

Alexander Kohut, *Aruch Completum*, 8 Vols. and Suppl., Vienna, 1878–92.

Marcus Jastrow, *A Dictionary of the Targumim, the Talmud Babli and Yerushalmi, and the Midrashic Literature*, Putnam's, 1903, 2 Vols.

J. Hamburger, *Real-Encyclopädie für Bibel und Talmud*, Vol. II, Strelitz, 1883; Suppl. I, Leipzig, 1886.

Samuel Krauss, *Griechische und lateinische Lehnwörter in Talmud, Midrasch und Targum*, Berlin, 1898–99.

W. Bacher, *Die Agada der Tannaiten*, Strassburg, 1884–90; *Die Agada der Babylonischen Amoräer*, Strassburg, 1878; *Die Agada der Palästinensischen Amoräer*, Strassburg, 1892–99.

I. H. Weiss, *Dor, Dor Vedorshav*, 2nd ed., New York, 1924.

L. Zunz, *Die Gottesdienstlichen Vorträge der Juden*, 2nd ed., Frankfort-on-the-Main, 1892.

Israel Bettan, *Studies in Jewish Preaching*, Hebrew Union College Press, 1939, Chap. I.

Morris Goldstein, *Thus Religion Grows: Story of Judaism*, Longmans, 1936, Chap. II.

Meyer Waxman, *A History of Jewish Literature*, Bloch, 2nd ed., 1938, Vol. I.

George F. Moore, *Judaism in the First Centuries of the Christian Era*, 3 Vols., Harvard Univ. Press, 1927, 1930.

REPRESENTATIVE WORKS ON JESUS, GIVING THE JEWISH BACKGROUND

I. Abrahams, *Studies in Pharisaism and the Gospels*, Cambridge, 1917, 1924.

B. H. Branscombe, *Jesus and the Law of Moses*, Hodder and Stoughton, 1930.

S. J. Case, *Jesus, a New Biography*, Chicago, 1927.

D. Chwolson, *Das letzte Passamahl Christi und der Tag seines Todes*, 2nd ed., Leipzig, 1908. A Jewish convert to Christianity, Chwolson retains a scholarly attitude.

S. S. Cohon, art., "The Place of Jesus in the Religious Life of His Day," in *Journal of Biblical Literature*, Vol. XLVIII, pp. 82–108.

G. Dalman, *The Words of Jesus: Considered in the Light of Post-Biblical Jewish Writings and the Aramaic Language*, Eng. trans., 1902.

Martin Dibelius, *From Tradition to Gospel*, Eng. trans., London, 1934.

H. G. Enlow, *A Jewish View of Jesus*, Bloch, 1920.

Gerald Friedlander, *Jewish Sources of the Sermon on the Mount*, London, 1911.

H. E. Goldin, *The Case of the Nazarene Re-opened*, Exposition Press, 1948.

M. Goguel, *The Life of Jesus*, Eng. trans., Macmillan, 1945.

Charles Guignebert, *The Jewish World in the Time of Jesus*, Eng. trans., Dutton, 1939; also, *Jesus*, Eng. trans., Knopf, 1935.

Joseph Klausner, *Jesus of Nazareth*, Heb. original, Jerusalem, 1922; 2nd ed., 1927; Eng. trans., Macmillan, 1925. The main studies of Jesus by modern Christian scholars are reviewed on pp. 71–106; by Jewish scholars, on pp. 106–124.

C. C. McCown, *The Search for the Real Jesus*, Scribner's, 1940.

C. G. Montefiore, *The Old Testament and After*, Macmillan, 1923; *Rabbinic Literature and Gospel Teachings*, Macmillan, 1930; *The Synoptic Gospels*, 2nd ed., Macmillan, 1931.

Pierre Van Paassen, *Why Jesus Died*, Dial, 1949.

H. L. Strack and P. Billerbeck, *Kommentar zum Neuen Testament aus Talmud und Midrasch*, 4 Vols., Munich, 1922–28.

Solomon Zeitlin, *Who Crucified Jesus?* Harper, 1942.

The Westminster Commentaries and International Critical Commentaries on the New Testament; also, standard introductions to the New Testament.

### THE EARLY RELATIONS BETWEEN JUDAISM AND CHRISTIANITY

Bernard J. Bamberger, *Proselytism in the Talmudic Period*, Hebrew Union College Press, 1939.

J. Bergmann, *Jüdische Apologetik im neutestamentlichen Zeitalter*, Berlin, 1908.

William G. Braude, *Jewish Proselyting in the First Five Centuries of the Common Era*, Brown Univ., 1940.

M. Friedlander, *Synagoge und Kirche in ihren Anfängen*, Berlin, 1908.

Paul Goodman, *The Synagogue and the Church*, London, 1908.

Joseph Klausner, *From Jesus to Paul*, Heb. original, Jerusalem, 1939; Eng. trans., Macmillan, 1943.

K. Kohler, *The Origins of the Synagogue and the Church*, New York, 1929.

J. Z. Lauterbach, art. "The Attitude of the Jew Towards the Non-Jew" in *Yearbook of Central Conference of American Rabbis*, Vol. XXXI (1921), pp. 186–222.

A. Marmorstein, art. "The Background of the Haggadah," in *Hebrew Union College Annual*, Vol. VI (1929), pp. 141–205; also, "Judaism and Christianity in the Middle of the Third Century," *ibid.*, Vol. X (1935) pp. 223–263.

C. G. Montefiore, *Judaism and Saint Paul*, Goschen, 1914.

W. O. E. Oesterley and H. Loewe, *Judaism and Christianity*, 3 Vols., Macmillan, 1937.

James Parkes, *The Conflict of the Church and the Synagogue*, Soncino Press, London, 1934; also *Judaism and Christianity*, Univ. Chicago Press, 1948.

H. J. Schoeps, *Jüdisch-Christliches Religionsgespräch in 19 Jahrhunderten*, Berlin, 1937.

WRITINGS OF THE CHURCH FATHERS

*The Apocryphal New Testament*, ed. M. R. James, Oxford, 1924.

*Didascalia Apostolorum*, in "Horae Semiticae," No. 2; Eng. trans., London, 1903.

*Patrologia Graeca*, ed. by J. P. Migne and others, 176 Vols., Paris, 1857–99.

*Patrologia Orientalis*, ed. by René Graffin, 25 Vols., Paris, 1907–43.

*Patrologia Latina*, ed. by J. P. Migne and others, 221 Vols., Paris, 1844–1902.

*The Apostolic Fathers*, ed. J. B. Lightfoot and J. R. Harmer, Macmillan, 1891.

*The Ante-Nicene Fathers*, T. & T. Clark, Edinburgh, n.d., 20 Vols.

*The Ante-Nicene Fathers* (to 325), ed. Roberts and Donaldson, Buffalo, 1886–87.

*Nicene and Post-Nicene Fathers*, ed. P. Schaff, New York, 1886–90.

*Nicene and Post-Nicene Fathers: Second Series*, ed. Schaff and Wace, Scribner's, 1890.

*The Fathers of the Church*, ed. by Ludwig Schopp, 1st of proposed 72 Vols., Cima Publ. Co., 1946.

M. Friedlander, *Patristische und talmudische Studien*, Vienna, 1878.

L. Ginzberg, *Die Haggada bei den Kirchenvatern*; Part I, Amsterdam, 1899; II, Berlin, 1900; III, Warsaw (Poznansky Memorial), 1927; IV, New York, 1929; V, Vienna (Chajes Memorial), 1933.

Amos B. Hulen, art. "The 'Dialogues with the Jews' as Sources for the Early Jewish Argument Against Christianity," in *Journal of Biblical Literature*, 1932, pp. 58–71.

S. Krauss, "The Jews in the Works of the Church Fathers," in *Jewish Quarterly Review*, old series, Vol. V (1893), pp. 122–157; Vol. VI (1894), pp. 82–99; 225–261.

George F. Moore, art. "Christian Writers on Judaism," in *Harvard Theological Review*, 1921, pp. 197–254.

Bishop Murawski, *Die Juden bei den Kirchenvätern und Skolastikern*, Berlin, 1925.

A. L. Williams, *Adversus Judaeos: A Bird's-Eye View of Christian Apologiae until the Renaissance*, Cambridge, 1935. Comprehensive account of Christian Anti-Jewish polemics.

HISTORICAL BACKGROUND OF THE PERIOD

Heinrich Graetz, *Geschichte der Juden von den ältesten Zeiten bis auf die Gegenwart* (1848), Leipzig, 11 Vols.; last ed., 1900–09; Hebrew trans. by S. P. Rabinowitz contains added material on Russia and Poland, and corrections and notes by A. Harkavy; Eng. trans., Jewish Pub. Soc., 5 Vols. and 1 Vol. Index, 1891–95, continues history to 1870, but lacks the footnotes and notes of the original later ed. and corrections of Harkavy.

One-volume histories of the Jewish people by Margolis and Marx, Jewish Pub. Soc., 1927; by A. L. Sachar, Knopf, 1948 ed.; by S. Grayzel, Jewish Pub. Soc., 1947.

H. St. J. Thackeray, English trans. of *Works of Flavius Josephus*, Putnam's, 1926–43; W. W. Whiston, Eng. trans., E. P. Dutton & Co., Inc., N. Y., Kegan Paul and Routledge, London, 1906, used here.

Joseph Derenbourg, *Essai sur l'histoire et la géographie de la Palestine d'après le Talmud et les autres sources rabbiniques*, France, 1867.

M. S. Enslin, *Christian Beginnings*, Harper, 1938.

L. Finkelstein, *The Pharisees: The Sociological Background of Their Faith*, Jewish Pub. Soc., 1938.

Foakes Jackson and K. Lake, *The Beginnings of Christianity*, New York, 1920–33.

M. Friedlander, *Die religiösen Bewegungen innerhalb des Judenthums im Zeitalter Jesu*, Berlin, 1905.

S. Funk, *Die Juden in Babylon 200–500*, Berlin, 1902, 1908.

M. Joel, *Blicke in die Religionsgeschichte zu Anfang des zweiten christlichen Jahrhunderts*, Berlin, 1880–83.

J. Juster, *Les Juifs dans l'Empire Romain*, Paris, 1914.

Joseph Klausner, *Historiah Yisraelith*, Jerusalem, Vols. II–IV, 1924–25.

E. Meyer, *Ursprung und Anfang des Christentums*, 3 Vols., Stuttgart, 1921–23.

Robert H. Pfeiffer, *History of New Testament Times*, Harper, 1949.

Emil Schürer, *The History of the Jewish People in the Time of Jesus Christ*, 5th German ed., 1920; Eng. trans., 5 Vols., Edinburgh, 1901.

Abba H. Silver, *A History of Messianic Speculation in Israel*, Macmillan, 1927.

## II. THE POST-TALMUDIC PERIOD

Encyclopedias as in Section I.

The works named in Section I which continue the account of Jewish history and also of the relationship between the Church and the

Synagogue into the centuries subsequent to 500 c.e. belong to the literature of this Post-Talmudic period as well.

For this later period there should be added the following:

G. F. Abbott, *Israel in Europe*, Macmillan, 1907.

F. Baer, *Die Juden in christlichen Spanien*, 2 Vols., Berlin, 1929–36.

A. Berliner, *Censur und Confiskation hebräischer Bücher im Kirchenstaate*, Frankfort-on-Main, 1891.

Joseph S. Bloch, *Israel and the Nations*, Berlin, 1922; Eng. trans., Berlin-Vienna, 1927.

Solomon Grayzel, *The Church and the Jews in the XIIIth Century*, Dropsie College, Philadelphia, 1933.

H. Graetz, art. giving history of attacks on the Talmud, from Donin to the time of the Frankists, in *Monatsschrift für Geschichte und Wissenschaft des Judenthums*, 1885, pp. 529–541.

A. M. Hyamson, *A History of the Jews in England*, Macmillan, 1907.

S. Katz, *The Jews in the Visigothic and Frankish Kingdoms of Spain and Gaul*, Cambridge, Mass., 1937.

D. Kaufman, art. "Informers of the Middle Ages," in *Jewish Quarterly Review*, old series, Vol. XIII (1896), pp. 217–238.

Guido Kisch, *The Jews in Medieval Germany*, Univ. of Chicago Press, 1949.

S. Krauss, *Studien zur Byzantinisch-Jüdischen Geschichte*, Vienna, 1914.

Ferdinand Lot, *Le Fin du Monde Antique et les Débuts du Moyen Age*, Paris, 1927.

Jacob R. Marcus, *The Jew in the Medieval World: A Source Book, 315–1791*, Sinai Press, 1938.

Louis I. Newman, *Jewish Influences on Christian Reform Movements*, Columbia Univ. Press, 1925.

James Parkes, *The Jew in the Medieval Community*, London, 1938.

Ulisse Robert, arts. on confiscation of Jewish mss. in France in middle of 13th century, in *Revue des Etudes Juives*, Vol. 3, pp. 214, 216, 223.

W. Popper, *Censorship of Hebrew Books*, New York, 1899; also art. "Censorship of Hebrew Books" in *Jewish Encyclopedia*, Vol. III, pp. 642–652.

Cecil Roth, *The History of the Jews of Italy*, Jewish Pub. Soc., 1946; also, *A History of the Jews in England*, Oxford, 1941.

## A. ON THE TOLEDOTH YESHU

*Toledoth Yeshu*,[36] appearing also under the title *Maase Talui*,[37] of various dates and places of publication, or with no identification on the title page.

E. N. Adler, art. "Un fragment araméen du Toldot Yéschou," in *Revue des Etudes Juives*, Vol. 61 (1910), pp. 126–130.

Richard von der Alm, *Die Urtheile heidnischer und jüdischer Schriftsteller der vier ersten christlichen Jahrhunderte über Jesus und die ersten Christen*, Leipzig, 1864. Comments on its origin and nature.

Gershom Bader, *Helkath Mehokek*,[38] Cracow, 1891. Combines Hebrew version with Christian accounts.

S. Baring-Gould, *The Lost and Hostile Gospels*, England, 1874.

E. Bischoff, *Ein jüdisch-deutsches Leben Jesu*, Leipzig, 1895. Yiddish translation, using German print.

R. Dunkerley, *The Unwritten Gospel*, London, 1925.

Robert Eisler, *The Messiah Jesus and John the Baptist*, Paris, 1930; Eng. trans. by A. H. Krappe, London, 1931.

L. Ginzberg, prints a Genizah version of the Toledoth Yeshu in *Ginze Schechter*, Jewish Theological Seminary, 1928, Vol. I, pp. 324–338.

J. Guttmann article on Jesus in *Encyclopedia Judaica*, Berlin, 1932, Vol. IX, pp. 77–79.

R. Travers Herford, in J. Hastings' *Dictionary of Christ and the Gospels*, Edinburgh, 1908, Vol. 2, pp. 876–882.

Joseph Klausner, *Jesus of Nazareth* (Eng. trans.), Macmillan, 1925, pp. 47–54. Bibliography, synopsis, and discussion.

S. Krauss, *Das Leben Jesu nach jüdischen Quellen*, Berlin, 1902, presents 3 Hebrew versions from mss. and adds fragments of still other versions. Most comprehensive discussion.

S. Krauss, art. "Une nouvelle recension hébraique du Toldot Yêsû," in *Revue des Etudes Juives*, Vol. 3, new series (1938), pp. 65–88; two other text fragments edited in *R.E.J.*, old series, Vol. 62 (1911), pp. 28 ff.; pp. 240–247. He discussed these findings in *Monatsschrift für Geschichte und Wissenschaft des Judenthums*, Vol. LXXVI (1932), pp. 586 ff.; Vol. LXXVII (1933), pp. 44 ff.

S. Krauss, art. "Jesus in History and Legend," in *The New Era*, Vol. VI (1904–5), pp. 19–27, 153–162; "Jesus in Jewish Legend" in *Jewish Encyclopedia*, New York, 1907, Vol. VII, pp. 170–173.

Raymund Martini, *Pugio Fidei*, publ. Paris, 1651 f. This Spanish

Dominican translated the *Toledoth Yeshu* into Latin in the 13th century.

E. B. Nicholson, *The Gospel According to the Hebrews*, London, 1879.

Alfred Resch, *Toledot Yeshu Hamoshiach*, translated from Greek into Hebrew, Leipzig, 1898.

Hugh J. Schonfield, *According to the Hebrews*, London, 1937. English translation, textual critique, and interpretation.

J. C. Wagenseil, *Tela ignea Satanae*, Altdorf, 1681; gives a Hebrew version, translates into Latin, refutes, and surveys the earlier literature on it.

## B. DISPUTATIONS AND POLEMICS OF THE MIDDLE AGES

The Original Sources are given in the text and notes.

The fullest compilation in Hebrew of Jewish Polemics and Disputations is in the *Otzar Vikkuhim*, by J. D. Eisenstein, New York, 1928.

A listing of the main sources in the field of Jewish Polemics is given in *Otzar Vikkuhim*, pp. 23–28; also in the *Jewish Encyclopedia*, Vol. X, p. 109; original sources for polemics in Spain, indicated in *The Jews in Spain*, by A. Neuman, Jewish Publ. Soc., 1942, Vol. II, pp. 353–370.

Literature Supplementary to the references in Section I on the relations between Judaism and Christianity, extending beyond 500 C.E.:

I. Broydé, art. "Polemics and Polemical Literature" in *Jewish Encyclopedia*, Vol. X, pp. 102–109.

J. D. Eisenstein, *Otzar Vikkuhim*, New York, 1928; The Introduction gives in outline the history of the Jewish polemics, pp. 6–22.

M. Friedlander, *Geschichte der jüdischen Apologetik*, Zurich, 1903.

Robert Gordis, *The Jew Faces a New World*, Behrman, 1941.

I. Graeber, *Jews in a Gentile World*, Macmillan, 1942.

A. Jellinek, art. "Zur Geschichte der Polemik gegen das Christentum," in *Orient* X (1847).

M. Lifschitz-Golden, *Les Juifs dans la Littérature Française du Moyen Age*, Columbia Univ., 1935.

Isadore Loeb, *La Controverse religieuse entre les Chretiens et Juifs en Moyen Age*, Paris, 1888; arts., "La Controverse sur le Talmud," in *Revue des Etudes Juives*, Vol. 1–3; "La Controverse de 1263 a Barcelona," Vol. 15; "Polemistes Chretiens et Juifs en France et Espagne," Vol. 18.

C. H. Moehlman, *The Christian-Jewish Tragedy*, Rochester, 1933.

H. Pflaum, *Die religiöse Disputation in der Europäischen Dichtung des Mittelalters*, Geneva, 1935.

J. Trachtenberg, *The Devil and the Jews; The Medieval Conception of the Jew and Its Relation to Modern Antisemitism*, Yale, 1943.

M. Waxman, *A History of Jewish Literature*, Bloch, 1933; Vol. II, Chap. X, on Polemics and Apologetics.

T. Weiss-Rosmarin, *Judaism and Christianity: The Differences*, Jewish Book Club, N. Y., 1943.

I. Ziegler, *Religiöse Disputationen im Mittelalter*, Frankfort-on-Main, 1924.

## C. REFERENCES IN KARAISM

W. Bacher, art. on "Inedited Chapters of Jehudah Hadassi's 'Eshkol Hakkofer,'" in *Jewish Quarterly Review*, old series, Vol. VIII (1896), pp. 431–444; also art. on Kirkisani in Vol. VII (1895), pp. 687–710.

Jacob Mann, *Texts and Studies*, Cincinnati, 1931, Vol. II.

Moses Mocatta, *Isaac ben Abraham Troki's "The Faith Strengthened,"* Eng. trans., England, 1851.

Leon Nemoy, art. "Al-Qirqisānī's Account of the Jewish Sects and Christianity," in *Hebrew Union College Annual*, Vol. VII (1930), pp. 317–397.

M. Waxman, *A History of Jewish Literature*, Bloch, 1938, Vol. I, Chap. XIII.

## D. THE RECORD IN JEWISH PHILOSOPHY

The original sources are given in the text and notes.

Julius Guttmann, *Die Philosophie des Judentum*, Munich, 1935.

I. Husik, *A History of Mediaeval Jewish Philosophy*, 2nd ed., Macmillan, 1930.

D. Neumark, *Geschichte der jüdischen Philosophie des Mittelalters*, Vols. I, II, Berlin, 1907, 1910; in Hebew, Vol. I, 1921; Vol. II, 1929.

M. Steinschneider, *Jewish Literature*, German ed., Frankfort, 1905; Hebrew trans., Warsaw, 1923, Chap. XII.

M. Waxman, *A History of Jewish Literature*, Bloch, 1933; Vol. II, Chap. V.

*Special Works on Individual Philosophers*

W. Bacher, art. in *Jewish Quarterly Review*, old series, Vol. VII (1895), pp. 687–710.

Jacob Mann, art. "An Early Theologico-Polemical Work," in *Hebrew Union College Annual*, Vols. XII–XIII (1937–38), pp. 411–459.

A. Marmorstein, art. on David al-Mukammas in *Monatsschrift für Geschichte und Wissenschaft des Judenthums*, 1922, pp. 48 f.

S. S. Cohon, "Saadia Gaon," *Journal of Jewish Bibliography*, Vol. III, No. 4, 1942.

J. Guttmann, *Religionsphilosophie des Saadia*, Göttingen, 1882.

H. Malter, *Life and Works of Saadia Gaon*, Jewish Publ. Soc., 1921.

Samuel Rosenblatt, *Saadia Gaon: The Book of Beliefs and Opinions*, Eng. trans., Yale Univ. Press, 1948.

Moise Ventura, *La Philosophie de Saadia Gaon*, Paris, 1934.

J. Guttmann, *Die Philosophie des Solomon ibn Gabirol*, Göttingen, 1889.

I. Zangwill, *Selected Religious Poems of Solomon ibn Gabirol*, Jewish Pub. Soc., 1923.

M. Hyamson, *Duties of the Heart* (*Hoboth Halebaboth*) *by Bahya Ibn Pakuda*, Eng. trans., Bloch, 1949.

Nina Salomon, *Selected Poems of Jehudah Halevi*, Jewish Pub. Soc., 1924.

S. S. Cohon, art. "Jehuda Halevi" in *American Jewish Year Book*, Vol. 43 (1941–42), pp. 447–488.

Isaak Heinemann, *Jehuda Halevi*, Oxford, 1947.

Hartwig Hirschfeld, *Kitab Al Khazari*, Eng. trans., London, 1931.

J. Guttmann, *Die Religionsphilosophie des Abraham ibn David aus Toledo*, Göttingen, 1879.

A. Cohen, *The Teachings of Maimonides*, Routledge and Kegan Paul, Ltd., London, 1927.

I. Epstein, *Moses Maimonides*, London, 1935.

M. Friedlander, *The Guide for the Perplexed*, Eng. trans., London, 1904.

A. Hershman, *Code of Maimonides; Book Fourteen, Book of Judges*, Eng. trans., Yale Univ. Press, 1949.

D. Yellin and I. Abrahams, *Maimonides*, Jewish Pub. Soc., 1903.

S. Zeitlin, *Maimonides*, Bloch, 1935.

N. Adlerblum, *A Study of Gersonides*, Columbia Univ. Press, 1926.

D. Neumark, art. "Crescas and Spinoza," in *Central Conf. of American Rabbis Year Book*, Vol. 18 (1908), pp. 277–319.
M. Waxman, *The Philosophy of Don Hasdai Crescas*, Columbia Univ. Press, 1920.
H. A. Wolfson, art. "Crescas on the Problem of Divine Attributes," in *Jewish Quarterly Review*, new series, Vol. VII, pp. 1–44, 175–221.
I. Husik, *Sefer Ha-'Ikkarim by Joseph Albo*, Hebrew and English, 5 Vols., Jewish Pub. Soc., 1929–30.

R. H. Elwes, *Philosophy of Benedict de Spinoza*, trans., Tudor, 1936.
M. Waxman, art. on "Baruch Spinoza's Relation to Jewish Philosophic Thought and to Judaism," *Jewish Quarterly Review*, new series, Vol. XXIX.
H. A. Wolfson, *The Philosophy of Spinoza*, 2 Vols., Harvard U. Press, 1934.

## E. JESUS IN RELATION TO THE TOTALITY OF JEWISH LIFE

The Traditional Prayer Book for Weekdays, Sabbath, Holy Days, Festivals and Private Devotions.
*The Shulhan Aruch*, arranged by Joseph Caro, first ed. with Moses Isserles additions, 1578.
I. Abrahams, *Historical and Explanatory Notes to the Authorized Daily Prayer Book*, London, Revised ed., 1922.
I. Abrahams, *Jewish Life in the Middle Ages*, Jewish Pub. Soc., 1896; 2nd ed., London, 1932.
Leo Baeck, *The Essence of Judaism*, Schocken, 1948.
Israel Bettan, *Studies in Jewish Preaching*, Hebrew Union College Press, 1939.
E. R. Bevan and C. Singer, *The Legacy of Israel*, Oxford, 1927.
S. S. Cohon, *Judaism, A Way of Life*, Union of American Hebrew Congregations, 1948.
Lewis N. Dembitz, *Services in Synagogue and Home*, Jewish Pub. Soc., 1898.
I. Elbogen, *Der jüdische Gottesdienst in seiner geschichtlichen Entwicklung*, Leipzig, 2nd ed., 1931.

L. Finkelstein, ed., *The Jews: Their History, Culture and Religion*, 2 Vols., Harper, 1950.

Solomon B. Freehof, *The Small Sanctuary: Judaism in the Prayerbook*, Union of American Hebrew Congs., 1942.

M. Friedlander, *The Jewish Religion*, London, 2nd ed., 1900.

Morris Goldstein, *Thus Religion Grows: Story of Judaism*, Longmans, 1936.

Ernest Jacob, arts. "Judaism and Christianity in the Middle Ages," "Agreements and Differences," in *Universal Jewish Encyclopedia*, Vol. 3, pp. 184–186.

Morris Joseph, *Judaism as Creed and Life*, Bloch, 4th ed., 1920.

K. Kohler, *Jewish Theology, Systematically and Historically Considered*, Macmillan, 1918.

Isaac Landman, art. "Christians, Judaism's Attitude Toward," in *Universal Jewish Encyclopedia*, Vol. 3, pp. 187–191.

Jacob Mann, art. "Changes in The Divine Service of the Synagogue Due to Religious Persecutions," in *Hebrew Union College Annual*, Vol. IV, 1927, pp. 241–310.

S. Schechter, *Studies in Judaism*, Jewish Pub. Soc., 3 Vols., 1896, 1908, 1924.

Milton Steinberg, *Basic Judaism*, Harcourt Brace, 1947.

L. Zunz, *Die Gottesdienstlichen Vorträge der Juden*, 2nd ed., 1892.

# NOTES

## CHAPTER I
### Pages 1–15

Works cited in the Literature Analysis are named here
in abbreviated form

1. This is discussed in detail in Chapter IV.
2. Strack, *Introduction*, p. 79. Printings free of censorship are: Bomberg, 1520–23; 1531; Justinian, 1548. First censored printing: Basle, 1578–80. First partial restoration of censored matter: Amsterdam, 1644–48.
3. *Ibid.*, p. 279, n. 27. It should be added that the authenticity of this document has been debated.
4. *Ibid.*, p. 86. Also, Strack names Gershom of Soncino as the first Jewish printer to practise voluntary censorship. For further information on censorship, see articles on this subject in the *Jewish Encyclopedia* and *Universal Jewish Encyclopedia*, and the literature there cited.
5. Strack, *Introduction*, p. 203.
6. Given in detail in Literature Analysis.
7. See p. 247.
8. See p. 254.
9. But not of the *Minim*, which is a separate subject, as will be seen in Chap. II, Sec A, #4.
10. *Jewish Quarterly Review*, old series, Vol. XVII, p. 171.
11. P. 407.
12. Pp. 9–11.
13. *Pharisaism: Its Aim and Its Method*, 1912; *The Pharisees*, 1924.
14. *Judaism in the First Centuries of the Christian Era.*
15. *Conflict*, pp. 148–150, 194.
16. *Journal of Biblical Literature*, Vol. LI (1932), pp. 58–71.
17. *Ibid.*, p. 63.
18. *Ibid.*, p. 64.
19. *Ibid.*, p. 64.
20. "Christian Writers on Judaism," in the *Harvard Theological Review*, Vol. XIV (1921), p. 200.
21. *Dialogue Between a Christian and a Jew*, Marburg, 1899, pp. 3–4.
22. Parkes, *op. cit.*, pp. 61, 80–81, 109–115.

23. *Einleitung in die drei ersten Evangelien*, Berlin, 1905, p. 113.

24. *From Jesus to Paul*, p. 3; *Jesus of Nazareth*, p. 363.

25. Fully discussed in Chapter IV.

26. W. Bacher merely wrote a review on Herford's book; J. Klausner summed up his conclusions as an introductory portion of *Jesus of Nazareth*, without giving the texts, the detailed discussions or the material of the Amoraim; S. Zeitlin and Louis Ginzberg have made pointed comments and corrections, but in scattered form; S. Krauss was concerned primarily with the Toledoth Yeshu. See Literature Analysis for fuller discussion.

27. Their respective works are described in Literature Analysis.

28. Published by Macmillan in 2 Vols., 1910, 1919.

29. See the expounding of this thought in C. G. Montefiore and H. Loewe, *A Rabbinic Anthology*, pp. xii–xiii.

30. Dates, 1808–1874. *Das Leben Jesu* (written 1835–36).

31. Dates, 1809–1882. *Christus und die Cäsaren* (1877).

32. Dates, 1856–1933. Includes Talmudic references.

33. Dates, 1850–1934. *The Pre-Christian Jesus* (1906).

34. Dates, 1865–1935. Includes Talmudic references. *Die Christusmythe* (1909).

35. Published 1923; *Le Mystère de Jésus*.

36. Published 1926; *Jesus: A Myth*.

37. Karlsruhe—translated into English by Joseph McCabe, London, 1912, p. 1.

38. b.c.e. signifies Before the Christian Era; c.e. is Christian Era.

39. In *De Providentia*, 2, 64, Philo tells of his pilgrimage to the Temple in Jerusalem.

40. It should be noted that some part of the Josephus items regarding Jesus is regarded by many as genuine; see Chap. II, Summary.

41. VIII, 3.

42. "The Halaka in the Gospels and its Relation to the Jewish Law at the Time of Jesus"—*Hebrew Union College Annual*, Vol. I, pp. 372–373.

43. *The Search for the Real Jesus*, p. 206.

44. In 1903 Herford (*ibid.*, p. viii) expressed his hope that the material he had assembled would supply Christian scholarship with the desired knowledge of what rabbinical literature contained regarding the origins of Christianity.

45. For example, Ben Stada and Balaam identifications with Jesus: see Section B in Chapter II.

46. For example, B. Sanhedrin 43a; Gittin 56b–57a; B. Sanhedrin 106a; B. Yoma 66b.

47. Vol. 6, pp. 87–88.

48. The Lindsey Press, London, 1928, p. 201.

49. B. Sanhedrin 43a: see Chap. III, Section A, #1.

50. P. vii. Reprinted with permission of copyright owners, The Jewish Publication Society of America.

51. *Kommentar zum Neuen Testament aus Talmud und Midrasch.*

52. C. G. Montefiore, *Some Elements of the Religious Teaching of Jesus*, London, 1910; *Rabbinic Literature and Gospel Teaching*, London, 1930.

53. W. O. E. Oesterley and H. Loewe, *Judaism and Christianity.*

54. P. 106, n. 27.

55. As is shown in Chapter IV and the Literature Analysis, there is additional material now available.

56. "We shall make no use of the statements of the Amoraim," p. 20.

57. There are, of course, separate studies such as the research into the Toledoth Yeshu by Samuel Krauss and the compilation of disputations and polemics by J. D. Eisenstein.

## CHAPTER II
### Pages 17–104

1. Herford, *op. cit.*, p. 18; also, Strack, *Introduction*, p. 9.

2. Assuming that everything regarding Jesus is not entirely mythical.

3. Variant dates: Goguel, *Jesus*, p. 232, places birth some time before death of Herod in 4 B.C.E., as indicated by Matthew, and, on p. 228, places death at 28 C.E.

4. Strack, *Introduction*, p. 65; the Palestinian Talmud was not really "completed."

5. B. B. Metz. 86a. סוף הוראה.

6. Strack, *Introduction*, p. 71.

7. *Ibid.*, p. 118.

8. A Baraitha passage is identified by one of these introductory words, meaning "it is taught" or "the rabbis teach": תנו רבנן, תני, תניא, והתניא, כדתניא, תני פלוני. Many Baraithoth of the Palestinian Talmud have no introductory expression wherewith to identify them. A full listing of external identifying expressions of Baraithoth is given by M. Higger, in *Proceedings of American Academy for Jewish Re-*

*search*, Vol. IX (1939), pp. 51–55. Higger has assembled the Baraithoth in his *Ozar Habaraitot*, 5 Vols., New York, 1938–1942.

9. Meaning "addition" or "supplement."

10. For a discussion of the complicated problem of the Tosefta composition and date see Strack, *Introduction*, pp. 75–76 and the notes pertaining thereto.

11. Analysis of the Midrashim is in Part II of Strack's *Introduction*. These three contain the sayings of the Tannaim, although ultimate compilation was by the Amoraim.

12. Used by Laible and Herford.

13. *Ibid.*, p. 29.

## CHAPTER II    SECTION A    #1

1. As is demonstrated in Section B of this chapter.

2. והתניא means more than "and it has been taught"; it is a cue-word, designating a Baraitha tradition.

3. F adds: and on the eve of the Sabbath.

4. ישו is an abbreviation for ישוע or יהושע. Mu adds: the Nazarene.

5. Mu adds: Yeshu the Nazarene.

6. The Hebrew כשף implies: to whisper charms; see Jastrow, *Dictionary*, Vol. I, p. 676; Levy, *Dictionary*, Vol. II, p. 459.

7. Herford's "deceived" is not altogether accurate. The Hebrew היסית, gives the sense of "stirring up"; see Jastrow, *Dictionary*, Vol. I, p. 583. "Entice," meaning to "attract" or "allure," seems the most exact translation.

8. *E.g.*, M. Friedlander, in *Die religiösen Bewegungen* insists that there is nothing genuine in the Talmud, of early date, regarding Jesus.

9. His approximate dates are 37 or 38 to 100 C.E.

10. *Antiquities*, XX.X.1.

11. *Op. cit.*, XV.IX.3,1,4.

12. *War*, II.XX.4.

13. *Op. cit.*, VI.VIII.3.

14. *Life* of Josephus, 22.

15. Millar Burrows, *What Mean These Stones?* American Schools of Oriental Research, New Haven, 1941, ¶¶9, 65, 193, tells how much temporary excitement was created by discovery of an ossuary with the name "Jesus son of Joseph." But the excitement faded when it was realized that these names were as common as William or Henry in the America of today; that in archeology there is no direct, but only general confirmation, on the historicity of Jesus. In this connec-

tion it is interesting to learn (Jack Finegan, *Light from the Ancient Past*, Princeton U. Press, 1946, pp. 371, 408) that the oldest picture of Jesus of Nazareth is dated at the middle of the second century, found in the Catacomb of Priscilla at Rome; the second oldest, from the first part of the third century, was found in the Church at Dura-Europos in the Syrian desert.

16. Matthew 26:64; Mark 14:62; similarly, Luke 22:69.

17. John 19:7. In the above quotation from Mark, Jesus replies affirmatively to the question, "Art thou the Christ, the Son of the Blessed?"

18. Matthew 27:37; Mark 15:26; Luke 23:37–38; John 19:19.

19. See Chap. II, Sec. A, #2, #3, #4.

20. יהושע. Krauss, *op. cit.*, p. 250, mentions the suggestion of Elias Levita that since the ישוע spelling of the word means "savior," the last letter was left off, to remove the possibility of such a thought being associated with Jesus. Our answer: then why was not the יהושע spelling retained?

21. יוסי from יוסף, see Jastrow, *Dictionary*, Vol. I, p. 570. Another illustration is אשתמוע (Josh. 21:14) becoming אשתמה (Josh. 15:50).

22. This is in disagreement with Strack, *Jesus, etc.*, p. 18, n. 2; however, he is correct in the view that the three letters of the name do *not* constitute an abbreviation made up of the initial letters of the words ימח שמו וזכרו ("may his name and memory be erased"), although this manipulation of words may have suggested itself in later times when Christians persecuted Jews.

23. Based on the Greek of Matthew 2:23, John 19:19 for Nazareth— Ναζωραῖος—which Lauterbach (*op. cit.*) indicates, would be a *nomen agentis*, not a person of a city, Nazareth. See also M. Lidzbarski, *Mindäische Liturgien*, Berlin, 1920, pp. XVI ff.; also *Ginza, Der Schatz oder das grosse Buch der Mindäer*, Göttingen, 1925, p. IX. Goguel, *Jesus*, pp. 66, n. 1, 193–198, quotes use of *netzer* to refer to protecting deity created by Jewish Gnostics.

24. See Herford, *op. cit.*, p. 52, n. 2.

25. Mark 15:42; Luke 23:54; John 19:31, 42.

26. John 19:14.

27. Matthew, Chaps. 25–26; Mark, Chaps. 14–15; Luke, Chaps. 22–23.

28. D. Chwolson, *Das letzte Passamahl, etc.* He explains that there were those who believed (contrary to the view of Hillel which in time was the accepted one) that Pesah does not take precedence over Sabbath requirements; therefore, when Passover Eve came on Sabbath Eve, there were those who sacrificed the Paschal lamb on the evening

preceding, in order not to take a chance of violating the Sabbath at twilight of Sabbath Eve. בין הערבים was regarded as בין השמשות.

29. Laible, *op. cit.*, pp. 81–83; Klausner, *op. cit.*, p. 28, 326; Zeitlin, *Chajes Memorial Volume*, p. 302; also, *Who Crucified Jesus?* p. 161, and note 20.

30. Mark 15:61; Matthew 26:63; Luke 22:67, 70.

31. Mark 15:62; Matthew 26:64; Luke 22:69.

32. M. Sanhedrin VII,5.

33. H. Danby, art., "The Bearing of the Rabbinical Criminal Code on the Jewish Trial Narratives in the Gospels," in *Journal of Theological Studies*, Vol. XXI (1919), pp. 51–76; also, *Tractate Sanhedrin, Mishnah and Tosefta*, London, 1919, pp. ix–xii. See also Klausner, *op. cit.*, p. 343.

34. Klausner, *op. cit.*, p. 334.

35. J. Z. Lauterbach, art., "The Pharisees and Their Teachings" in *Hebrew Union College Annual*, Vol. VI (1930), p. 74, n. 7; also Klausner, *op. cit.*, pp. 343–344.

36. Herford, *Judaism in the New Testament Period*, p. 211.

37. See art., "Pseudo-Messiahs," in *Jewish Encyclopedia*.

38. Margolis and Marx, *History*, pp. 213–215; Graetz, *History*, Vol. 2, pp. 409 ff.

39. S. Zeitlin, *Who Crucified Jesus?* p. 168.

40. Ps. 110:1.

41. Mark 15:2; Matthew 27:11; Luke 23:3; John 18:33, 37.

42. Mark 15:26; Matthew 27:37; Luke 23:38; John 19:19.

43. See Klausner, *Jesus of Nazareth*, pp. 339–355; and H. G. Enelow, *A Jewish View of Jesus*; Emil G. Hirsch, *The Crucifixion*, 1921; C. Guignebert, *Jesus*, Part III, Chaps. III, IV; S. Zeitlin, *Who Crucified Jesus?* Chap. X; Pierre Van Paassen, *Why Jesus Died*, 1949.

44. Mark 3:22; Matthew 9:34; 12:24.

45. *Dialogue with Trypho*, C. 69.

46. L. Blau, *Das altjüdische Zauberwesen*, Budapest, 1898.

47. B. Sanhedrin 17a; B. Menahoth 65a.

48. Verses 1–6.

49. A phrase signifying that this viewpoint is the law.

50. M. Sanhedrin VI,4. כל הנסקלין נתלין דברי רבי אליעזר והחכמים אומרים אינו נתלה אלא המגדף והעובד עבודה זרה. Bacher (in *JQR* review of Herford) corrects the last two words, as here indicated, instead of the later reading כוכבים ומזלות (worship of "stars and constellations").

51. Matthew 5:17.

52. See fuller discussion of "Jewishness of Jesus," in Klausner, *op. cit.*, pp. 363–368.

53. Matthew 24:11.

54. Matthew 24:24; similarly, I Timothy 4:1.

55. *Antiquities*, XX.VIII.6.

56. *War*, II.XIII.4; there is also a reference to the deluder, Theudas, *Antiquities*, XX.V.1 (Acts 5:36).

57. *I.e.*, ‏והדיח את ישראל‎.

58. Matthew 27:63; John 7:12, 47; speaks of a "deluder."

59. M. Sanhedrin VII,10 differentiates as follows: "The *massith* speaks in a loud voice, the *maddiah* in a low voice." In B. Sanhedrin 43a both terms are used.

60. See also Chwolson, *op. cit.*, p. 88, n. 1.

61. M. Sanhedrin VI,4.

62. Goguel, *The Life of Jesus*, p. 72, presents another opinion as to why one part of this passage mentions stoning; another part, hanging. Lauterbach, *op. cit.*, states that this Baraitha could not refer to crucifixion but rather exposing the body in hanging after death (as explained in Sifre to Dt. 21:22) and that the Baraitha follows the tradition expressed by R. Eliezer that all who are stoned are hanged; thus, it would not be necessary to prove Jesus a blasphemer, for this would be his punishment as an enticer too. There is merit in this view. In any event, had the Jews executed Jesus, the Gospels certainly would have recorded the fact, and would not have placed the onus upon Rome. We must conclude that the confused author of the Baraitha was reconstructing what might have happened from the standpoint of Jewish law. He must have had a theological objective in mind, even as the New Testament is conditioned by theological objective.

63. Pp. 147–148.

64. This Baraitha is introduced as contradictory to that preceding it, which tells of the herald walking before the convicted person and making proclamation only at the time of punishment.

65. Herford, *op. cit.*, p. 88, thinks the part about the forty days is fictitious, suggested possibly by the forty days' interval between the crucifixion and the ascension, taken from the Gospels, or Dalman's suggestion of Jesus' forty days fast in the wilderness, or Laible's thought of forty days fasting ending with Easter. Schonfield, *op. cit.*, p. 158, believes this detail is introduced to contradict the mention in *Acts of Pilate*, 2 to 9, that a number of Jews did come forward to

Pilate, in defense of Jesus. Lauterbach, *op. cit.*, holds that the author of the Baraitha regarded Jesus as a "rebellious teacher" (M. Sanhedrin XI,4), in which case there would be a delay of forty days between the sentence and the punishment at Pesah time, but that the author of the Baraitha is confused since Jesus was not a rebellious teacher, and there is no instance of a herald making vocal proclamation for forty days other than for such a case. See also N. Brüll, *Jahrbücher*, VII, p. 96; disapproves view of Joel, *op. cit.*, p. 58.

66. Matthew 26:65; 27:23; Mark 15:1; 13–14; Luke 22:71; 23:15–23.

## CHAPTER II    SECTION A    #2

1. A separate Baraitha; not part of the preceding one as Herford states, *op. cit.*, p. 91.

2. See Chap. III, Sec. A, #1. Strack, *Jesus etc.*, errs in giving the entire passage, including the Baraitha opening, in the Amoraic section.

3. Enumerated in Matthew 10:2–4; Mark 3:16–19; Luke 6:14–16; Acts 1:13.

4. Luke 1:10.

5. As in Genesis, Chap. 10.

6. *Op. cit.*, pp. 29, 283–4.

7. Mark 1:16–20; 2:14; Matthew 4:18–22; 9:9; Luke 5:1–11, 27.

8. *Contra Celsum*, i, 62.

9. Pp. 159–160.

10. M. Aboth II, 8.

11. B. Sanhedrin 14a; B. Ab. Zarah 8b.

12. See Bacher, *op. cit.*

13. *Op. cit.*, p. 93.

14. *Ibid.*, p. 92; Klausner, *op. cit.*, pp. 29–30 and footnotes.

15. Vogelstein differentiates between disciple and apostle; *Hebrew Union College Annual*, Vol. II, pp. 99–125.

## CHAPTER II    SECTION A    #3

1. B. Ab. Zarah 27b adds: son of R. Ishmael's sister.

2. *Ibid.*, is added: Jacob the *Min* of Kefar Sechanya.

3. R. Elazar ben Damah.

4. B. Ab. Zarah 27b reads: I will bring you a text from the Torah showing that it is permitted.

5. *Ibid.*, is substituted: for your body is clean and your soul has

gone forth in purity and you have not transgressed the words of your colleagues, who have said, "Whoso, etc."

6. Eccles. 10:8.

7. Ben Damah.

8. And not die; apparently this verse is what Ben Damah did not live to quote, to justify, by the Scripture, every effort to save one's life.

9. Lev. 18:5.

10. See Chap. III, Sec. A, #2.

11. This Midrash, being post-Tannaitic, is discussed in Chap. III, Sec. A, #2.

12. See Bacher, *Tannaiten*, I, pp. 186, 232, 240–271, for biography; also Strack, *Introduction*, p. 112.

13. Also shown as nephew in B. Menahoth 99b.

14. *Op. cit.*, pp. 105, 145.

15. *Op. cit.*, pp. 99–100, n. 3.

16. Based on conclusions in Chap. II, Sec. A, #4. R. Eliezer is supposed to have met the same Jacob: it had to be before 117 when Eliezer died, as Herford says (*Universal Jewish Encyc.*, Vol. 6, p. 87); the year 130 would be too long afterwards for Jacob to be active, especially if we take 95 as date of Eliezer's arrest.

17. See *supra*, Sec. A, #1.

18. See Graetz, *Geschichte*, I, pp. 312–313; also, Klausner, *op. cit.*, pp. 47, 105, 111.

19. Mark 7:32–35.

20. Mark 8:23–25.

21. John 9:6–8.

22. See *supra*, Sec. A, #1.

23. פַּנְטִירִי, פַּנְטִירָא, פַּנְדֵּרָא, פַּנְדִּירָא, פַּנְטֵּרָא (see Jastrow, *op. cit.*, Vol. II, p. 1186).

24. *Op. cit.*, p. 39.

25. Πενθερός.

26. Παρθένος.

27. *Op. cit.*, pp. 23–24.

28. Schonfield, *op. cit.*, p. 143; Eisler, *op. cit.*, p. 408.

29. Vol. II, p. 43.

30. ϱ becomes ר

31. v becomes ב

32. Julius Lewy, Professor of Semitic languages at the Hebrew Union College, accepts the cogency of this linguistic argument.

33. *Op. cit.*, p. 40.

34. Parkes, *Conflict*, Chap. V.

35. *Jesus, etc.*, Preface, also p. 21, n. 3.

36. *Ibid.*; this view is favored by Eisler, *op. cit.*, p. 408.

37. See Laible, *op. cit.*, pp. 19–25; also Dalman's note to p. 21; Krauss, *op. cit.*, p. 276, n. 13.

38. In *Refutation*, *i*, 28, 32.

39. See Williams, *Adversus Judaeos*, pp. 79–82.

40. See *Literature Analysis* for articles by Krauss, Hulen, Moore, regarding Jews in the works of the Church Fathers; also, see reservations by Williams, *Adversus Judaeos*, and Parkes, *Conflict*, regarding the historicity and reliability of the early Dialogues.

41. *Op. cit.*, p. 39.

42. *Op. cit.*, p. 23.

43. *Op. cit.*, p. 25

44. Πάνθηρ.

45. *Op. cit.*, p. 23. Paulus Cassel, *Aus Literatur und Geschichte*, Berlin, 1885, pp. 334–337, holds that, as ridicule, the Greek *parthenos* (virgin) was deliberately distorted to *panther*, to compare Mary's indiscretions with those of the panther. Perles, art. in *Magyar Zsido Szemle*, 1889, pp. 193–200, denies that Jewish literature represents the panther as lustful; Goldfahn (in *Jüdisches Literaturblatt*, XX, 1891, p. 151) quotes B. Kiddushin 70a, Midr. Ps. to Ps. 80:14 and to Ps. 78:45 to show the error of Perles' denial; nevertheless, Lauterbach, *op. cit.*, is correct in disallowing Cassel's interpretation on the grounds that this was too early a date for such a meaning to be read in, that the Amoraim took Pandira as the name of the *father*, that the Church would not have adopted the name Panther if it were insulting.

46. Herford, *op. cit.*, p. 39; Schonfield, *op. cit.*, p. 144. Among other untenable guesses: Perles, in above citation, suggests ὕπανδρος which means "a dissolute woman"; A. S. Kamenetzki, *Sefer Hayovel shel Hadoar*, New York, 1927, p. 322, and in *Hatekufah*, 1923, pp. 511–512, indulges in strange mutations of the word in seeking its origin.

47. A. Deissmann, *Light From the Ancient East*, Eng. trans., Doran, 1927, pp. 73–74. He is accepted by Eisler, *op. cit.*, p. 408 and Plate XXX; Schonfield, *op. cit.*, p. 144.

48. *Orientalische Studien* in a volume dedicated to Theodor Nöldeke, Gieszen, 1906, pp. 871 ff.

49. Klausner, *op. cit.*, p. 23, n. 16; Goguel, *op. cit.*, p. 74.

50. See N. Bentwich, *Hellenism*, Jewish Pub. Soc., 1919; M. Radin,

*The Jews Among the Greeks and Romans*, Jewish Pub. Soc., 1915; the *Works of Josephus*; Enslin, *op. cit.*, Chap. V, "In the Tideway of Greek Thought."

51. *Antquities*, XIX.VIII.1.

52. Pp. 144–150.

53. Epiphanius, *Haereses*, 78; see also Klausner, *op. cit.*, p. 23; Herford, *op. cit.*, p. 39, n. 2; *cf.*, Matthew 1:15; Luke 3:24.

54. Williams, *Adversus Judaeos*, pp. 155–156.

55. *Oratio in circumcisionem Domini*, P. Graeca, 97.

56. *De fide orthodoxa*, P. Graeca, 94.

57. *Vita Mariae*, P. Graeca, 120.

58. Chaps. 27, 28. See Williams, *op. cit.*, pp. 184–185.

59. B. Yebamoth 62b: בני בנים הרי הם כבנים.

CHAPTER II     SECTION A     #4

1. Rather than "old man," because זקן implies "an elderly honored leader."

2. Which word seems a more exact translation for בטלים than "idle" or "vain."

3. Erroneously trans. by Laible (p. 36), "The judge is faithful towards me"; also by Herford (p. 138), "Faithful is the judge concerning me."

4. *I.e.*, R. Akiba.

5. שוק means "street," but implies "a market" (where, among other things, harlots are for hire), see Jastrow, *op. cit.*, II, p. 1541.

6. Dt. 23:19.

7. Laible and Herford mistakenly give this as the answer instead of the continuation of the question.

8. Variant translation: But I answered, "No."

9. Micah 1:7.

10. *I.e.*, the exposition of Scripture.

11. Prov. 5:8.

12. *I.e.*, the hated authority of the Roman government.

13. The translation of this phrase differs from Herford and Strack (Laible and Klausner do not translate this passage); it is based on Jastrow, *op. cit.*, II, p. 974, and I, p. 542. Part of the problem is the question of the correct original text. However, a significant difference in meaning can be given by the variant translations.

14. Town mentioned by Josephus (*Life*, 51), north of Jotapata in

Galilee, seat of R. Hananya Tradion; home of R. Joshua. See Jastrow, *op. cit.*, II, p. 992. The spelling of the town is slightly different from the one mentioned in the Baraitha version of this same incident.

15. Prov. 5:8.

16. Prov. 7:26.

17. It is, therefore, surprising that Herford deals with them primarily in the *Minuth* portion of his study, when they are far more valuable as Jesus-texts.

18. Strack, *Introduction*, p. 306, n. 10.

19. Aboth II, 8 f.

20. *Op. cit.*, I. 537.

21. *Die religiösen Bewegungen*, pp. 191–192, 206–207, 215–221.

22. Art. in *Jewish Quarterly Review*, 1923.

23. *Op. cit.*, pp. 63–66. Some doubt is expressed, but the incident is sorrowfully accepted.

24. *Op. cit.*, pp. 140–145.

25. *Jesus, etc.*, footnote to the German translation of this text, #4, a, b.

26. *Jesus of Nazareth*, pp. 37–44.

27. See Chap. II, Sec. A, #3.

28. Galat. 1:19; Josephus, *Antiquities*, XXIX.I.

29. Klausner, *op. cit.*, p. 125.

30. M. S. Enslin, *Christian Beginnings*, p. 387; other views are here discussed.

31. Pp. 295–298.

32. Persecution related by Eusebius (*Ecc. Hist.*, III.32), on authority of Hegesippus.

33. See Chap. II, Sec. A, #3, n. 2.

34. Koheleth R. I, 8. ‎אדם גדול כמותך.

35. *Hagoren*, IV, 34 n.

36. As Bacher believes: *Jewish Encyclopedia*, Vol. V, pp. 560–561.

37. L. Finkelstein, *Akiba*, Covici-Friede, 1936, p. 153; the historic reconstruction is given in pp. 223–225.

38. The ban and subsequent return of the colleagues are told in: B. Baba Metsia 59b; B. Sanhedrin 68a, 101a; P. Shabbath II:6.

39. See discussion of Toledoth Yeshu, Chap. IV, Sec. A.

40. Pierson Parker thesis in Pacific School of Religion Library, Berkeley, Calif., *A Partial Reconstruction of the Gospel According to the Hebrews*, 1934, p. 162.

41. Compare Mark 12:35–37; Luke 20:41–44; Matthew 22:41–45.

42. Compare Matthew 15:17; Mark 17:18–19.

43. B. P. Grenfell and A. S. Hunt, *Fragment From an Uncanonical Gospel—From Oxyrhynchus,* Oxford Univ. Press, 1908, p. 17.

44. Second half of *Christianity in Talmud and Midrash,* and second half of *Jesus, etc.*

45. מין.

46. Gen. 1:21, 24; 6:20; 7:14; Lev. 11:14; Dt. 14:13–15; Ez. 47:10.

47. Referring to Dt. 8:8.

48. *Ibid.,* pp. 362–364.

49. Levy, *op. cit.,* Vol. III, p. 104a.

50. Quoted and discussed by Herford, *op. cit.,* pp. 362–365.

51. Nu. 15:39, where it refers to going astray from the commandments of God.

52. Eccles. 7:26.

53. Ps. 63:12.

54. Besides Herford and Strack, bibliography on *Minim* would include: Graetz, *Gnosticismus und Judenthum,* 1846; M. Friedlander, *Der vorchristliche jüdische Gnosticismus,* 1898; *idem, Die religiösen Bewegungen innerhalb des Judenthums im Zeitalter Jesu,* 1905; M. Joel, *Blicke in die Religionsgeschichte,* 1880; A. Büchler, in *Judaica, Festschrift zu Hermann Cohens, etc.,* 1912, and *Monatsschrift,* Vol. 76 (1932), pp. 412–456; A. Marmorstein, *Religionsgeschichtliche Studien,* 1910; R. T. Herford in *Kohut Memorial Volume,* 1935, pp. 359–369; I. Elbogen, *Der jüdische Gottesdienst,* pp. 36 ff., 51; Jost, *Geschichte des Judenthums und seiner Sekten,* 3 Vols., Leipzig, 1857–59. S. Hahn, in *Magyar Zsidó Szemle,* 1936–1938, pp. 267–275; K. Kohler, *Origins, etc.;* Bacher, in *Revue des Etudes Juives,* Vol. XXXIII, pp. 38 ff.; F. C. Grant, *The Earliest Gospel,* 1943; *Journal of Biblical Lit.,* Vol. LXIII (1944); pp. 313–316, Vol. LXVII (1948), pp. 305–318; *Orient. Lit.,* Vol. 2, p. 825, Vol. 4, p. 204, Vol. 5, p. 1, Vol. 6, p. 620; *Monatsschrift,* Vol. 19, p. 163; *Jewish Quarterly Review,* old series, Vol. IX, p. 515; also the Jewish Encyclopedias, Dictionaries and Histories on *Minim.*

55. See above literature; Kohut's *Aruch Completum,* Vol. 5, pp. 168–9, assembles various views.

56. *Op. cit.,* pp. 249, 332, 368.

57. *Ibid.,* pp. 376–381.

58. *Festschrift,* p. 271 ff.

59. Mann, *Hebrew Union College Annual,* Vol. XII–XIII, pp. 422, 431.

60. See Chap. IV, Sec. B.

61. Herford gives detailed critique of Friedlander in *op. cit.*, pp. 368–376.

62. *Gnosticismus*, pp. 71–74; *Bewegungen*, pp. 191–192, 206–207, 215–221.

63. *Hebrew Union College Annual*, Vol. VI (1930), p. 183; Vol. X (1935), p. 255.

64. פושעי ישראל. *Studien* I, pp. 26–35; *Hebrew Union College Annual*, Vol. X, pp. 223–263.

65. *The Earliest Gospel*, Abingdon-Cokesbury, 1943, pp. 92–93.

66. *Journal of Biblical Lit.*, Vol. LXVII (1948), pp. 305–318.

67. M. Megillah IV, 8, 9.

68. This method he supposes as a symbol of the installation of the high priest, as in Lev. 21:10.

69. *Major Trends in Jewish Mysticism*, Schocken, 2nd ed., 1946, p. 359, n. 24.

70. *Conflict*, p. 94.

71. B. Berachoth 28a. See Singer and Abrahams, *Companion to the Daily Prayer Book*, pp. LXIV–LXV; Graetz, *Geschichte*, Vol. IV, n. 11; Herford, *op. cit.*, pp. 125–137; Trachtenberg, *op. cit.*, p. 182.

72. H. Leitzmann, *Geschichte der alten Kirche*, 1932, I, p. 297; *Journal of Biblical Lit.*, Vol. LXV (1946), art. by L. Wallach, "A Jewish Polemic Against Gnosticism," pp. 395–396; *ibid.*, art. by H. A. Fischel, "Jewish Gnosticism in the Fourth Gospel," pp. 157–175; *Jewish Encyclopedia*, Vol. XI, p. 372.

73. Art. in *Encyc. Britannica*, 11th ed., Vol. 12, p. 152; *idem, Hauptprobleme der Gnosis*, Göttingen, 1911; Marmorstein, *Hebrew Union College Annual*, Vol. X, pp. 228–230; art., "Gnosticism," *Hastings Encyc. of Religion and Ethics*, Vol. VI, pp. 231–242; *Ante-Nicene Fathers*, Vol. VIII, pp. 69–70 (Introd. to pseudo-Clementines).

74. *Origins of the Synagogue and the Church;* see also, Walker, *op. cit.*, pp. 55–56.

75. See Montefiore and Loewe, *Anthology*, pp. 624–627.

76. Parkes, *Conflict*, pp. 78–96.

77. Bousset, *Encyc. Britannica*, as above.

78. See *Rabbinic Anthology*, p. 668, n. 26.

79. See *Rabbinic Anthology*, pp. 161–162; Schechter, *Studies*, Vol. I, p. 190.

80. *E.g.*, B. Hullin 13b.

81. See Jastrow, *op. cit.*, I, p. 16.

82. See *Rabbinic Anthology*, pp. 251, 627; Marmorstein, *Religionsgeschichte*, pp. 11 ff.

83. ערלים is used in medieval Jewish lit.; see J. Mann, *Hebrew Union College Annual*, Vol. II, p. 274, n. 18.

CHAPTER II    SECTION A    #5

1. *I.e.*, the Gospel.
2. Strack, *Introduction*, p. 115.
3. *Ibid.*, pp. 121–122.
4. Herford translates: "the women's house," *op. cit.*, p. 146.
5. Soncino translates: "another book."
6. Matthew 5:17.
7. 71 to 73 C.E. would be a probable date of the episode; see Herford, *op. cit.*, p. 148.
8. *Op. cit.*, p. 155, n. 1; also pp. 162–165; *see* Klausner, *op. cit.*, p. 72, n. 1.
9. As in T. Shabbath XIII, 5; P. Shabbath 15c; B. Shabbath 116a.
10. *Op. cit.*, II, 40 n.
11. *Bewegungen*, pp. 188–202.
12. As in B. Hullin 13a; T. Hullin II, 20.
13. *La lingua ebraica nel Cristianesimo primitivo*, Florence, 1905, p. 9.
14. *Op. cit.*, p. 72.
15. Montefiore and Loewe, *op. cit.*, p. 605. See discussion by L. Ginzberg, *Journal of Biblical Lit.*, Vol. XLI, pp. 121–123.
16. *Op. cit.*, pp. 137–155.
17. בי נצרפי. See Herford, *op. cit.*, pp. 165–171, for various interpretations.
18. *Jesus, etc.*, pp. 79–80.
19. See Jost, *op. cit.*, II, 40 n.; Löw, *Hehalutz*, II, pp. 100–101. *Be Abidan* are named also in B. Shabbath 152a; B. Ab. Zarah 17b; *Be Nitzraphi* in B. Erubin 79b, 80a.
20. *Bewegungen*, p. 201.
21. *Journal of Biblical Lit.*, Vol. LXIII, p. 315.
22. *Op. cit.*, Chaps. X–XIII; See Strack, *op. cit.*, pp. **15–17.**
23. *Studies*, Vol. I, p. 157.
24. *Op. cit.*, p. 45.
25. *Op. cit.*, I, p. 27.
26. Herford, *op. cit.*, pp. 148–149.
27. Based on Nu. 27:8.

28. Probably of a figurine of gold.

29. In *Chajes Memorial Volume*, pp. 304–305.

30. "Place no stumbling block before the blind."

31. See Pesikta De Rab Kahana, #122; P. Yoma 38; Midr., Lev. R. XXI.

32. *E.g.*, B. Sanh. 33, "R. Tarphon said, thy ass is gone, Tarphon," means, "I shall have to make compensation for an error in judgment."

33. *E.g.*, Krauss, Herford, Strack, Klausner, Lauterbach, Nicholson, Güdemann, Graetz.

34. See Klausner, *op. cit.*, p. 45.

35. Parker, *Ancient Citations* ms.; Krauss, *New Era*, pp. 152–162.

36. Güdemann, *Religionsgeschichtliche Studien*, pp. 69–70; Herford, *op. cit.*, pp. 150–151; Klausner, *op. cit.*, pp. 45–46.

37. *Op. cit.*

## CHAPTER II   SECTION B   #1

1. כשף, the Hebrew term, implies sorcery or casting of spells by whispering. Jastrow, *op. cit.*, I, p. 676.

2. There is a question as to whether the charms or formulas for magic were scratched tattoo-like upon the flesh (not skin)—or the secret inscribed on something and inserted into the flesh which was cut open.

3. שוטה can be translated "madman," or "fool."

4. Laible translates: "The son of Stada was son of Pandera"; *op. cit.*, p. 8. Herford translates: "Ben Stada is Ben Pandira"; *op. cit.*, p. 35—which Bacher corrects: "Ben Stada? Was he not the son of Pandira?"

5. Klausner translates the confused ending as follows: "Ben Stada—is he not Ben Pandera? R. Hisda said, The husband was Stada, Pandera was the paramour. Was not the husband Pappus ben Yehuda? His mother was Stada. Was not his mother Miriam M'gadd'la N'shaya?" etc.; *op. cit.*, p. 22, n. 9.

6. Strack, *Introduction*, p. 127; Bacher, *Amoräer*, pp. 61–71; *Jewish Encyc.*, VI, pp. 422 f.

7. *I.e.*, his magic.

8. Herford translates the variant reading נאבד, "destroy."

9. *I.e.*, not a permanent marking.

10. To sin through idolatry.

11. See Jastrow, *op. cit.*, I, p. 583.

12. Court-house.

13. Pointed out by S. Krauss, *op. cit.*, pp. 186–188, 274–277.

14. B. Gittin 90a; see Strack, *Introduction*, p. 113.

15. II, p. 972.

16. See *Aruch Completum* and J. Levy, *Wörterbuch*, *s.v.* Wrong identification also by P. Cassel, *op. cit.*, pp. 338–341; A. S. Kaminetzki, *Hatekufah*, XVIII (1923), pp. 311 ff.

17. *Op. cit.*, pp. 7–19.

18. *Op. cit.*, p. 37.

19. P. 345, n. 1; maintains this position in *Universal Jewish Encyc.*, Vol. 6, pp. 87–88.

20. On the passage, B. Shabbath 104b.

21. *Vikkuah Rabbenu Yehiel*, ed. S. Grünbaum, Thorn, 1873, pp. 4–5.

22. *Essai sur l'histoire de la Paléstine*, Paris, 1867, pp. 468–471.

23. *Blicke in die Religionsgeschichte*, II, p. 55.

24. In S. A. Horodetski's Hebrew periodical, *Hagoren*, Berdichev, 1903, IV, pp. 33–37.

25. *Op. cit.*, review of Herford's book.

26. *Jewish Encyclopedia*, Vol. IV, p. 50.

27. *Jesus, etc.*, p. 29, #d, note 1.

28. *Jesus of Nazareth*, pp. 20–23.

29. Louis Ginzberg, *Journal of Biblical Lit.*, Vol. XLI, p. 121.

30. *Op. cit.*

31. Vol. on *Sanhedrin*, p. 456, n. 5.

32. Löwy, in Rahmer's *Literaturblatt*, VII, No. 4, p. 15.

33. Matthew 13:55; Josephus, *Antiquities* XX.IX.1.

34. Also named in Matthew 10:3, Mark 3:18, Luke 6:15.

35. See Grünebaum, in *Literaturblatt*, VII, No. 8, p. 20.

36. בן סוטרא in the former; בן סטרא in the latter.

37. סרטא; given in his manuscript on this passage.

38. Reifman makes the same emendation (*Halebanon*, V, No. 8, Paris, 1868, p. 116) but still applies the name to Jesus. N. Brüll, *Jahrbücher*, VII, p. 95, emends it to בן סירטא and also refers it to Jesus.

39. Offered by Eisler, *op. cit.*, p. 178; Schonfield, *op. cit.*, pp. 114–123; also, Hans J. Schoeps, art. "Simon Magus in der Haggada?" *Hebrew Union College Annual*, Vol. XXI (1948), pp. 257–275.

40. *Homilies*, 2:22; *Recognitions*, 1:72, 2:7, 2:14, 3:63. There are opposing views as to whether "Simon" mentioned in Josephus (*Antiquities* XX.VIII.6) is Simon Magus: see *Jewish Encyc.*, "Simon Magus."

41. *Hagoren*, IV (1903), pp. 33–37.

42. *Op. cit.* (1903), p. 345.

43. *Antiquities* XX.VIII.6. Parallel ref. in *The Jewish War*, II.XIII.5, mentions that 30,000 men were deluded by him.

44. Acts 21:38.

45. As we see in Chaps. III, IV.


## CHAPTER II   SECTION B   #2

1. Ps. 55:23.

2. Strack, *Introduction*, p. 119.

3. Joshua 13:22.

4. The sentence that follows is Amoraic, to be discussed later.

5. *I.e.*, Nu. 22 to 24.

6. *Op. cit.*, pp. 77–78.

7. Isaiah Horowitz in שֵלָ"ה, Furth, 1764, p. 362a.

8. Nu. 23:19.

9. Nu. 24:23.

10. *Jesus, etc.* (Comment on M. Sanh. X, 2), p. 26, n. 2.

11. Also *Jüdische Zeitschrift für Wissenschaft und Leben*, Breslau, VI, pp. 31–37.

12. *Op. cit.*, pp. 53–62.

13. Vol. VII, p. 171.

14. *Op. cit.*, p. 67.

15. *Ibid.*, p. 66.

16. *Ibid.*, p. 71.

17. *Op. cit.*, p. 33.

18. Perles emends the reading to פנחס פליסטאה as a rough adaptation of Pontius Pilate: *Monatsschrift*, 1872, pp. 266–267.

19. See *Aruch Completum*, *s.v.*; the word is divided בלא עם. See B. Sanhedrin 105a.

20. Bacher, *Tannaiten*, II, 506, n. 2.

21. Strack, *Introduction*, p. 117.

22. *E.g.*, B. B. Bathra 14b; P. Pesah. 3c. *Jewish Quarterly Review*, Vol. XVII, p. 177.

23. *Zeitschrift*, VI, pp. 36–37.

24. *Pirke Aboth*, New York, 1925, pp. 140–141; *Universal Jewish Encyc.*, Vol. 6, p. 88.

25. Schoeps, *op. cit.*, second section, does indeed apply many of the items to Simon Magus.

26. Revelation 2:14–15. See H. P. Chajes, *Markus Studien*, Berlin, 1899, p. 25.

27. Lauterbach, *op. cit.*, arrives at the same conclusion.

28. *E.g.*, 2 Peter 2:15; Jude 11; Revelation 2:14.

29. *Journal of Biblical Literature*, Vol. XLI (1922) beginning p. 121; also quoted as note to Soncino trans. of B. Sanhedrin 106b.

30. Variations are found for this passage in the 2nd Targum to Esther 3:1, printed in Venice in 1518.

31. In *Jesus, etc.*, pp. 45–46.

32. *E.g.*, J. Levy, *Dict. of the Targumim*, Vol. I, Leipzig, 1867, p. 330.

### CHAPTER II     SECTION B     #3

1. Klausner, *op. cit.*, p. 35, printing error in 1944 ed. gives wrong section-number.

2. Bacher, *Tannaiten*, I, pp. 409–424; Strack, *Introduction*, p. 114; Klausner, *op. cit.*, p. 36.

3. B. Arachin 11b; Sifre to Nu., #116, ed. Friedmann, p. 53a, b.

4. See Strack and Billerbeck, *op. cit.*, on *Peloni*, I, p. 38.

5. *Revue des Etudes Juives*, I (1881), p. 293.

6. Vol. VII, p. 170.

7. *Op. cit.*, p. 32.

8. *Op. cit.*, pp. 43–45.

9. *Op. cit.*, pp. 35–36.

10. I.ix.1, 32–33; Origen wrote c. 248, quoting Celsus of c. 178 c.e.

11. *E.g.*, Tractate Kallah 51a.

12. Josephus wrote of nearly every detail of his times; why is there scarcely mention of Jesus, if he were prominent? In all his writing there are two scant references and their genuineness is challenged.

13. See *Antiquities* V.VIII.2–3; see also Eisler, *op. cit.*, Append. XV.

14. M. Aboth III, 12.

15. *Chajes Memorial Volume*, p. 300.

16. לסוד should be translated "whitewashing," not "founding."

17. Herford's trans., "founding his sepulchre," selects words which would deliberately indicate Jesus; *op. cit.*, p. 46; corrected by Bacher, *Jewish Quarterly Review*, *op. cit.*

18. *I.e.*, parry with counter-questions. Grammar is *Hiphil*; not (as Herford translates) *Kal*, to mean "they differed on them."

19. Strangely, this passage is missing in Laible's compilation. The Baraitha explained by Graetz, *Geschichte*, IV, p. 194, n. 5.

20. *Op. cit.*, pp. 36–37.

21. Regarding Hyrcanus, for example, see Josephus, *Antiquities*, XIII.X.5–7; regarding Alexander Jannaeus, *ibid.*, XIII.XIII.5.

22. *Against Apion*, I. 7.

23. *Die Worte Jesu*, p. 4, n. 2.

24. *Jewish Quarterly Review* review of Herford.

25. *Yoma* volume, p. 310, n. 10. It mentions *Pharisaism in Transition* by B. Z. Boksor, pp. 18 ff., which maintains that *peloni* as a reference to Jesus can hardly be supported by facts.

26. *E.g.*, M. Sanhedrin, III, 7; B. Sanhedrin 29a.

27. Art. "Philo in Rabbinic Literature," *Journal of Biblical Lit.*, Vol. LIII (1934), pp. 144–149.

28. *I.e.*, the menstrual period; see Lev. 15:32.

29. *I.e.*, meeting-place.

30. An uncovered head was a sign of disrespect and impudence. See J. Z. Lauterbach art. "Should One Cover the Head When Participating in Divine Worship?" *C.C.A.R. Yearbook*, Vol. XXXVIII (1928).

31. *Tractate Kallah Rabbati*, New York, 1936, ed. Higger.

32. So, Ibn Yarhi in his commentary to this Tractate: see Higger, *op. cit.*, Introd., p. 25. Laible, in particular, becomes quite exercised: *op cit.*, pp. 33–39. It is thought the Toledoth Yeshu is based on this passage; discussion Chap. IV, Section A.

33. As is seen in Chap. III.

34. Laible agrees that, originally, Jesus may not have been meant. Herford, Bacher, Strack, Klausner, Zeitlin (*Jewish Quarterly Review*, Vol. XXXIV, p. 120). believe there is no historical value in this.

35. P. 311, n. 36.

36. P. 30.

## CHAPTER II    SECTION B    #4

1. Mu ms. adds "the Nazarene."

2. *I.e.*, between Jannaeus and the rabbis.

3. *I.e.*, Yehoshua and Jesus.

4. אכסניא means "inn"—but also "inn-keeper." This is a pun on the two meanings.

5. "Bleary and half-closed"—perhaps, near-sighted.

6. This number, to emphasize severity.

7. Important prayer in worship.

8. Until he had completed the prayer which should not be interrupted.

9. *I.e.*, that I may have looked upon her, with certain thoughts, because of her beauty.

10. Similarly.

11. Lauterbach suggests it might mean: he *departed* from Judaism, as in יצא לתרבות רעה; or, he *departed* from the world, as in אול מן עלמא.

12. See Strack footnote to the passage in *Jesus, etc.*, p. 32, n. 1; refers to Josephus, *Antiquities* XIII.XIV.2.

13. Soncino Talmud in English; *Sanhedrin* Vol., p. 736, n. 2.

14. *Jewish Quarterly Review*, Vol. VII, p. 687; see also *Jewish Encyclopedia*, Vol. VII, p. 171.

15. See Chap. IV, Sec. A; also Krauss, *Leben Jesu*, pp. 65, 118, 147.

16. See Herford, *op. cit.*, pp. 50–54.

17. See Anonymous (but really G. R. S. Mead), *Did Jesus Live 100 B.C.?* Theosophical Pub. Soc., London, 1903; A. Schweitzer, *Von Reimarus zu Wrede: Eine Geschichte der Leber-Jesu-Forschung*, Tübingen, 1906, p. 326; M. Goguel, *Jesus the Nazarene, Myth or History*, Appleton, 1926.

18. *Jewish Quarterly Review, op. cit.*

19. *Jesus, etc.* (footnote to B. Sanhedrin 107b), p. 33.

20. *Op. cit.*, pp. 24–27.

21. In *Chajes Memorial Volume*, pp. 303–304.

22. Frankel, Graetz and Lauterbach deny validity of the passage.

23. Probably taken from B. Sanhedrin 43a.

24. *Jesus im Thalmud*, pp. 41–45, Laible argues well that the name of Jesus throughout the Babylonian Talmud version is interpolated; Klausner, *op. cit.*, p. 27; H. P. Chajes, *Hagoren*, IV, p. 34, n. 2; see also Mechilta, *Yithro*, Amalek #81, ed. Friedmann, p. 55a, b.

25. Compare B. Moed Katan 16a, 7b; B. Ab. Zarah 40a; Paltoi Gaon, *Teshuboth Hageonim*, Lyk, 1864, No. 10, p. 8.

26. Strack, *Jesus, etc.*, footnote to B. Sanh. 107b.

27. S. Grünbaum, *Vikkuah Rabbenu Yehiel mi-Paris*, 1873, p. 5; with the reading *lebinatha*, "bricks," one may contrive a theory that one brick was put across the other, to form a cross.

28. See Chap. IV, Sec. B.

29. Ed. 1785, II, p. 12b.

30. Ferrara ed. 1551, p. 67a.

31. Cited by Eisenmenger, 1892 ed., I, p. 231.

32. II, Chap. 59.

33. Ed. by A. Neubauer, in *Medieval Jewish Chronicles*, Oxford, Eng., 1887, Vol. I, p. 53.

34. ‫קבלת אמת‬.
35. Colossians 4:11.
36. See Chap. I, *supra*.
37. *Op. cit.*
38. ‫ספרים חיצונים‬. P. Sanhedrin X, 1 or 28a; B. Sanhedrin 100a.
39. See *Yuhasin*, p. 103 *s.v.* ‫;אבוה‬ Rashi to B. Hagigah 15a, *s.v.* ‫;באמבטי‬ also Steinschneider ed. of ‫אלפא ביתא דבן סירא‬, Berlin, 1858, pp. 16b, 17.
40. Matthew 2:13–15.
41. Perhaps because Yehoshua means "savior," and is the fuller form of Yeshu.

## CHAPTER II   SECTION B   #5

1. Dt. 21:23.
2. Bacher, *Tannaiten*, II, pp. 1–69; Strack, *Introduction*, p. 115.
3. *Op. cit.*, p. 87.
4. Matthew 27:37, 39, 42, 43.
5. Jastrow, *op. cit.*, II, p. 1282.
6. Herford cannot explain it. His reference to Pinhas the robber as a name for Pontius Pilate has no bearing on this; identification with Pontius is disproven, anyway.
7. In *Jewish Quarterly Review*, Vol. XVII, p. 176.
8. In *Jesus, etc.*, p. 19, #b (wrongly marked #a), n. 2.
9. Lev. 25:35.
10. *Literaturblatt* (Rahmer), XIV (1885), No. 42, p. 165.
11. Matthew 15:13; John 13:17.
12. *Op. cit.*
13. B. Gittin 43a; B. Pesahim 42a; B. Kethuboth 49a; B. Shabbath 21b, 88; B. Betzah 33a; B. Sotah 14a, 39a.
14. Sifra, *Behar* VI (Weiss ed., 109c).
15. See Bacher, *Tannaiten*, I, p. 64–66, regarding Paturi.
16. *Die Juden in Babylonien*, p. 94, n. 2.
17. See Soncino Talmud in English, *Sanhedrin* volume, p. 417, n. 4.
18. Strack, *Introduction*, p. 115.
19. "Jose" (Yose) is a shortened form of "Joseph" (Yosef).
20. See J. Levy, Koback's *Jeshurun*, IV, p. 4; A. Lewin, Rahmer's *Literaturblatt*, VIII (1879), No. 32, p. 127.
21. Sidon, as in *Literaturblatt*, VIII, No. 47, p. 186, n. 20.
22. B. Sanhedrin 56a.
23. M. S. Rens, *Literaturblatt*, VIII, No. 39, p. 157.
24. Munich ms., Palestinian Talmud; Sifra, Chap. 18 of *Emor*.

25. יוסה.

26. A. Kohut, *Jewish Quarterly Review*, o.s., Vol. III (1891), pp. 552–554.

27. Soncino Talmud in English, *Sanhedrin* volume, p. 378, n. 2.

28. *Ibid.*, p. 553.

29. Ex. 15:26.

30. Excepting passage, B. Shabbath 67a top.

31. אני יהוה רפאך.

32. יהושע.

33. *Journal of Biblical Lit.*, Vol. XLI (1922), pp. 123–124.

34. See also the Talmud dictionaries on גמטריא.

35. See I. Abrahams, *Companion to Prayerbook*, on *Alenu*, pp. lxxxvi–lxxxviii; also Elbogen, *op. cit.*

36. *Rabbinic Anthology*, pp. 366–367; see also Popper, *Censorship of Hebrew Books.*

## CHAPTER II    SECTION C

1. Art. "A Unitarian Minister's View of the Talmudic Doctrine," *Jewish Quarterly Review*, o.s., Vol. II (1890), p. 463.

2. P. 12.

3. *Op. cit.*, pp. 115–117.

4. *Hebrew Union College Annual, op. cit.*

5. *Hebrew Union College Annual*, Vol. XXI (1948), pp. 275–330.

6. Jewish Pub. Soc., 1917, p. 39.

## CHAPTER II    SECTION C    #1

1. G. F. Moore, *Judaism*, Vol. I, p. 364, states that Gentile Christianity is founded on a doctrine of two powers. However, it is his opinion (p. 365; and Note 111 in Vol. III) that Tannaitic arguments against two powers are equally relevant to heathen polytheists, Jewish Dualists and Christian apologists. He gives Tannaitic allusions to God's unity in Vol. I, pp. 360–367.

2. As Herford believes; *op. cit.*, p. 293.

3. אמת ויציב. See M. Ber. II. Midr. Gen. R. XCVIII.3 traces the Shema to Abraham.

4. *Op. cit.*, p. 20.

5. *De Abrahamo* 24:119 ff. On Philo's ideas of internal unity or simplicity of God, see Wolfson, *Philo*, Vol. II, pp. 152–158.

6. Amos 4:13.

7. Ps. 69:22.

8. Dan. 7:9.

9. Dan. 7:10.

10. Ex. 20:2.

11. Dt. 32:39.

12. Dt. 32:39.

13. Matthew 28:18; II Corin. 13:14.

14. Williston Walker, *A History of the Christian Church*, Scribner's, 1934, pp. 69–70, 74–75, 114–119, 179–180.

15. S. Krauss, art. "The Doctrine of the Trinity," *New Era*, Vol. VI, pp. 470–477.

16. *E.g.*, Herford, pp. 261–266; Lauterbach, *op. cit.*; Cohen, *Everyman's Talmud*, pp. 4–6; Montefiore and Loewe, *op. cit.*, p. 9; Kohler, *op. cit.*, pp. 23, 26; Schechter, *Aspects*, p. 40, n. 1.

17. Hebrews 1:1, 2.

18. See Herford, *op. cit.*, pp. 264–266, for fuller discussion.

19. Passage is Gemara, but Ishmael was a contemporary of Judah the Nasi.

20. Shimeon ben Azai is of R. Akiba's time. Cognate passages are Sifra 4c (ascribed to Yose ben Halafta) and Yalkut Shimeoni § 604.

21. *E.g.*, the interpretation of Ps. 110:1 in Matthew 22:41–44; many instances in Justin, *Dialogue*.

### CHAPTER II    SECTION C    #2

1. Gen. 6:2.

2. One reading is אלהין ("god"); another, אלהיא ("gods").

3. Ex. 17:6.

4. Ps. 15:13.

5. חסד means: mercy, loving kindness, grace.

6. Is. 63:7.

7. Ps. 89:1.

8. Ps. 89:2. Jewish Pub. Soc. Bible translation: "For I have said: For ever is mercy built."

### CHAPTER II    SECTION C    #3

1. Chap. XI.

2. Vol. II, pp. 323–377.

3. See also J. Greenstone, *The Messiah Idea in Jewish History*.

4. *I.e.*, "A star (kochab) shall come forth out of Jacob."

5. *Viz.,* you will be long dead.
6. Parkes, *op. cit.,* pp. 78, 93.
7. *Tannaiten,* II, 222, n. 4.
8. *Op. cit.*
9. *Op. cit.,* pp. 207–209.
10. Midrash Rabbah on Canticles 2:13, p. 17c; Derech Eretz Zuta 100, 10; Baraitha, B. Sanhedrin 97a.
11. B. Sanhedrin 97b.
12. עקבות. Jastrow translates our passage: in the period preceding the Messiah.
13. Ben Yose.
14. B. Sanhedrin 99a.
15. See A. H. Silver, *Messianic Speculation in Israel* for further detail.

## CHAPTER II     SECTION C     #4

1. A miraculous "Heavenly Voice."
2. *I.e.,* in Halachah his view prevails.
3. Dt. 30:12.
4. Ex. 23:2. This is not literal, but a Midrashic interpretation.
5. Note 97; pp. 690–693.
6. Vol. I, pp. 376–379; Vol. II, p. 349. On *Bath Kol,* Vol. I, pp. 85, 237–238, 421–422; Vol. II, pp. 234, 348, 353.
7. So understood by Schechter, *Aspects,* pp. 6–7.
8. So understood by Montefiore, *Synoptic Gospels,* Vol. II, p. 201.
9. See *Rabbinic Anthology,* p. 692.
10. See art. "The Significance of Miracles for Talmudic Judaism," *Hebrew Union College Annual,* Vol. XX (1948), pp. 363–406.
11. *E.g.,* Mechilta, *Bahodesh, Yithro,* #4, p. 216; Sifre to Dt., *Haazinu,* #306, p. 131b.
12. John 1:17 compares Moses and Jesus; see also Mark 9:2–8.

## CHAPTER II     SUMMARY

1. *E.g.,* Herford, *op. cit.,* p. 71; Klausner, compare "the impudent one" in *Jesus of Nazareth,* p. 30, with *Jesus to Paul,* p. 311.
2. *Op. cit.,* pp. 4–5.
3. *Life of Jesus,* pp. 201–204.
4. *Jewish Sources of the Sermon on the Mount,* London, 1911, p. xxii; see Klausner, *Jesus,* p. 27, n. 27, regarding M. Friedlander.

5. See Sec. A, #1 and Sec. A, #3.

6. See Sec. A, #1.

7. See Sec. A, #2.

8. See Sec. A, #4.

9. See Sec. A, #5.

10. See Sec. A, #3.

11. See Zeitlin, *Who Crucified Jesus?*; Guignebert, *Jesus.*

12. Refutation i.28: "Mary was turned out by her husband, a carpenter by profession, after she had been convicted of unfaithfulness. Cast off by her spouse, and wandering about in disgrace, she then in obscurity gave birth to Jesus by a certain soldier Panthera."

13. Herford, *op. cit.*, pp. 27–31.

14. Quoted as Appendix II in Laible's *Jesus Christ in Talmud.*

15. *Op. cit.*, pp. 18–19.

16. Mattathias, however, is mentioned casually in B. Megillah 11a, B. Shabbath 21a, Midr., Ex. R. II. 15.

17. *Journal of Biblical Literature*, Vol. XLI, p. 121. See Schechter, *Aspects*, pp. 4–5.

18. Schechter, *Aspects*, pp. 6–8, alludes to damage to our knowledge by loss of older documents.

19. *Einleitung in die drei ersten Evangelien*, Berlin, 1905, p. 113.

20. *The Jewish Encyclopedia*, Vol. IV, p. 50.

21. This is according to Whiston's translation. Slight variations in translation are given by Klausner, *op. cit.*, pp. 55–56, 58, and Goguel, *op. cit.*, p. 77.

22. *E.g.*, Schurer, *op. cit.* (German 3rd ed.), pp. 547–548, 581; Guignebert, *op. cit.*, pp. 17–21; S. Zeitlin, *Jewish Quarterly Review*, n.s., Vol. XVIII (1927–8), pp. 231–255 (in book form, *Josephus on Jesus*, Dropsie College, 1931).

23. Burkitt and Harnack, for example, do.

24. *E.g.*, Klausner, *Jesus of Nazareth*, pp. 55–60; T. Reinach, *R.E.J.*, Vol. XXXV, 1897, pp. 13–14; Eisler, *op. cit.*, at length; Goguel, *op. cit.*, pp. 75–82. There are differences in opinions as to how the passage should be reconstructed. Klausner's opinion is indicated here.

25. Published for first time, in Russia, 1866–1869; also called *Halôsis.* For bibliography, see n. 24 *supra*; Goguel, p. 82, n. 2; *Universal Jewish Encyc.*, Vol. 6, p. 211.

26. There could be a relationship with Toledoth Yeshu; see Chap. IV, Section A.

27. *Annales* XV.44.

28. *Epistle* X.96.

29. *Life of Claudius*, 25, 4. Was this Jesus? Eisler believes it referred to Simon Magus (I, pp. 132 ff.). Goguel, *op. cit.*, pp. 91–93, includes among the pagan sources, Thallus the Samaritan (d. before 60 C.E.), of whom Tertullian wrote, "Thallus, in the third book of his history, calls this darkness an eclipse of the sun, but in my opinion he is wrong"; but *is* this a source?

30. See B. Bamberger, "The Dating of Aggadic Materials," *Journal of Biblical Lit.*, Vol. LXVIII (1949), pp. 115–123.

31. For further discussion in this regard, see *Der vorchristliche jüdische Gnosticismus*, pp. 71–74; *Der Antichrist*, pp. xix–xx; *Die religiösen Bewegungen*, pp. 191–192, 206–207 n, 215–221; Klausner, *op. cit.*, pp. 18–54; Goguel, *op. cit.*, pp. 184–200; Zeitlin, *Chajes Memorial Volume*, p. 295.

32. *E.g.*, Goguel, *op. cit.*, p. 161. Klausner, *op. cit.*, pp. 67–70, differs somewhat.

33. *Jesus of Nazareth*, pp. 125–126.

34. *Op. cit.*, pp. 141–142, 156–157.

35. *Op. cit.*, pp. 385–387, 399–400, 411–412, 422–424, 451.

35a. See Goguel, *Jesus*, pp. 184–185.

36. Celsus says: "Since then, these persons can perform such feats, shall we of necessity conclude that they are sons of God?" (*Contra Celsum*, Bk. I, pp. 67–68); "It was not as a teacher of new religious principles nor as a new lawgiver, but as a wonder-worker, that Jesus won fame and influence" (Kohler, in *Jewish Encyc.*, Vol. VII, p. 167; see also p. 171). We know that Shimeon ben Yohai's magic was approved, as in healing the daughter of Antoninus Pius. S. W. Baron tells that the chief officers of the synagogue, in the Roman period, until the time of Constantine, led opposition to Jesus and the Apostles, and dabbled in magic healing (*The Jewish Community*, Vol. I, p. 103).

37. *History of the Jews*, Vol. 2, p. 156. Reprinted with permission of copyright owners, The Jewish Publication Society of America.

38. *Harvard Theological Review*, Vol. 16, p. 96; takes position differing with the main interpretation in Klausner's *Jesus of Nazareth*. This would help explain, too, why (as Zeitlin points out in the *Chajes Memorial Volume*, p. 306) the Halachah in Mishnah Yadaim refers to the legalistic controversy between Judah of Galilee, a contemporary of Jesus, and the Pharisees—but not of Jesus. See Cohon, art. in *Journal of Biblical Lit.*, 1929, which interprets Jesus as an *Am-Haaretz Hassid*.

39. As reported by Jack Finegan, *Light from the Ancient Past*, p. 58. Based on E. L. Sukenik, "The Earliest Records of Christianity," *American Journal of Archaeology*, 1947, pp. 351–365.

40. Harold R. Willoughby, *Journal of Biblical Lit.*, Vol. LXVIII (1949), pp. 61–65.

41. See Kohler, *Origins*, chapter on "Paul and the Heathen Church."

# CHAPTER III
### Pages 105–139

1. Strack, *Introduction*, p. 203.
2. See *op. cit.*, p. 20.

## CHAPTER III     SECTION A     #1

1. Part in parenthesis is added in Munich code.
2. Dt. 13:9.
3. Chap. II, Sec. A, #1.
4. Strack, *Introduction*, p. 128; Bacher, *Bab. Amoräer*, pp. 93–97.
5. *Op. cit.*, p. 83.
6. *Jewish Quarterly Review*, o.s., Vol. XVII.
7. Vol. 6, p. 88—"was one for whom aught in his favor could be said."
8. *Op. cit.*, p. 87.
9. *Legatio ad Gaium* 38, #299 ff.
10. *Antiquities* XVIII.III.1; *War* II.IX.4; *Antiquities* XVIII.IV.1, 2.
11. *Op. cit.*, pp. 89–90.
12. *Jesus, etc.*, p. 18, n. 8. Lauterbach, *op. cit.*, indicates the Talmud would say ממשפחת דוד or מבית דוד if Davidic descent were meant.
13. Hinted by Bacher, *Jewish Quarterly Review*, Vol. XVII.
14. Mark 14:1.
15. Luke 23:7–8.
16. This would be implied by קרוב למלכות (as used in B. B. Kama 83a); Lauterbach, however, applies this meaning to Pilate's friendship for Jesus. Yet, since a Jewish practice is discussed would not the application be rather to the quasi-Jewish authority, Herod? Lauterbach's own preference is based on the fact that Ulla lived at the time when the Emperor Constantine had accepted Christianity as the official religion and that, therefore, assuming the friendly relations between the civil authority and Christianity to have existed even in the

time of Jesus, the delay of forty days was because of Jesus' influence with the government.

17. See Ginzberg, *Legends,* Vol. VI, p. 479.

18. Ps. 42:3.

19. Ps. 41:6.

20. Ex. 23:7.

21. Ps. 10:8.

22. Is. 11:1.

23. Is. 14:19.

24. Ex. 4:22.

25. Ex. 4:23.

26. Ps. 100:1.

27. Ps. 50:23.

28. See Chap. II, Sec. A, #2.

29. *Op. cit.,* pp. 73–76.

30. *Op. cit.,* p. 94.

31. *Jesus, etc.,* p. 43, n. 1.

32. *Op. cit.,* p. 30.

33. There are those who regard this entire passage as Baraitha, but the Aramaic of this latter part would seem to make it Amoraic: the author agrees with Klausner on this.

34. *Jewish Quarterly Review,* Vol. XVII.

35. בני instead of בוני ; נקי instead of נקאי; מתי instead of מתאי.

36. Based on suggestion of V. Burch, Schonfield presents this theory; *op. cit.,* pp. 153–157.

37. Huldreich ed., p. 35. See discussion of Toledoth Yeshu in Chap. IV, Sec. A.

CHAPTER III    SECTION A    #2

1. See Jastrow, *op. cit.,* I, p. 175. Herford translates: "something stuck in his throat."

2. Eccles. 10:5.

3. Strack, *Introduction,* p. 120; Bacher, *Pal. Amoräer,* I, pp. 124–194.

4. See Chap. II, Sec. A, #3.

5. מן.

6. משום.

CHAPTER III    SECTION A    #3

1. Herford wrongly translates: "this world."

2. Herford wrongly translates: "join thyself."

3. Lament. 1:5.

4. Dt. 23:7.

5. See Ginzberg, *Legends*, Vol. VI, p. 145; also Strack *Jesus, etc.*, p. 41, n. 6 (refers to Nu. 31:16).

6. Klausner, *op. cit.*, pp. 34–35, and Zeitlin, *Chajes Memorial Volume*, pp. 298–299, regard the date early; not so Strack or Herford.

7. *Jesus, etc.*, p. 41, n. 8; he gives B. Erubin 63a to validate his argument.

8. *Op. cit.*, p. 34. Strangely, Herford uses this instance of proximity of the names of Balaam and Jesus to infer that Balaam sometimes means Jesus; *op. cit.*, pp. 69–70.

9. Ginzberg, *Legends*, Vol. VI, pp. 123–124, 144; he names specifically B. Sanh. 106b.

10. *Chajes Memorial Volume*, pp. 298–299.

11. See Chap. V, Sec. A; also, Krauss, *Leben*, pp. 84–88.

12. See Marmorstein, *Hebrew Union College Annual*, Vol. X (1935), p. 228, n. 22.

13. Quotes are from Ps. 144:14.

14. Ps. 91:10.

15. *Op. cit.*, p. 52.

16. *Op. cit.*, p. 61.

17. See קדח in *Aruch Completum*. Against him, Jesus, not Manasseh, is meant.

18. Suggested by Herford, *op. cit.*, p. 59.

19. II, p. 1315.

20. Strack, *Introduction*, pp. 125, 127.

CHAPTER III    SECTION B    #1

1. Ex. 23:17.

2. Prov. 13:23.

3. *de Spectaculis*, XXX; *P. Latina*, I, p. 662.

4. Bacher, *Bab. Amoräer*, pp. 61–71; *Jewish Encyc.*, Vol. 6, pp. 422–423.

5. Bacher, *Tannaiten*, I, pp. 289, 324–327; *Jewish Encyc.*, Vol. IX, p. 512.

6. Lauterbach in his discussion does not accept מגדלת שער נשיא to mean "women's hairdresser." He refers to the Toledoth Yeshu which says of Mary that "before she married" she had long hair; it is understood that after she married her hair would not be seen, whether

short or long. "Hairdresser" would not apply, for what would prevent her from being a hairdresser after marriage? (Would it be proper to follow this profession after marriage?)

7. Krauss, *op. cit.*, pp. 274–275; R. Hananel comment on מאי מגדלת in Tosafoth to B. Kid. 49a; Midr. Echah. R. II (p. 44a Horeb ed.).

8. Reported by Irenaeus and Hippolytus; see *Jewish Encyclopedia*, Vol. XI, pp. 372–373; Schonfield, *op. cit.*, pp. 115–116; Schoeps, *Hebrew Union College Annual*, Vol. XXI.

9. Luke 8:2.

10. B. Gittin 90a.

11. Strack, in *Jesus, etc.*, p. 34, #a, n. 5, goes into the attempt of Jacob ben Meir (Tosafist) to explain away the anachronisms of the later Talmudic confusion as to the date of Jesus.

12. *From Jesus to Paul*, p. 255. Quote from E. Renan, *Les Apôtres*, Paris, 1866, p. 13.

13. Herford, *op. cit.*, pp. 47–48.

14. See Jastrow, *op. cit.*, I, p. 406; II, p. 876. Even Strack, *Jesus, etc.*, translates: "carpenters." Soncino transl., *Sanhedrin*, p. 725, n. 5, mentions that this may refer to the mother of Jesus.

15. Strack, *Introduction*, p. 132.

16. *Jewish Quarterly Review*, Vol. XVII.

17. Dt. 5:4.

18. Strack, *Introduction*, p. 125. This is Hiyya II.

19. Herford, *op. cit.*, pp. 304–305; also Laible, *op. cit.*, pp. 50–51. Strack, *Jesus, etc.*, also translates this way; p. 37, #10, #b; also n. 2.

20. ברא דוניתא.

21. Chap. II, Sec. A, #3.

22. A note, p. 101a.

### CHAPTER III    SECTION B    #2

1. Nu. 24:23.

2. Strack, *Introduction*, p. 122.

3. Herford, *op. cit.*, pp. 75–76; Laible, *op. cit.*, p. 61.

4. It became dangerous only when Christianity had become the State religion; see Chapter IV, Section B.

5. Strack, *Introduction*, p. 124.

6. See Herford, *op. cit.*, pp. 77–78.

7. Chap. II, Sec. A, #4.

8. Chap. III, Sec. A, #3, n. 9.

9. Sifre #357, p. 150a.

10. *Rabbinic Anthology*, p. 576, n. 7, pp. 652–653.
11. Midr., Numbers Rabbah XIV.20.

### CHAPTER III    SECTION B    #3

1. See Herford, *op. cit.*, pp. 95–96.
2. B. Kethuboth 51b; P. Terumoth 46b; Midr., Gen. R. #76.
3. Chap. II, Sec. A, #2.
4. *Geschichte*, IV, p. 295 and n. 28; also see Jastrow, *op. cit.*, II, p. 930.
5. Ginzberg, *Legends*, Vol. IV, p. 337, suggests Jesus connotation.
6. *Ibid.*, Vol. VI, pp. 426–427.
7. Ps. 139:17.
8. By Duschak, in Rahmer's *Literaturblatt*, VI (1877), No. 51, p. 203.
9. I Corin. 15:45.
10. Mark 15:34.
11. Midrash, Gen. R. XVIII.6; XXXI.9.
12. I Corin. 15:45.
13. Ginzberg correction for המירס which he regards as an error.
14. "The Definition of the Jewish Canon and the Repudiation of the Christian Scriptures," art. in *Essays in Modern Theology and Related Subjects*, New York, 1911.
15. The only ms. for this part of P. Talmud. See Ginzberg, *Journal of Biblical Lit.*, Vol. XLI, p. 121; also, in *Jewish Encyc.*, Vol. II, p. 677. לעגא instead of לעגה.
16. Midr. Eccles. R. XII.12. לעגא.
17. *Rabbinic Anthology*, pp. 605, 667 n., 20j.
18. See *supra*.

### CHAPTER III    SECTION C    #1

1. Dt. 4:32.
2. אלהים is plural form, meaning God. So in the other quotations.
3. Literally פקרו means "express skepticism," in the sense of breaking through the orthodox view.
4. Gen. 1:26.
5. Gen. 1:27.
6. *I.e.*, you have given an inadequate answer.
7. "God, God, the Lord"—three designations for divinity.
8. Josh. 22:22.

9. Ps. 50:1.
10. Josh. 24:19.
11. Continuation of above verse.
12. Dt. 4:7.
13. *Rabbinic Anthology*, p. 11.
14. *Adversus Judaeos*, Books I, II, III.
15. Prov. 24:21.
16. Zech. 13:8.
17. *Ibid.*
18. Dt. 4:4.
19. ‏עושה עצמו אלוה‎.
20. While G. F. Moore does not accept Tannaitic statements as alluding unquestionably to Christianity, he does so accept the debates as of the third century, especially with Abahu; Vol. I, p. 365; Vol. III, p. 116, n. 110.

### CHAPTER III    SECTION C    #2

1. Nu. 23:19.
2. Chap. II, Sec. B, #2. Ginzberg calls this an anti-Christian passage; *Legends*, VI, p. 133.
3. Strack, *Introduction*, p. 125; Bacher, *Pal. Amoräer*, II, pp. 88–142.
4. *Op. cit.*, pp. 62–64.
5. *Jesus, etc.*, p. 37, #10, #a, n. 2. Refers to John 10:30, 33; 14:12.
6. As in Daniel 7:17, 14; Matthew 16:27; 26:64.
7. Daniel 3:25; Jewish Pub. Soc. translation.
8. *Jesus, etc.*, p. 76, #23, #a, n. 1.
9. Ex. 20:2.
10. Herford's translation omits the important word "son."
11. Is. 44:6 for all these quotes.
12. Eccles. 4:8.
13. Strack, *Introduction*, p. 128; Ginzberg, *Legends*, Vol. VI, pp. 418–419, sees here a Jewish reply to claim of the Church Fathers that the Daniel expression "son of God" refers to Jesus.
14. Midr. Ps., on Ps. 55:22; p. 147a, #6, Buber ed.
15. Midr. Ps., on Ps. 119:123; p. 250b, #55, Buber ed.

### CHAPTER III    SECTION C    #3

1. Is. 60:2.
2. *Op. cit.*, p. 277.

3. See Chap. IV, Sec. B.

4. See Chap. II, Sec. C, #3.

5. Cohen, *Everyman's Talmud*, p. 367, regards this as a "skeptical note."

6. *Jewish Theology*, p. 386.

7. B. Sanhedrin 97b.

8. B. Sanhedrin 97a.

9. *Ikkarim* 4:42.

10. *Responsa* II, ¶356.

11. *Aspects*, pp. 345–346.

12. Midr. Ps., on Ps. 106:1.

13. Midr., Dt. R. V.11, on Dt. 17:14.

14. Chapter II, Section C, #3.

15. לְבָן changed to לְבֵּן. See, however, Soncino, *op. cit.,Sanhedrin*, Vol. II, p. 656, n. 5.

16. *E.g.*, B. Shabbath 31a end; Tanna Debe Eliyahu, p. 128.

17. B. Berachoth 34b; B. Shabbath 63a; B. Taanith 64a.

18. Midr. Ps., on Ps. 10:12; p. 66b; B. Megillah 11a; B. Sanhedrin 97b.

19. B. Baba Bathra 12b; B. Sukkoth 52a; see *Everyman's Talmud*, p. 370, n. 1.

20. Midr., Lev. R., XXXVI.2; Tanhuma, *Re'eh* #4; B. Pesahim 88a; etc. See *Everyman's Talmud*, pp. 375–377.

## CHAPTER III    SECTION C    #4

1. Ps. 145:1.

2. The textual evidence is Is. 51:14, 15—after "his bread fails not" we read "I am the Lord thy God who stirreth up the sea."

3. *Viz.*, the partition between God and man.

4. Dt. 30:11, 12.

5. See particularly A. Guttmann, *op. cit.*

6. See comments, *Rabbinic Anthology*, pp. 156–159.

## CHAPTER III    SUMMARY

1. Strack, *Introduction*, p. 34, #a, n. 1.

2. Chap. III, Sec. A, #1.

3. See Chap. II, Sec. B, #1.

4. Otherwise, Toledoth Yeshu would also speak of Ben Stada.

5. "The Attitude of the Jew Towards the Non-Jew," *C.C.A.R. Yearbook*, Vol. XXXI (1921), p. 188. See also p. 186.

6. Chap. III, Sec. A, #2.

7. Chap. III, Sec. A, #3.

8. Chap. III, Sec. B, #1.

9. Chap. III, Sec. B, #2.

10. Chap. III, Sec. B, #3.

11. *Universal Jewish Encyclopedia*, Vol. 3, p. 181.

12. Klausner, *From Jesus to Paul*, pp. 310–311, 600, believes there *are* references to Paul. Even what he regards as possible hints are erased by the corrective criticism of S. Zeitlin, *Jewish Quarterly Review*, n.s., Vol. XXXIV (1943–44), p. 120. A new study relating Paul to the rabbis is: W. D. Davies, *Paul and Rabbinic Judaism*, S.P.C.K., London, 1948.

13. Chapter III, Section C.

## CHAPTER IV
### Pages 141–227

1. See Morris Goldstein, *op. cit.*, Book II (Rabbinic Judaism); also George F. Moore—*Judaism in the First Centuries of the Christian Era*.

2. Leopold Lucas, in *Zur Geschichte der Juden im IV Jahrhundert*, Berlin, 1910, presents in collected form the statements of the Church Fathers regarding the Jews. See also the translation of their writings in the *Ante-Nicene; Nicene and Post-Nicene Fathers*.

3. Pp. 2–4; see also Graetz, *History*, Vol. 2, pp. 561–564.

4. Graetz, *op. cit.*, pp. 566–572; Marcus, *op. cit.*, pp. 3, 4–5.

5. Ed. by Mommsen and Meyer, Berlin, 1905. Summarized and indexed, together with other legislation, 300–800, affecting Jews, *op. cit.*, pp. 379–391.

6. Especially Codex Justinianus, in Corpus Juris Civilis, ed. by Kreuger and Mommsen, Berlin, 1886; summarized by Parkes.

7. Graetz, *op. cit.*, pp. 613–617, 626; Marcus, *op. cit.*, pp. 3–5; Parkes, *Judaism and Christianity*, pp. 115–124.

8. Graetz, *op. cit.*, Vol. 2, pp. 13–16; Marcus, *op. cit.*, pp. 6–7.

9. As translated by Parkes, *Conflict*, p. 392.

10. Parkes, *ibid.*, translates it, "the Mishnah."

11. Jacob Mann, art. on "Changes in Divine Service," *Hebrew Union College Annual*, Vol. IV, pp. 241–310; Eppenstein, *Contribution and History of Liturgy in Gaonic Times*, p. 24; Davidson, Introduction, *Machzor Yannai*.

CHAPTER IV    SECTION A

1. ספר תולדות ישו.
2. מעשי תלוי "Deeds of the One Who Was Hanged."
3. מעשי דאותו ואת בנו "Deeds of That One and His Son."
4. מעשי ישו "Deeds of Jesus."
5. Migne, *P. Latina*, CIV, Coll. 77–100; summarized in English, Williams, *Adversus*, pp. 352–353.
6. Migne, *P. Latina*, CXVI, 141–184; Williams, *op. cit.*, pp. 355–365; Graetz, *Geschichte*, Vol. 5, pp. 237–242. Similar material is reported by Klausner, *op. cit.*, p. 51, in *Contra Judaeos*, by Hrabanus Mauras, Archbishop of Magenta in 847.
7. In Schechter collection at Oxford University. Edited, published, discussed by Ginzberg, Krauss, Adler.
8. S. Krauss, in *Jewish Encyclopedia*, Vol. VII, p. 173.
9. He calls it *Fabula de Christi Miraculis Judaica; id est Maligna.* See later discussion of Martini, *infra*, pp. 204–205.
10. *Victoria adversus impios Ebreos*; publ. 1520, Justiniani, Paris.
11. אבן בוחן.
12. *Vom Schem Hamphoras und vom Geschlecht Christi*, in *Werke*, Wittemberg.
13. *I.e.*, "Fiery Darts of Satan"; published at Altdorf.
14. *Historia Jeschua Nazareni*, Leyden.
15. In *Revue des Etudes Juives*, Vol. III, new series (1938), pp. 65–88. He was given the ms. by son of Ph. Munk of Boskovitz, Moravia (d. 1885), to whom it had belonged. This article prints the Hebrew portion. Krauss identifies the two versions here as belonging to the Slavonic type.
16. *Op. cit.*, pp. 32–34.
17. An English translation based on the Hebrew Codex in the Strassburg Univ. Library is given by Schonfield, *op. cit.*, pp. 35–61. A Hebrew version combining the six mss. printed by Krauss in *Leben Jesu* is given by Eisenstein, *op. cit.*, pp. 227–235.
18. Different texts give differing dates. The chronology of the Toledoth is confused in many instances. This date follows the tradition of Jesus a century earlier.
19. Some versions say: Pappos ben Yehudah (as in the Talmud); in others, the roles of Yohanan and Joseph are switched.
20. Obviously based on the Talmud story: Tractate Kallah 51a.
21. Variant: Jerusalem.

302    *Jesus in the Jewish Tradition*

22. Stone which, according to legend, God cast into the water, to establish the foundation of the world. אבן שתיה. See Ginzberg, *Legends*, Vol. V, pp. 14–16.

23. Variant: dogs.

24. Is. 7:14.

25. Ps. 2:7; he quoted also Ps. 2:1–2; Hos. 2:4.

26. Is. 11:1.

27. Ps. 1:1.

28. Dt. 18:20.

29. They quote Is. 11:4; Jerem. 11:4 which describe the Messiah Jews expect.

30. Variant: horsemen. Eisler, in *Messiah Jesus*, p. 112, says the original reading was the similar Hebrew word which means "Pharisees" rather than "horsemen."

31. Variant: Yeshu caused to live many other inanimate objects made of clay.

32. A repetitious passage is here omitted.

33. Is. 14:13.

34. Compare this with ability of Satan to fly, according to legend; Ginzberg, *Legends*, Vol. V, pp. 84–85. Regarding Balaam flying, Vol. VI, p. 144. Simon Magus also flew in a contest with Peter, as discussed in Chap. II, Sec. B, #1. The Zohar tells of defilement of Jesus and Mohammed.

35. Ps. 69:21; Is. 1:6; Is. 57:3; 53:4; Dan. 9:26 are quoted here by Yeshu as prophecies of his torment.

36. Variant: he went to Egypt and there learned the secret of sorcery, this time not by God's power, but Judah mingled among his disciples and filched it from him; Yeshu, therefore, had to return to Jerusalem to attempt to regain the Name.

37. Variant: Pappa ben Retsitsetha.

38. As in Sanhedrin 43a. Wagenseil, *op. cit.*, p. 17, mentions twelve apostles; Huldreich, *op. cit.*, p. 35, names Matthia, Elikum, Mordecai, Thoda, Johannos. See *supra*, Chap. III, Sec. A, #1.

39. Dt. 21:23. The cabbage stalk is referred to in II Targum to Esther 7:9.

40. With reference to Ps. 49:16.

41. R. Tanhuma lived four hundred years after Jesus. This is another indication of how garbled all this is.

42. Variant: for which they had to pay the gardener thirty pieces of silver.

43. "Kepha" is Aramaic for "rock," which in Greek is "Peter." Variant: Elijah (probably Paul is meant).
44. Isaiah 1:14.
45. Variants (which do not use the name Simeon) add here: Elijah the Nazarenes call Paul.
46. John 6:42.
47. Agnes L. Smith, *The Old Syriac Gospels*, London, 1910, p. 2.
48. Klausner, *op. cit.*, pp. 67, 234.
49. Ephesians, Chap. 18 (I. 57), quoted from *The Historical and Linguistic Studies in Literature related to the New Testament*, Allan Hoben, Univ. of Chicago Press, Vol. I, 1909.
50. Matthew 1:19.
51. Apocryphal Gospels: E. Hennecke, *Neutestamentliche Apocryphen*, Tübingen, 1904; M. R. James, *Apocryphal N.T.*, Oxford Univ. Press, 1924; R. Hoffmann, *Das Leben Jesu nach den Apocryphen*, Leipzig, 1861. Uncanonical Gospels: E. Nestle, *Novi Testamenti Graeci, Supplementum*, Leipzig, 1896, German trans. by E. Preuschen, Giessen, 1905; Baring-Gould, *op. cit.*
52. Chap. 2, verses 3-6.
53. Chaps. 13-16.
54. *Dialogue*, LXXVIII.
55. *Contra Celsum*, Bk. I, 28, 32. See discussion *supra*, Chap. II, Sec. A, #3.
56. 2:43-50.
57. *Gospel of Thomas* α, 6:1.
58. *Ibid.*, 19:2-4.
59. Chap. II, Sec. B, #3.
60. *E.g.*, Mark 1:23-42; Luke 2:12-26; 7:15-16; Matthew 8:2-4; 9:2-8; John 5:1-16.
61. *Op. cit.*, 2:2-5.
62. *Cf.* B. Sanhedrin 106b; B. Sotah 47b; see *Jewish Encyclopedia*, Vol. VII, p. 171.
63. See Trachtenberg, *op. cit.*; especially p. 230.
64. Published London, 1897; pp. 236, 392.
65. *New Era*, Vol. VI, p. 27.
66. See *supra*, n. 21.
67. B. Shabbath 104b; B. Sanhedrin 67a; see *supra*, Chap. II, Sec. B, #1.
68. Chap. III, Sec. B, #1.
69. 1:1.

70. B. Sanhedrin 43a. See Chap. II, Sec. A, #1.

71. *Ibid.*, #2.

72. Matthew 27:64.

73. Verses 29–30.

74. 13:1.

75. Justin's *Dialogue*, CVIII: Eusebius, *Hist. Eccl.*, IV. 18. See also Clementine *Refutations* I.42.

76. Verse 24.

77. *De Spectaculis*, XXX.

78. Krauss, *Revue des Etudes Juives, op. cit.*

79. Acts 9:26–30; 22:17–21; Galat. 1:18–21.

80. Chap. II; also Literature Analysis.

81. See refs. to the *Minim, supra*; also n. 114, *infra.*

82. "Lettres sur les Juifs," in *Oeuvres*, i, 69, p. 36.

83. *Op. cit.*, p. 53.

84. *The Historic Christ*, 1933, p. 19.

85. *Leben Jesu*, pp. 246–248.

86. *Monatsschrift*, 1933, p. 55. He argues here against Bernard Heller and E. Bischoff who deny that there is an *Ur-Toledoth*.

87. *Op. cit.*, p. 30.

88. *Ibid.*, p. 227.

89. *Op. cit.*, p. 225.

90. *Op. cit.*, p. 52.

91. *Josephus on Jesus.*

92. Goldstein, *op. cit.*, pp. 159–164, 169.

93. *Monatsschrift*, 1933, pp. 57–58.

94. Discussion and sources given by Williams, *op. cit.*, pp. 339–347; Trachtenberg, *op. cit.*, pp. 65; 231, n. 19.

95. Queen Helena is generally identified as Salome (or Saline, mistakable as Helene) Alexandra, wife of Alexander Jannaeus; or, Helene, wife of Simon Magus; or Queen Helena of Adiabene, who embraced the Jewish religion (Josephus, *Antiquities*, XX.II. 1–5). As for the contest of magic power, the closest analogy is the story of Simon Magus.

96. In *Compendium of History*; see Williams, *supra.*

97. *Op. cit.*, i, pp. 66–67.

98. Parkes, *op. cit.*, pp. 245–255.

99. *Ibid.*, p. 252.

100. Opening of Chap. IV.

101. *Op. cit.*, p. 53.

102. As in *Patrologia Orientalis*. See Parkes, *op. cit.*, Chap. 8;

Williams, *op. cit.*, Books II, III.

103. Eisler, *op. cit.*, p. 111.

104. *According to the Hebrews.*

105. Origen, *op. cit.*, Bk. II, 13.

106. *Op. cit.*, p. 27.

107. Especially close to Matthew.

108. *Op. cit.*, p. 63.

109. *Monatsschrift*, 1933, p. 54. Use of the phrase "Gospel of the Hebrews," we could assume, meant for Krauss the lost "Gospel According to the Hebrews."

110. *Revue des Etudes Juives*, 1938, pp. 65 f.; refers to Parkes' mention in *Judaism and Christianity*, Vol. II, p. 131 n., that Schonfield was about to publish a book proving this; when the book appeared it did not claim conclusive proof but rather recommended the theory as a likely one, requiring further study.

111. *The Four Gospels and Our Translated Gospels.*

112. Enslin, *op. cit.*, p. 381.

113. *Ibid.*, p. 502.

114. The story in the Toledoth of how Simeon Kepha separated Christianity from Judaism and thus brought peace within Israel, it is interesting to observe, is found also in A. Jellinek, *Beth Hamidrash*, 2nd ed., Jerusalem, 1938, Vol. V, pp. 60 ff.; Vol. VI, pp. 11 ff.

115. Kraus, *Revue des Etudes Juives*, 1938, pp. 65–88.

116. *Ibid.*

117. Krauss, *Das Leben*, p. 237.

118. *Jews and the Church in the XIIIth Century*, p. 29.

119. A garbled version in Hebrew, printed in New York City, which came to the writer's attention, did in fact state in the Preface that it was put in print and circulated in order to counteract the missionizing among the Jews which the author regarded as particularly zealous.

120. *Jewish Encyclopedia*, Vol. VII, p. 170.

121. *History*, Vol. 5, p. 185.

122. *Op. cit.*, pp. 53–54.

123. See Chap. IV, Sec. C.

## CHAPTER IV    SECTION B

1. *Op. cit.*, p. 422.

2. The *Otzar Vikkuhim* is an excellent Hebrew compilation as far

as it goes. The most recent (1938) German study on the theme is by H. J. Schoeps; it is reviewed by S. S. Cohon in *Jewish Quarterly Review*, new series, Vol. XXIX (1938), p. 330.

3. *Op. cit.*, p. 245.

4. Marcus, *op. cit.*, pp. 20–21.

5. Williams, *op. cit.*, Chap. XXII; also p. 363; Migne, *P. Latina*, CXXI, pp. 478–514; J. Aronius, *Regesten zur Geschichte der Juden im fränkischen und deutschen Reiche bis zum Jahre 1273*, 1902, #103.

6. Kirkisani's work is dated 937, which is also the first half of the tenth century, but he was a Karaite, and will be discussed later.

7. For explanation of Genizah, see *supra*.

8. J. Mann, art. in *Hebrew Union College Annual*, Vol. XII–XIII (1937–38), pp. 411–459; gives text and interpretation.

9. Dt. 14:1; Ex. 4:22; Is. 48:16.

10. See W. Bacher, in *Jewish Quarterly Review*, old series, Vol. VII (1895), pp. 687–710. See also Marmorstein, *Monatsschrift* (1922).

11. *Ishrun Makalat*.

12. There are those who deny that Saadia is dependent on Al-Mukammas.

13. *Universal Jewish Encyclopedia*, Vol. 6, p. 319.

14. A. H. Silver, *op. cit.*, pp. 55–56. Nemoy, *Hebrew Union College Annual*, Vol. VII, p. 383.

15. *Kitab al-anwar*.

16. Al-Mukammas disagreed with the order in which he placed the origin of Christianity.

17. Chap. II, #7.

18. See Nemoy, *op. cit.*, p. 331, n. 45; other errors, see p. 335, n. 67; p. 361, n. 215; p. 337.

19. *I.e.*, the story of his being the excommunicated disciple of Yehoshua b. Perahiah.

20. As in B. Shabbath 104b.

21. Nemoy, *op. cit.*, p. 364, n. 229.

22. Supposedly the founder of the Sadducees; like the Sadducees, Kirkisani states, Jesus forbade divorce.

23. *I.e.*, Jesus; so Nemoy, *op. cit.*, interprets. Quoted from his translation, p. 365.

24. Bacher, *Jewish Quarterly Review*, old series, Vol. VIII (1896), pp. 431–444. Censored part was printed also by Harkavy in *Altjüdische Denkmäler aus der Krim*.

25. See L. Zunz, *op. cit.*, pp. 154–162; Eisler, *op. cit.*; S. Zeitlin, *Josephus on Jesus.*

26. *Jewish Encyclopedia*, Vol. VII, pp. 445–446.

27. *Universal Jewish Encyclopedia*, Vol. 6, p. 317.

28. אמונות ודעות in Hebrew; was written originally in Arabic. Rosenblatt, *op. cit.*, gives excellent English translation; quoted here.

29. Treatise II.

30. Literally: go forth to heresy.

31. Chapter III of this Treatise.

32. Entire Treatise on Creation must be read for the complete argument.

33. Henry Malter, art. "Saadia Gaon's Messianic Computation," *Journal of Jewish Lore and Philosophy*, Vol. I (1919), pp. 45–61, discusses calculations for Messiah date.

34. Nehemiah 8:8.

35. Every Bible translation is necessarily an interpretive work.

36. B. Shabbath 104b; see *supra*, Chap. II.

37. B. Sanhedrin 103a; see *supra*, Chap. III, Sec. B, #3.

38. B. Sanhedrin 106a; see *supra*, Chaps. II, III.

39. B. Abodah Zarah 16b, 17a; see *supra*, Chap. II, Sec. A, #4.

40. B. Berachoth 12a. תלמידי ישו.

41. M. Sotah 9:15 תהפך למינות Rashi says נמשכים אחר טעותו של ישו ותלמידיו נקרא מינים; see also B. Baba Bathra 25a.

42. B. Sanhedrin 17a. ובעלי כשפים המסיתין ומדיחין בכשפיהם כגון הנוצרי.

43. Chap. III, Sec. B, #3.

44. *Sefer Haberith*, included in *Milhemeth Hobah* collection, Constantinople, 1910.

45. *Vikkuah* (וכוח), also included in above collection. David Kimhi's abbreviated name is *Radak*.

46. *Teshuboth Lenotzrim*.

47. *Sefer Hakuzari* in the Hebrew translation.

48. I:4.

49. I:5.

50. II:2; IV:1, 15.

51. III:65.

52. II:56.

53. I:8.

54. Isaiah 52:13 ff.

55. IV:22.

56. For easy reference see his *Selected Poems*, Eng. trans., Jewish Pub. Soc., 1924; also S. S. Cohon, art. on "Judah Halevi" in *Universal Jewish Encyclopedia*, Vol. 6, pp. 225–229.

57. IV:23.

58. Listed in *Universal Jewish Encyclopedia*, Vol. 7, pp. 294–295. Good bibliography on Maimonides: pp. 295–296.

59. *E.g.*, Thomas Aquinas.

60. Zeitlin, *Maimonides*, pp. 45–46; see J. Mann, in *Hatekufah*, 1928.

61. *Ibid.*, p. 219, Chap. VI, n. 1a (as per ms. in Jewish Theological Sem. library).

62. *H. Akkum* IX:4; see Zeitlin, *Maimonides*, p. 15; S. Liberman, *Kiryath Sefer*, XV (1938), p. 60.

63. *E.g.*, Tosafoth to B. Sanhedrin 63b; Isserles, *Shulhan Aruch*, Orah Hayim, 156; see Kohler, *op. cit.*, p. 429.

64. *H. Melachim* XI:3–4. Translation as in A. Cohen, *The Teachings of Maimonides*, pp. 224–245; see A. Hershman, *Code of Maimonides*, pp. xxii–xxiv, 239–240, 310.

65. Daniel 11:14.

66. Zeph. 3:9.

67. *Responsa* (*Kobets Teshuboth Harambam*) ed. Lichtenberg, 1859, Vol. I, 14b.

68. B. Sanhedrin 106b.

69. *Ibid.*, Vol I, p. 34a, b.

70. Sifra, *Ahare Moth*, #143.

71. *Responsa, ibid.*, Vol. II, pp. 23d, 24.

72. M. Waxman, *op. cit.*, Vol. I, p. 314.

73. *Op. cit.*, p. 76.

74. For details see Husik, *op. cit.*, Chapter V.

75. *Cf.* Israel Zangwill translations, Jewish Pub. Soc., 1923.

76. Chap. I, entirely.

77. Main trends are outlined in Husik, *op. cit.*, p. 200.

78. *Emunah Ramah*; originally in Arabic.

79. Husik accepts this as a definite fact; *ibid.*, p. 226.

80. *Guide*, I:35.

81. *Guide*, I:45. *Yad, H. Yesode Hatorah*, I:7.

82. *Guide*, I:58.

83. *Guide*, I:36.

84. *Guide*, II:45; *Commentary*, Introd. to *Helek; Yad, H. Yesode Hatorah*, VIII. A. Cohen, *op. cit.*, p. 325, n. 24, relates this to Christianity and Mohammedanism.

85. *Commentary*, Introd. to *Helek; Yad, H. Yesode Hatorah*, IX. A. Cohen, *op. cit.*, p. 157, names this a definite allusion to Christianity.

86. *Responsa* II, 6c–7a; *Yad, H. Melachim*, XI–XII; *H. Teshubah*, VIII–IX; *Commentary*, Introd. to *Helek*.

87. *Commentary*, Introd. to *Helek*, which is to M. Sanhedrin X.

88. Elbogen, *op. cit.*, pp. 87 ff.

89. *Op. cit.*, p. 90.

90. *Milhamoth Adonoi*; in Bodleian Library, Oxford; also, Breslau, Germany.

91. Migne, *P. Latina*, CLVII, 535–672.

92. As Williams, telling of this, readily concedes; *op. cit.*, p. 237, and n. 1.

93. All but the conclusion of this disputation is printed by Wagenseil, *op. cit.*; given in Hebrew by Eisenstein, *op. cit.*, pp. 81–86.

94. See *supra*, Chap. III.

95. See *supra*, Chap. II.

96. Graetz, *op. cit.*, Vol. 3, p. 577, is astonished. He says Yehiel was honest but inaccurate. Yet we now know that Graetz himself was misled by some of the Talmudic references.

97. Marcus, *op. cit.*, pp. 145–150; also, in 1205, Pope Innocent III declared, "they publicly insult Christians by saying that they (Christians) believe in a peasant who had been hung by the Jewish people. Indeed, we do not doubt that He was hung for us, since He carried our sins in His body on the cross, but we do not admit that He was a peasant either in manners or race" (See Grayzel, *XIII Century*, p. 107).

98. The disputation is recorded in *Milhemeth Hobah*, 1710; by Wagenseil, *op. cit.*; a better edition in Hebrew by Steinschneider, *Sefer Vikkuah Haramban*, Berlin, 1860; I. Loeb, *R.E.J.*, 1887, pp. 1–18; Eisenstein, *op. cit.*, pp. 86–94. Discussion in Schechter, *Studies*, Vol I, pp. 125–130; Hamburger, *op. cit.*, Vol. III, pp. 53–56; Williams, *op. cit.*, pp. 244–247; Graetz, *History*; Neubauer, *The Expositor*, Vol. VII, pp. 98 ff.

99. Jewish Pub. Soc. Bible translates: "As long as men come to Shiloh."

100. B. Sanhedrin 58; Midrash R., Lamentations I.51.

101. Schechter, *op. cit.*, Vol. I, p. 106, comments that this was not said to flatter the king; the same view that the messianic belief is of minor significance in Judaism is repeated elsewhere by Nahmanides, where the possibility of flattery is no factor.

102. Possibility suggested by Scholem, *op. cit.*, p. 128.

103. שילייא.

104. *Op. cit.*, I, p. 121. Reprinted with permission of copyright owners, The Jewish Publication Society of America.

105. Marcus, *op. cit.*, pp. 41–42.

106. However, Peter Niger, a Dominican of the fifteenth century,

claimed Martini to have been a Jew to the age of forty: *cf.* Wolf, *Bibliotheca Hebraea,* 1727, iii, 900; Williams, *op. cit.,* p. 248.

107. "Bridle for the Jews."

108. "Dagger of Faith," published in 1278.

109. See Williams, *op. cit.,* p. 249, n. 4.

110. Williams, *op. cit.,* pp. 228–232.

111. *Ezer Hadath.*

112. G. Belasco on Ibn Pulgar in *Jewish Quarterly Review,* old series, Vol. XVII (1905), pp. 26–56; also *The Support of Faith,* 1906.

113. *Eben Bohan.*

114. *Ezer Ha-emunah.*

115. Known also as *Efodi.*

116. Williams, *op. cit.,* pp. 267–276; further refs. given in p. 267, n. 2, 3.

117. Printed by Z. A. Poznanski, Budapest, 1913; given by Eisenstein, *op. cit.,* pp. 260–288; contents outlined by Waxman, *op. cit.,* pp. 542–544.

118. "Refutation of Christian Dogmas"; Hebrew trans. by Joseph ibn Shemtob. Pub., Salonika, 1860; reprinted in substance by Eisenstein, *op. cit.,* pp. 288–310.

119. See Margolis and Marx, *History,* p. 411.

120. Eisenstein, *op. cit.,* pp. 236–260, does, in fact, combine Isaac Troki, Lipmann and the two older *Nitzahon* documents. *Sefer Hanitzahon* is outlined by Waxmann, *op. cit.,* Vol. II, pp. 545–551.

121. It was believed, probably in error, that while still a Jew, Lorki had defended Judaism against Paul of Burgos. See *Jewish Encyclopedia,* Vol. VI, p. 551; Vol. X, pp. 105–106; Steinschneider, *Jewish Literature,* 1857, p. 20; Graetz, on Lorqui.

122. Geronimo's arguments are given by Williams, *op. cit.,* pp. 261–266.

123. These two are in the Eisenstein collection of disputations.

124. More complete summary of his philosophy, see Husik, *op. cit.,* Chap. XV.

125. More complete summary of his philosophy, *ibid.,* Chap. XVII.

126. See Cohon, *Christianity and Judaism Compare Notes,* p. 64.

127. See Husik, *op. cit.,* pp. 406–407.

128. See English translation by Husik. Phrases reprinted with permission of copyright owners, The Jewish Publication Society of America.

129. T. Sanhedrin XIII, 2; Maimonides, *Yad, H. Teshubah* III:5; *H. Eduth* XI:10; *H. Melachim*, VIII:11.

130. Neubauer, *Expositor*, 1888, p. 190; Williams, *op. cit.*, Chap. XLVII; Graetz, *History*.

131. See Scholem, *op. cit.*, pp. 308–312.

132. Marcus, *op. cit.*, p. 159; Grayzel, *History*, pp. 423–424.

133. See Strack, *Introduction*, p. 84.

134. See Roth, *History of the Jews of Italy*, pp. 100, 142, 162, 303–304, 411.

135. The dates are modified by Jacob Mann, *Texts and Studies*, Vol. II.

136. Williams, *Christian Evidences*, 1910, 1919.

137. Included in Eisenstein, *op. cit.*, pp. 170–184.

138. *Ibid.*, pp. 184–193.

139. *Ibid.*, pp. 193–200.

140. This portion is not available in English, excepting in the doctoral dissertation of Lou H. Silberman, in the library of the Hebrew Union College.

141. *Ibid.*, pp. 201–221.

142. "Judaism Uncovered."

143. Strack, however, defends Eisenmenger. See *Introduction*, pp. 87–88.

144. Preface to *Seder Olam*, 1757, letter to Council of the Four Lands, quoted from *Universal Jewish Encyc.*, Vol. 3, p. 190. The entire text is translated, about the same, by Oscar Z. Fasman in *Judaism in a Changing World*, ed., Leo Jung, New York, 1939, pp. 121–136.

## CHAPTER IV    SECTION C

1. *Studies*, Vol. I, p. 104. Reprinted with permission of copyright owners, The Jewish Publication Society of America.

2. Pp. 264–265.

3. Dt. 4:40.

4. ‫קבלת עול מלכות שמים‬.

5. ‫קבלת עול מצות‬.

6. The *Shulhan Aruch* is the standard compilation, its authority recognized universally; with exception that Ashkenazic Jewry (of Polish and German tradition) accept the annotations added by Moses Isserles.

7. ‫שאלות ותשובות‬.

8. ‫מנהגים‬.
9. ‫תקנות‬.
10. For further study, see reading recommended in Section E of Literature Analysis.

## CHAPTER V
### Pages 229–242

1. S. Krauss, *Jewish Encyclopedia*, Vol. VII, p. 173.
2. S. H. Kraines and E. S. Thetford, *Managing Your Mind* (copyright and published) Macmillan, 1943, p. 142.
3. *Jewish Encyclopedia*, Vol. VII, p. 170.
4. *The New Era*, Vol. VI, p. 20.
5. *Studies*, Vol. I, p. 197.
6. *Cf.* I. Sonne, *Hebrew Union College Annual*, Vol. XXI (1948), p. 11.
7. Pp. 189–191.
8. *Viz.*, Jewish compassion.
9. P. 306. Specific literature is cited.
10. There are various theories on date and manner of origin of the ghetto: see Abrahams, *Middle Ages*, Chap. IV; also, *Universal Jewish Encyclopedia*, art. "ghetto."
11. See Abrahams, *op. cit.*, p. 66, also n. 2.
12. *Ibid.*, p. 409.
13. Summarized in *Universal Jewish Encyclopedia*, Vol. 3, pp. 187–191; Kohler, *op. cit.*, pp. 426–432; Abrahams, *op. cit.*, pp. 413–429; *Jewish Encyclopedia*, Vol. V, pp. 615–626.
14. T. Sanhedrin XIII, 2.
15. *Op. cit.*, II:5.
16. *Op. cit.*, IV:23.
17. *Yad, H. Melachim* XI, 4.
18. *E.g.*, by Nahmanides, *Derashah*, 5, ed. Jellinek; Rashi, Tosafoth to B. Ab. Zarah 2a, 57b; B. Sanhedrin 63b. *Shulhan Aruch, Yoreh Deah*, 148:12.
19. Translated by I. Zangwill and I. Davidson, Jewish Pub. Soc., 1923, p. 86. The poem continues with exaltation of the role of Israel. Reprinted with permission of copyright owners, The Jewish Publication Society of America.
20. Chap. 956.
21. *Yad, H. Melachim* X, 12.

22. Sermon 88, p. 26; as translated by Bettan, *op. cit.*, p. 189. The thought is similar to Maimonides, *Responsum 58.*

23. *Yoreh Deah*, 251:1; 335:9; 347:1.

24. *Hoshen Mishpat*, Chaps. 366–369.

25. *Yoreh Deah*, 267:27.

26. *Orah Hayim*, 224:7.

27. *The Religions of Democracy*, by Finkelstein, Ross and Brown; Devin-Adair, 1941.

28. S. S. Cohon and H. F. Rall, Macmillan, 1927.

## LITERATURE ANALYSIS

1. The Gaonic period ends in 1040.

2. See discussion for this division in the Eras of Jewish History: Morris Goldstein, *Thus Religion Grows: Story of Judaism*, pp. 262 ff.

3. Published in Philadelphia, Pa., 1917.

4. The Mishnah text in Babylonian Fragments, dated in the ninth century, found in the Genizah recovery of ancient mss. may yield further information when properly edited; it is discussed by P. Kahle, in *Hebrew Union College Annual*, Vol. X (1935), pp. 185–223; Vol. XII–XIII (1938), pp. 275–325.

5. ספר דקדוקי סופרים.

6. It covers: 1. Zeraim. 2. Moed. 4. Nezikin (lacking Tractate Aboth). 5. Kodashim (only Tractates Zebahim and Menahoth, Hullin; lacking the ten others).

7. For further analysis, see Strack, *Introduction*, pp. 82–83; also, S. Schechter, *Studies in Judaism*, Third Series, Jewish Pub. Soc., 1945, p. 300, n. 21.

8. קונטרס למלאות חסרונות הש"ס.

9. קבוצת ההשמטות.

10. ספר השבת אבדה

11. קונטרס אומר השכחה.

12. A copy may be seen at the Jewish Theological Seminary, New York City; referred to by Strack, *Introduction*, p. 280.

13. Fuller details, giving the description of these works, their history, the literature on them and an enumeration of the lesser Midrashim, are to be found in Strack, *Introduction*, pp. 201–234; 331–349; the articles on Midrash and the individual Midrashim in the *Jewish Encyclopedia* and the *Universal Jewish Encyclopedia*; L. Zunz, *Die*

*Gottesdienstlichen Vorträge der Juden*; I. H. Weiss, *Dor Dor Vedoreshav*; Israel Bettan, *Studies in Jewish Preaching*, Chapter I.

14. Literary references on individual items are indicated in these notes.

15. *Christianity in Talmud and Midrash*, p. 35, n. 1.

16. *Jewish Quarterly Review*, o.s., Vol. XVII, p. 175.

17. *Op. cit.*, p. 174.

18. In the Preface to *Jesus, etc.*

19. *E.g.*, מדגלא instead of מגדלא on p. 401; לפביהם instead of לפניהם and בך instead of בן on p. 402; צוה instead of צואה on p. 404.

20. *E.g.*, indirect references other than those emphasizing God's unity.

21. *E.g.*, those dealing with God having a son, etc.

22. *E.g.*, B. Yoma 66b, B. Gittin, 56b, 57a, B. Sanhedrin 43a, B. Ab. Zarah 27b.

23. As indicated in Chapter I.

24. *Op. cit.*, p. 172.

25. Discussed and shown in Chapter II.

26. 1848–1922, founder of the Institutum Judaicum in Berlin, Germany.

27. *E.g.*, J. Berachoth 3c; Midr. R. to Dt. 6:4.

28. These works are more fully described later in this chapter. See also Moore, Hulen and Krauss as indicated in this chapter, Section C.

29. See Chap. I.

30. *E.g.*, B. Shabbath 116a, b; B. Ab. Zarah 16b, 17a.

31. *E.g.*, Pesikta Rabbati 100b, 101a; B. Sanhedrin 106a.

32. *E.g.*, Midr., Lev. R. IV.6; indirect references.

33. P. 18.

34. P. 20

35. P. 20.

36. תולדות ישו.

37. מעשי תלוי.

38. חלקת מחוקק.

# INDEX